The Magic Menu Cookbook

75 EXCITING MEALS TO ENTERTAIN YOUR FAMILY AND FRIENDS

Marion Dee Longarini

Kathleen   C.   Nichols

Edmond   C.   Longarini

PRENTICE-HALL, INC., *Englewood Cliffs, N.J.*

The Magic Menu Cookbook: 75 Exciting Meals to Entertain Your Family and Friends
by Marion Dee Longarini, Kathleen C. Nichols, Edmond C. Longarini

© 1970 by Edmond C. Longarini

Copyright under International and Pan American
Copyright Conventions

Library of Congress Catalog Card Number: 70-98384

Printed in the United States of America   *T*

ISBN-0-13-545046-2

Prentice-Hall International, Inc., London
Prentice-Hall of Australia, Pty. Ltd., Sydney
Prentice-Hall of Canada, Ltd., Toronto
Prentice-Hall of India Private Ltd., New Delhi
Prentice-Hall of Japan, Inc., Tokyo

Foreword

This book is written for, and dedicated to, all new brides; and to those experienced homemakers who find it difficult to prepare complete dinners in a timely and efficient manner.

Each menu presented in this book includes a list of all ingredients to serve four or six guests, a list of utensils needed, a timetable to follow, as well as complete cooking instructions. In addition, menus are arranged according to their cost and ease of preparation.

It is our hope that, by utilizing this book and other volumes to follow, anyone can become an admired and often complimented chef who can, with utmost confidence, remark ". . . and then I cooked!"

Marion Dee Longarini
Kathleen C. Nichols
Edmond C. Longarini

Introduction

Although there are a great many cookbooks available, containing every imaginable type of recipe, very few of them, if any, offer a simple and complete format for the preparation of an entire dinner. Most include recipes for every course, but they are listed in different chapters, with the result that much effort is expended in searching and planning. Some recipes list ingredients to serve four, some to serve six, and others to serve eight or more. And very few recipes state the full time required for preparation of a particular dish, making it extremely difficult to have meals ready on time.

By offering complete menus, standardized ingredient lists, timetables for step-by-step preparation of the entire meal, and detailed cooking instructions, this book is designed to free you from tedious calculations and planning. Each menu presented has been preplanned and pretested, but to be sure of obtaining the best results, it is recommended that the following steps be taken in the preparation of each menu:

A. *Selection of a menu*   Each of the menus presented will contain recipes for each course of the meal including dessert. Since tastes vary greatly as to the amount of sweetness desired in each meal, the desserts indicated may be omitted entirely if desired, or replaced with a simple sherbet or ice cream.

The menus have been arranged according to their cost, simplicity, and impressiveness. There are three separate divisions:

CHAPTER ONE—Relatively inexpensive and simple meals, appropriate for informal family dinners.

CHAPTER TWO—Dinners of moderate cost that are suitable for casual entertainment of business associates and friends.

CHAPTER THREE—Although not necessarily classified as "gourmet" or formal dinners, these are a little more costly, require a little more effort, and are a little more impressive. They are appropriate for the entertaining of bosses, VIP's, and discriminating dinner guests.

After selecting the chapter that is most appropriate for the occasion, check the ingredients in each recipe to determine that all foods are in season and available; look at the timetable to make sure there is sufficient time to prepare the dinner; and make the final selection of the menu.

B. *Selection of the wine* The first item listed on each menu represents the premium quality American wine that will complement the dinner to be served. For those who prefer a less expensive wine, a Standard American Wine Selection Chart appears on pages 246 through 248. For those who prefer to make their own selection of premium American wines or European wines, those selection charts appear on pages 249 through 257.

In order to acquaint the inexperienced host and hostess with the history and customs in the serving of wines, a brief introduction to wines is presented in Chapter Five.

C. *Ingredient list* The ingredients required in each recipe are listed for serving four and six.

There are some recipes that cannot be cut down to serve four and these are listed in the six column only.

In order to conserve space, abbreviations have been used in the ingredient lists, and a table of these abbreviations appears on page xii.

Since food products are packaged by many different companies in varying weights, measures, and sizes, it is impossible to compile a standard list of sizes or weights for each item. If you cannot obtain the exact weight or size specified in the ingredient list, use the closest weight or size available.

The spices are listed in amounts that would not be objectionable to the average taste. Except for pies, cakes, and breads, most of the ingredient amounts may be varied slightly to suit individual tastes.

Utensils made by different manufacturers carry varied designations and come in many sizes; select the utensil that is the closest dimension or size to the one specified.

Frozen foods may be substituted for fresh foods in most cases.

D. *Timetable* The timetable for each menu has been prepared and tested to properly indicate the time that each phase of work should be started to have dinner ready to serve at 8:00 P.M. Adjustments may be penciled in to serve dinner earlier or later than specified. Items that may be prepared in advance and refrigerated are marked with an asterisk (*). In order to provide enough time for cocktails, last minute primping, or socializing, it is suggested that all items marked with an asterisk be prepared in advance. Dishes that may be partially prepared in advance, refrigerated, and baked just before serving, will require about fifteen minutes more cooking time than specified in the instructions.

E. *Instructions* The instructions for the preparation of each recipe appear directly opposite the list of ingredients for that recipe. It is recommended that the instructions be read completely before starting the cooking procedure, to ensure that everything is well understood. A glossary of terms appears on page xiv.

A double slash mark (//) has been used to designate the stopping point in the preparation of a recipe, when a portion of the recipe can be prepared in advance.

CHAPTER FOUR contains recipes for a few simple hors d'oeuvres that may be served before dinner.

Contents

CHAPTER ONE   *Family meals*

CHAPTER FOUR *Hors d'Oeuvres*

CHAPTER FIVE *Introduction to Wines*

LIST OF ABBREVIATIONS

approx . . . approximately

bnch . . . . . bunch(es), a measurement of some vegetables

C . . . . . . cup(s), a standard measuring cup (8 ounces)

clv . . . . . . clove(s), a segment of garlic, etc.

env . . . . . envelope(s), of gelatin, spice mixes, yeast, etc.

hd . . . . . . head(s), of lettuce, cabbage, etc.

in . . . . . . inch(es), standard measurement

lb . . . . . . pound(s), measurement of weight (16 ounces)

lrg . . . . . large

med . . . . . medium

MSG . . . . monosodium glutamate, an ingredient that accents flavor

oz . . . . . . ounce(s), standard measurement

pkg . . . . . package(s), of cake mixes, frozen foods, etc.

pt . . . . . . pint(s), standard liquid measurement (16 ounces)

qt . . . . . . quart(s), standard liquid measurement (32 ounces)

sm . . . . . . small

tbl . . . . . . tablespoon(s), standard measurement (½ ounce)

tsp . . . . . . teaspoon(s), standard measurement (⅓ tablespoon)

TABLE OF EQUIVALENTS

Liquid:

60 drops . . . . 1 teaspoon
3 teaspoons . . . . 1 tablespoon
2 tablespoons . . . . 1 liquid ounce
4 tablespoons . . . . ¼ cup
16 tablespoons . . . . 1 cup
2 cups . . . . 1 pint
2 pints . . . . 1 quart
4 quarts . . . . 1 gallon

Dry Measure: 16 ounces . . . . 1 pound

Equivalents:

1 tablespoon butter . . . . 1 ounce
2 cups butter . . . . 1 pound
4 cups flour . . . . 1 pound
2 cups granulated sugar . . . . . . 1 pound
2⅔ cups brown sugar . . . . 1 pound
3½ cups powdered sugar . . . . . 1 pound
1 square baking chocolate . . . . . 1 ounce
7 to 8 eggs . . . . 1 cup
1 medium lemon . . . . 3 tablespoons juice
1 medium orange . . . . ⅓ to ½ cup juice
1 grated orange rind . . . . 1 tablespoon
1 can soup . . . . 1¼ cups

GLOSSARY OF TERMS

Barbecue . . . . To roast or broil over hot coals.

Baste . . . . . . To keep meat or other food moist by pouring melted fat, drippings, or sauce over food while roasting, baking, or barbecuing.

Beat . . . . . . To smooth a mixture with a brisk regular motion of a beating device (electric or hand beater).

Blanch . . . . . To rinse a food with scalding hot water.

Blend . . . . . . To mix two or more ingredients smoothly and inseparably together.

Broil . . . . . . To cook food by direct exposure to heat.

Brown . . . . . To cook a food until it turns brown.

Chill . . . . . . To place a food in a refrigerator until it becomes cold.

Colander . . . . A strainer for draining off liquids.

Combine . . . . To mix ingredients together.

Compote . . . . A fruit or food stewed or marinated in syrup.

Cream . . . . . To work to a smooth creamy mixture.

Dice . . . . . . To cut or chop into small cubes.

Dot . . . . . . To place small particles of butter or another ingredient on top of a food or dish.

Dredge . . . . . To coat a food with flour.

Drippings . . . . Fat and liquids that drip from cooking meat.

Drizzle . . . . . To sprinkle in fine drops.

Fold in . . . . . To mix foods without releasing air bubbles contained therein. This is accomplished by lifting a portion of the liquid or mixture from the bottom of the container, through the mixture, and up to the top, repeating the process until foods are blended.

Glaze . . . . . . A sugar or sugar syrup used to coat foods. Any type of thick liquid with which foods are coated.

Marinate . . . . To let a food stand in a seasoned mixture.

Meringue . . . . A mixture of sugar and beaten egg whites.

Mince . . . . . . To chop finely.

Pare . . . . . . To cut off the outer covering of skin of a fruit or vegetable.

Pasta . . . . . . An Italian word meaning *paste*. This word often describes any type of food preparation, made from flour, in the noodle or macaroni family.

Preheat . . . . . To heat an oven to a stated temperature before placing food in the oven to cook.

Puree . . . . . . A smooth, thick liquid made by pressing food through a fine strainer.

Reserve . . . . . To set aside and save for future use in a recipe.

Rind . . . . . . The thick outer coating of a food.

Sauté . . . . . . To cook food in a small amount of fat or grease, moving food around while cooking to keep it from browning or burning.

Scald . . . . . . To heat a liquid to just below its boiling point. When milk is scalded, a thin skin will form on top to indicate sufficient heating.

Section . . . . . To cut a fruit at the membranes after it has been peeled, leaving pieces as naturally divided.

Simmer . . . . . To cook a liquid at a temperature just below boiling. Small bubbles will rise slowly and the liquid will be relatively motionless.

Spoon . . . . . . To transfer liquids, or other foods, using a spoon.

Tear . . . . To pull apart into pieces.

Torte . . . . . . A round dessert, often in layers.

SPICES AND HERBS

Allspice . . . . A mildly sharp and fragrant spice made from the berry of a tropical American myrtaceous tree.

Basil . . . . An annual plant of the mint family. Leaves may be used fresh, dried, or ground.

Bay Leaf . . . . The leaf of a laurel tree.

Capers . . . . The pickled flower buds of a Mediterranean plant.

Caraway Seeds . . . . . . Seeds of a biennial herb of the carrot family.

Cayenne Pepper . . . . . . A very hot, biting condiment made from powdered pods and seeds of an African red pepper.

Celery Seeds . . . . Seeds of a small plant that closely resembles celery.

Celery Salt . . . . A mixture of ground celery seeds and salt.

Chili . . . . A hot pepper.

Chili Powder . . . . . . A mixture of ground red pepper and other spices.

Chives . . . . Similar to a green onion.

Cinnamon . . . . The aromatic inner bark of the *Cinnamonum* genus of trees, grown mostly in Ceylon. Available ground or in sticks.

Cloves . . . . The flower buds of a tree grown in the East Indies. Available either ground or whole.

Cream of Tartar . . . . . . Purified potassium bitartrate, used also as a baking powder ingredient.

Cumin Seeds . . . . Dried, slightly bitter fruit of the Cuminum Cyninum.

Curry Powder . . . . A yellow powder from India, composed of a variety of spices.

Dill Weed . . . . An annual herb grown mostly in India and used mainly for pickling and sauces.

Garlic . . . . A strong-flavored plant of the liliaceous family, the cloves of which are used for flavoring.

Garlic Salt . . . . A mixture of garlic and white salt.

Ginger . . . . The root of the reedlike plants of the genus *Zingiber,* native to the East Indies. Available as black ginger or candied ginger.

Marjoram . . . . A plant of the mint species.

Mint . . . . A fragrant annual plant, the leaves of which are used for seasoning.

Monosodium Glutamate . An ingredient that accents food flavors.

Mustard . . . . A pungent powder prepared from the mustard plant. Available dry, prepared, or in seed form.

Nutmeg . . . . The hard, aromatic seed of the fruit of the East Indian Myristica tree. Sold whole or ground.

Onion Salt . . . . A mixture of dried onion and white salt.

Oregano . . . . A plant of the mint family.

Paprika . . . . A sweet red pepper. Sold dried and ground.

Parsley . . . . An herb used in the flavoring of meats.

Pepper . . . . Made from the dried berries of the Piper Nigrum vine. Available whole (peppercorns) or ground.

Peppercorns . . . . Whole black pepper, the dried berries of the Piper Nigrum vine.

Pickling Spices . . . . . . Spices used to pickle foods.

Pimiento . . . . A garden pepper used as a vegetable or relish.

Poultry Seasoning . . . . . A mixture of spices used to flavor poultry.

Rosemary . . . . An evergreen Mediterranean

shrub, the leaves and flowers of which are used to flavor stews, sauces, and fish.

Sage . . . . A perennial mint, the leaves of which are dried and used as seasoning.

Seasoned Salt . . . . A mixture of spices and white salt.

Soy Sauce . . . . A sauce made from fermented soy beans.

Tabasco Sauce . . . . A hot, spicy sauce made from cayenne peppers.

Thyme . . . . An herb, the dried leaves of which are used as seasoning.

CHAPTER ONE
Family Meals

TIMETABLE

*3:00 pm	Prepare French Chocolate Pudding
*3:30	Prepare Spiced Fruit
*6:30	Prepare Beef and Spinach Casserole
7:00	Place casserole in oven at 350°
7:15	Prepare biscuits
7:40	Turn oven control to 450°
7:45	Remove casserole, cover to keep warm
7:45	Place biscuits in oven
8:00	Dinner is served

menu I

† A dry Claret wine; serve at cool room temperature (65°)   * May be prepared in the morning or the night before and refrigerated

---

FOR 4	FOR 6	INGREDIENTS

INSTRUCTIONS

BEEF AND SPINACH CASSEROLE

FOR 4	FOR 6	INGREDIENTS
10 in	12 in	Utensils: skillet
1½ qt	2 qt	baking dish
1½ pkg	2 pkg	frozen chopped spinach 10-oz pkg
1 sm	1 med	chopped onion
1 lb	1½ lb	ground beef
¾ C	1 C	precooked or instant rice
½ tsp	¾ tsp	garlic salt
¼ tsp	⅓ tsp	crushed oregano
¼ tsp	⅓ tsp	thyme
1 C	1½ C	small-curd cottage cheese
¾ C	1 C	golden mushroom soup
½ C	¾ C	shredded sharp Cheddar cheese

Defrost spinach. Chop onion. In the skillet, brown the meat and chopped onion together. Drain off grease. Add rice, garlic salt, oregano, and thyme. Place one-half of the spinach in the buttered baking dish. Add the meat mixture on top of the layer of spinach. Spoon the cottage cheese over the meat mixture, add a layer of the remaining spinach, pour the undiluted soup over all, and sprinkle with Cheddar cheese. / / Bake, uncovered, in preheated 350° oven for 45 minutes.

BAKING POWDER BISCUITS

med		Utensils: mixing bowl
med		cookie sheet
2 C		sifted flour
½ tsp		salt
4 tsp		baking powder
¼ C		shortening
¾ C		milk

Preheat oven to 450°. Sift flour onto waxed paper and measure. Add salt and baking powder. Then sift again into mixing bowl. Cut in the shortening with pastry blender or knife. Gradually add milk and make into soft dough. Place on floured board and knead lightly a few seconds. Roll out to ¾ inch thick and cut biscuits with a floured biscuit cutter. Place on greased cookie sheet and bake at 450° for 15 minutes.

SPICED FRUIT

1 qt	1 qt	Utensils: saucepan
med	med	mixing bowl
10-oz can	1-lb can	canned pear halves
10-oz can	1-lb can	canned peach halves
3 tbl	¼ C	brown sugar, firmly packed
¼ C	⅓ C	cider vinegar
2	3	cinnamon sticks
1 tsp	1½ tsp	whole cloves
½ tsp	¾ tsp	whole allspice

Drain the fruit syrup from each can into saucepan and place fruit in mixing bowl. Add sugar, vinegar, sticks of cinnamon, whole cloves, and whole allspice to the syrup. Boil for 5 minutes and pour over fruit in mixing bowl. Cover and refrigerate at least 4 hours before serving. / /. Remove fruit from marinade and place in small serving bowls.

FRENCH CHOCOLATE PUDDING

FOR 4 / FOR 6	INGREDIENTS	
med	Utensils: double boiler	
2 sm	mixing bowls	
1 C	semisweet chocolate pieces	
2	egg yolks	
¼ C	warm water	
1 C	heavy cream	
¼ C	powdered sugar	
½ tsp	cinnamon	

Melt the chocolate pieces in the top of double boiler over boiling water. In a small mixing bowl, beat the egg yolks with warm water and blend into chocolate. Remove from heat and refrigerate for 10 minutes; meanwhile, whip the cream with powdered sugar and cinnamon until stiff. Fold the cream into the chocolate mixture, then spoon into small dessert bowls. Refrigerate until ready to serve.

menu 2

Red Pinot†
Beef Bourguignon
Buttered Noodles
Green Peas
Fruit Salad
Chocolate Sundae

TIMETABLE

*3:15 pm	Prepare Beef Bourguignon
*4:00	Place beef casserole in oven at 325°
6:30	Add remaining ingredients to casserole, return to oven
*7:00	Prepare Fruit Salad
7:40	Prepare Buttered Noodles
7:45	Prepare Green Peas
7:50	Add dressing to salad
8:00	Dinner is served

After Dinner, prepare Chocolate Sundae.

† A dry Burgundy wine; serve at cool room temperature (65°)

* May be prepared in the morning or the night before and refrigerated

FOR 4	FOR 6	INGREDIENTS	INSTRUCTIONS

BEEF BOURGUIGNON

FOR 4	FOR 6	INGREDIENTS	
12 in	12 in	Utensils: skillet	
2 qt	3 qt	covered baking dish	
1 tbl	1 tbl	olive oil	
4 slices	6 slices	chopped bacon	
1¾ lb	2½ lb	stew beef, cut into pieces	
2 sm	2 med	sliced carrots	
1 sm	1 med	chopped onion	
¾ tsp	1 tsp	salt	
⅛ tsp	¼ tsp	pepper	
1 C	2 C	dry red wine	
10½ oz	10½ oz	canned beef consommé	
⅓ C	1 C	water	
1 tbl	2 tbl	tomato paste	
⅓ tsp	½ tsp	thyme	
1	1	bay leaf	
1	2	minced garlic cloves	
1½ tbl	2 tbl	flour	
8	12	pearl onions	
¾ lb	1 lb	chopped fresh mushrooms	

In the skillet, heat olive oil and sauté the bacon and beef until browned. Clean and slice carrots and add to skillet. Peel and chop onion and add to skillet. Cook mixture until browned, then drain off grease. Place mixture in baking dish and combine with the salt, pepper, wine, consommé, water, tomato paste, thyme, and bay leaf. Mince the garlic cloves and add to mixture. Cover and bake for 2½ hours in preheated 325° oven. Uncover casserole, remove ½ cup of liquid, gradually stir liquid into flour, then stir back into the casserole. Peel the onions, slice the mushrooms, and add both to the mixture. / / Cover and bake for at least one more hour.

BUTTERED NOODLES

FOR 4	FOR 6	INGREDIENTS
3 qt	4 qt	Utensil: saucepan
2 qt	2 qt	water
1 tsp	1½ tsp	salt
6 oz	8 oz	wide egg noodles
3 tbl	¼ C	butter or margarine
½ tsp	¾ tsp	salt
¼ tsp	¼ tsp	pepper

Bring water to a boil in saucepan. Add salt and noodles and cook, uncovered, for 8 to 10 minutes, or until noodles are tender. Drain noodles in colander and rinse with hot water. Place in serving bowl, add butter, salt, and pepper, and toss lightly.

GREEN PEAS

FOR 4	FOR 6	INGREDIENTS
1 qt	2 qt	Utensil: saucepan
½ C	¾ C	water
1 pkg	2 pkg	frozen peas, 10-oz pkg
1 tsp	2 tsp	sugar
½ tsp	1 tsp	salt
1 tbl	2 tbl	butter or margarine
¼ tsp	½ tsp	salt
⅛ tsp	¼ tsp	pepper

Bring water to a boil in saucepan, add frozen peas, sugar, and salt. Bring back to a boil, cover, and cook gently over reduced heat for 4 to 6 minutes, or until tender. Drain, stir in butter, salt, and pepper. Keep covered until ready to serve.

FOR 4	FOR 6	INGREDIENTS	INSTRUCTIONS

FRUIT SALAD

FOR 4	FOR 6	INGREDIENTS
med	lrg	Utensils: salad bowl
sm	sm	mixing bowl
¾ C	1 C	pineapple tidbits, 13½-oz can
¾ C	1 C	seedless green grapes
⅓ C	½ C	shredded mild Cheddar cheese
½ hd	¾ hd	lettuce

Drain pineapple tidbits, reserving required amount of syrup for dressing. Place pineapple in salad bowl. Add washed, halved grapes and shredded cheese. Wash and tear lettuce into bite-size pieces. Add to mixture. / / Just before serving, spoon salad onto serving plates and top with dressing.

Dressing

FOR 4	FOR 6	INGREDIENTS
¾ C	1 C	commercial sour cream
¼ C	⅓ C	pineapple syrup

In a small mixing bowl, stir the reserved pineapple syrup into sour cream.

CHOCOLATE SUNDAE

FOR 4	FOR 6	INGREDIENTS
sm	sm	Utensil: saucepan
½ C	¾ C	chocolate ice cream topping
1 pt	1½ pt	coffee or vanilla ice cream
¼ C	⅓ C	chopped pecans
4	6	maraschino cherries

Heat chocolate ice cream topping in saucepan until it just starts to bubble. Scoop servings of ice cream into sundae serving dishes, add 2 tablespoons of topping, sprinkle with 1 tablespoon of chopped pecans, and top with a maraschino cherry.

7

menu 3

Cabernet Rosét
Cheeseburger Deluxe
Corn Italienne
Roquefort Green Salad
Almond Ice Cream Balls

TIMETABLE

*5:00 pm	Chill wine
*6:00	Prepare Almond Ice Cream Balls
*6:45	Prepare salad and salad dressing
*7:15	Prepare Cheeseburger Deluxe
7:35	Broil cheeseburgers
7:35	Prepare Corn Italienne
7:55	Toss salad with dressing
8:00	Dinner is served

† A dry Claret rosé; serve chilled (45°)

* May be prepared in the morning or the night before and refrigerated

---

FOR 4	FOR 6	INGREDIENTS	INSTRUCTIONS

CHEESEBURGER DELUXE

FOR 4	FOR 6	INGREDIENTS
med	med	Utensil: mixing bowl
1 lb	1½ lb	lean ground beef
½ can	1 can	canned tomato soup
¼ C	⅓ C	finely chopped onion
2 tsp	1 tbl	prepared mustard
2 tsp	1 tbl	Worcestershire sauce
¾ tsp	1 tsp	prepared horseradish
1 tsp	1½ tsp	salt
4 to 6	6 to 8	hamburger bun halves
4 to 6	6 to 8	tomato slices
4 to 6	6 to 8	American cheese slices

In the mixing bowl, combine the ground beef, tomato soup, onion, mustard, Worcestershire, horseradish, and salt. / / Toast the bun halves in the broiler. Spread meat mixture evenly over toasted buns, covering edges completely. Broil about 4 inches from the flame for 12 to 14 minutes. Top each burger with a slice of tomato and a slice of cheese. Return to broiler and cook until the cheese melts.

8

FOR 4	FOR 6	INGREDIENTS

CORN ITALIENNE

8 in	8 in	Utensil: skillet
⅓ C	½ C	olive oil
3	4	minced garlic cloves
12 oz	1 lb	canned whole-kernel corn
1 tsp	1½ tsp	sweet basil
½ tsp	¾ tsp	salt
½ tsp	¾ tsp	pepper
⅓ C	½ C	grated Parmesan cheese
¼ C	⅓ C	sesame seeds
¼ C	⅓ C	chopped parsley

Heat the oil in skillet. Add garlic and sauté until lightly browned. Add the drained corn, basil, salt, and pepper, and toss well to blend. Sprinkle with cheese and sesame seeds. Cook until cheese has melted, and garnish with parsley just before serving.

ROQUEFORT GREEN SALAD

med	lrg	Utensil: salad bowl
1 med hd	1 lrg hd	lettuce
½ can	1 can	sliced carrots, 8¼-oz can
½ can	1 can	cut green beans, 8-oz can
1	2	sliced green onion

Wash and drain the lettuce. Break lettuce into salad bowl. Drain the carrots and beans and add to the lettuce. Slice the green onions into the bowl. / / Toss the salad with the dressing just before serving.

Dressing

sm	sm	Utensil: mixing bowl
2 oz	3 oz	Roquefort cheese
⅓ C	½ C	heavy cream
¾ tsp	1 tsp	salt
⅛ tsp	¼ tsp	pepper
2 tsp	1 tbl	lemon juice

Mash Roquefort cheese in mixing bowl. Add the cream, salt, pepper, and lemon juice. Blend until mixture is smooth. Cover and refrigerate until ready to serve.

9

ALMOND ICE CREAM BALLS

FOR 4	FOR 6	INGREDIENTS
2 qt	2 qt	Utensil: saucepan
1½ tbl	2 tbl	butter or margarine
⅓ C	½ C	sliced almonds
3 tbl	4 tbl	butter or margarine
⅓ C	½ C	brown sugar, firmly packed
1¾ C	2½ C	cornflakes
1 pt	1½ pt	vanilla ice cream

Melt the butter in saucepan. Add the almonds and stir over a low heat until browned. Remove almonds. Add more butter and melt in saucepan. Stir in the brown sugar, bring to a boil, and boil for 2 minutes. Remove from heat. Add the toasted almonds and cornflakes. Toss mixture lightly until cornflakes and almonds are coated with the brown sugar. Spread mixture on waxed papper and let cool. Roll scoops of ice cream in the cooled cornflake mixture, place balls on serving platter, and freeze until ready to serve.

menu 4

Chianti Wine†
Chili Corn Casserole
Sour Dough Bread
Pepper Salad
Crunchy Ice Cream Balls

TIMETABLE

*5:00 pm	Prepare ice cream balls and refrigerate
*6:30	Prepare salad and salad dressing and refrigerate
*6:50	Prepare bread and wrap in aluminum foil
*7:00	Prepare casserole
7:30	Bake casserole
7:40	Place bread in oven to warm
7:50	Toss salad with salad dressing
8:00	Dinner is served

† A dry red wine; serve at cool room temperature (65°)

* May be prepared in the morning or the night before and refrigerated

FOR 4	FOR 6	INGREDIENTS

CHILI CORN CASSEROLE

FOR 4	FOR 6	INGREDIENTS
10 in	12 in	Utensils: skillet
1½ qt	2 qt	baking dish
1 lb	1½ lb	ground beef
⅓ C	½ C	chopped onion
1 tbl	1½ tbl	salad oil
1 tsp	1½ tsp	salt
¼ tsp	⅓ tsp	pepper
1½ lb	2½ lb	canned chili with beans
½ pkg	1 pkg	corn chips, 11-oz pkg
1 C	1½ C	grated sharp Cheddar cheese

In a skillet, brown meat and onion in salad oil. Drain off the grease. Add salt, pepper, and chili with beans, mixing carefully. In the baking dish, arrange layers of chips, bean mixture, and cheese. Repeat until all ingredients are used, ending with a layer of cheese. / / Bake for 30 minutes in preheated 350° oven.

PEPPER SALAD

FOR 4	FOR 6	INGREDIENTS
med	lrg	Utensil: salad bowl
1 med hd	1 lrg hd	lettuce
1	2	chopped green onion
½ med	¾ med	sliced green pepper

Wash and drain lettuce and break into salad bowl. Chop the green onion, slice the green pepper, and add to the salad bowl. Refrigerate until ready to serve. / / Toss the salad with the salad dressing just before serving.

Dressing

FOR 4	FOR 6	INGREDIENTS
1 pt	1 pt	Utensil: glass jar
½ tbl	¾ tbl	sugar
½ tsp	¾ tsp	salt
¼ tsp	⅓ tsp	dry mustard
¼ tsp	⅓ tsp	celery seed (or celery salt)
(⅛ tsp)	(¼ tsp)	
½ C	¾ C	commercial sour cream
2 tbl	3 tbl	lemon juice

Combine the sugar, salt, dry mustard, celery seed, sour cream, and lemon juice in a glass jar and refrigerate until ready to serve. / / Shake vigorously and add to salad just before serving.

SOUR DOUGH BREAD

FOR 4	FOR 6	INGREDIENTS
sm	sm	Utensil: saucepan
2 tbl	3 tbl	butter or margarine
½ tsp	¾ tsp	garlic powder
½ loaf	¾ loaf	sliced sour dough or French bread

Soften butter in saucepan over low heat and mix in garlic powder. Spread mixture on bread slices, arrange slices back into loaf form, wrap in aluminum foil. / / Heat for 20 minutes at 350°.

CRUNCHY ICE CREAM BALLS

FOR 4	FOR 6	INGREDIENTS
sm	med	Utensils: shallow pan
8 × 8 in	8 × 8 in	baking pan
1 pt	1½ pt	vanilla ice cream
½ can	1 can	salted peanuts, 6½-oz can
½ can	1 can	chow mein noodles, 3-oz can

Scoop one ice cream ball for each serving (using about ¼ pint of ice cream for each ball) and place balls in a shallow pan in the freezing compartment. Crush the peanuts and chow mein noodles, combine them in a baking pan, and bake the mixture at 350° for 4 or 5 minutes. Let the mixture cool, then roll each ball in the mixture. Return the ice cream balls to the freezer and reserve any remaining peanut-noodle crumbs.

Sauce

FOR 4	FOR 6	INGREDIENTS
sm	sm	Utensil: saucepan
⅛ C	¼ C	light corn syrup
1½ tbl	3 tbl	water
1 tbl	2 tbl	butter or margarine
3 oz	6 oz	semisweet chocolate pieces

Combine corn syrup, water, and butter in a saucepan and bring the mixture to a boil over high heat. Remove from heat and stir in the chocolate pieces. Cool the sauce to lukewarm and spoon 2 tablespoons of sauce over each ice cream ball. Sprinkle any remaining peanut-noodle mixture over the top and return to freezer until ready to serve.

menu 5

TIMETABLE

*3:15 pm	Start cooking the corned beef if 5 pounds
*4:00	Prepare Pineapple Filled Cake
*4:15	Start cooking the corned beef if 3 pounds
*6:45	Prepare salad and salad dressing
*7:00	Prepare vegetables
7:15	Preheat oven to 200°
7:25	Place corned beef in oven
*7:25	Wrap rolls in foil
7:30	Place rolls in oven
7:30	Add potatoes, onions, and carrots to beef stock
7:40	Add cabbage to beef stock
8:00	Dinner is served

† A dry Burgundy wine; serve at cool room temperature (65°)

* May be prepared in the morning or the night before and refrigerated

---

FOR 4	FOR 6	INGREDIENTS
lrg	lrg	Utensils: deep kettle
9 × 9 in	9 × 12 in	baking pan
3 lb	5 lb	corned beef brisket, center cut
4	6	potatoes
4	6	small white onions
6	8	carrots
½ sm hd	1 sm hd	cabbage

INSTRUCTIONS

CORNED BEEF DINNER

Place the corned beef brisket in a deep kettle, cover with water, and bring to a boil. Reduce heat, cover, and simmer for 3 hours (for 3-pound brisket) or 4 hours (for 5-pound brisket). About 1 hour before serving, prepare the potatoes, onions, and carrots by peeling them and cutting into large pieces. / / About 40 minutes before serving, remove brisket from water reserve liquid in kettle, place in pan, and heat in preheated 200° oven. Bring reserved beef stock to a boil and add the potatoes, onions, and carrots. Lower heat and simmer, covered, for 10 minutes. Clean cabbage and cut into large wedges, add to other vegetables, and simmer for another 15 minutes.

13

TOMATO AND LETTUCE SALAD

FOR 4	FOR 6	INGREDIENTS
med	lrg	Utensil: salad bowl
1 med hd	1 lrg hd	lettuce
1 med	1 lrg	tomato
½ tsp	¾ tsp	dill weed

Wash lettuce and drain well. Cut the tomato into small wedges. Break lettuce into the salad bowl, add tomato wedges and sprinkle with dill weed. Cover and refrigerate until ready to serve. / / Toss salad with the salad dressing just before serving.

Dressing

FOR 4	FOR 6	INGREDIENTS
½ pt	½ pt	Utensil: glass jar
3 tbl	5 tbl	salad oil
1½ tbl	2 tbl	wine vinegar
1 sm	1 lrg	crushed garlic cloves
¼ tsp	⅓ tsp	salt
⅛ tsp	⅛ tsp	black pepper

Mix the salad oil, wine vinegar, garlic cloves, salt, and pepper in a glass jar and refrigerate until ready to serve.

SOUR DOUGH ROLLS

FOR 4	FOR 6	INGREDIENTS
4	6	sour dough rolls

Wrap each roll in aluminum foil. / / Heat for 30 minutes at 200°.

PINEAPPLE FILLED CAKE
Cake

	lrg	Utensils: mixing bowl
	2 9 in	cake pans
	1 pkg	white cake mix
	1⅓ C	water
	2	eggs

Preheat oven to 350°. In the mixing bowl, combine the cake mix, water, and eggs. Blend until smooth, then beat for 2 minutes. Pour into greased cake pans and bake for 25 to 30 minutes. Let cool, then gently split each layer in half. Spread the filling between each layer and assemble the cake. Spread frosting and keep refrigerated until ready to serve.

Filling

	1 qt	Utensil: saucepan
	1 pkg	vanilla pudding mix, 3¼-oz
	1½ C	milk
	½ C	drained crushed pineapple, 8½-ounce can

Prepare the pudding mix according to the directions on the package, *but reduce the milk to 1 ½ cups.* Chill pudding. Drain the crushed pineapple, reserving the liquid for Frosting. Fold in pineapple. Spread mixture between cake layers.

Frosting

	sm	Utensil: mixing bowl
	⅓ C	butter or margarine
	4 C	sifted powdered sugar
approx ¼ C		drained, crushed pineapple (left over from can used in filling)
approx 3 tbl		pineapple syrup (from can of crushed pineapple)

In the mixing bowl, blend the soft butter with one-half of the powdered sugar. Add the remaining powdered sugar and the drained, crushed pineapple. Add enough of the pineapple syrup to make mixture spreadable. Spread over sides and top of cake.

15

menu 6

TIMETABLE

*5:00 pm	Prepare and bake Apple Nut Dessert
6:20	Prepare and bake squash at 400°
7:00	Prepare Honey-Curry Chicken
7:15	Bake chicken
7:20	Prepare squash filling
7:40	Return squash to oven
7:40	Cook Brown Rice
7:45	Prepare rum sauce
8:00	Dinner is served

† A dry Burgundy wine; serve at cool room temperature (65°)

* May be prepared in the morning or the night before and refrigerated

---

FOR 4	FOR 6	INGREDIENTS
9 × 13 in	10 × 14 in	Utensils: baking pan
2 sm	2 sm	mixing bowls
3 lb	5 lb	chicken fryer parts
1 med	1 lrg	onion
1 tsp	1½ tsp	salt
½ tsp	¾ tsp	pepper
¾ tsp	1 tsp	ground ginger
2 tbl	3 tbl	butter or margarine
¾ C	1 C	dry white wine
¼ C	⅓ C	honey
2 tsp	1 tbl	curry powder

INSTRUCTIONS

HONEY-CURRY CHICKEN

Clean and dry the chicken parts. Thinly slice the onion and arrange on the bottom of a well-greased baking pan. Lay the chicken parts over the onion slices, skin side up. In a mixing bowl, combine salt, pepper, and ground ginger. Sprinkle spices over the chicken, dot with butter, pour wine over top, and bake in preheated 400° oven for 45 minutes. In a mixing bowl, combine the honey and curry powder. During the last 20 minutes of baking, baste chicken with honey-and-curry mixture several times. Pour the drippings from the pan over the rice when ready to serve.

16

BROWN RICE

FOR 4	FOR 6	INGREDIENTS
1 qt	2 qt	Utensil: saucepan
1½ C	2 C	water
½ tsp	¾ tsp	salt
1 C	1½ C	brown rice

Bring water to a rolling boil in a saucepan. Add salt. Stir in rice. Reduce heat, cover tightly, and steam for 15 minutes. Keep covered until ready to serve.

ACORN SQUASH WITH PINEAPPLE

FOR 4	FOR 6	INGREDIENTS
8 × 8 in	8 × 12 in	Utensils: baking pan
med	med	mixing bowl
2	3	acorn squash
4 tsp	2 tbl	butter or margarine
4 tsp	2 tbl	dry sherry wine
4 tsp	2 tbl	brown sugar, firmly packed
3 tbl	4 tbl	butter or margarine
⅓ C	½ C	drained, crushed pineapple, 8½-oz can
⅛ tsp	¼ tsp	nutmeg
¾ tsp	1¼ tsp	salt

Cut each squash in half and scoop out the seeds and fibers. Place squash halves into a greased baking pan. Add 1 teaspoon each of butter, wine, and brown sugar to the center of each half. Cover and bake at 400° for 45 minutes, or until tender. When baked, scoop the cooked squash out of the shells into a mixing bowl, leaving the wall of the squash shells about ¼ inch thick. Mash the squash and combine with the remaining butter, pineapple, nutmeg, and salt, beating until well blended. Spoon mixture back into shells and return to oven at 400° for 20 minutes.

FOR 4	FOR 6	INGREDIENTS

APPLE NUT DESSERT

	med	Utensils: mixing bowl
	9 × 13 in	baking pan
	½ C	butter or margarine
	2 C	sugar
	2	eggs
	2 C	flour
	2 tsp	baking soda
	½ tsp	salt
	½ tsp	nutmeg
	½ tsp	cinnamon
	1½ C	chopped nuts
	3 C	finely chopped tart apples

INSTRUCTIONS

Preheat oven to 325°. In a mixing bowl, cream butter and sugar until light and fluffy. Add eggs, one at a time, beating until blended. Sift flour onto a piece of waxed paper, measure, then sift again with baking soda, salt, nutmeg, and cinnamon. Add to the egg mixture, beating until smooth. Stir in the nuts and the finely chopped peeled apples. Spread into a greased baking pan and bake at 325° for 45 minutes, or until cake springs back when touched lightly in center.

Rum Sauce

FOR 4	FOR 6	INGREDIENTS
1 qt	1 qt	Utensil: saucepan
⅓ C	½ C	sugar
3 tbl	¼ C	butter or margarine
3 tbl	¼ C	light cream
1½ tbl	2 tbl	rum, light or dark

Combine sugar, butter, and light cream in a saucepan and simmer for 10 minutes. Stir in the rum, then pour, while hot, over the cake.

menu 7

TIMETABLE

*5:00 pm	Prepare Fruit Cocktail Pie
*6:15	Prepare salad and salad dressing
*6:30	Prepare Lima Bean Casserole
7:15	Bake Lima Bean Casserole at 350°
7:30	Prepare Apple Muffins
7:40	Heat oven to 400°
7:45	Remove Lima Bean Casserole
7:45	Bake Muffins
7:55	Add avocado to salad, add dressing, and toss
8:00	Dinner is served

† A dry Burgundy wine; serve at cool room temperature (65°)

* May be prepared in the morning or the night before and refrigerated

---

FOR 4	FOR 6	INGREDIENTS

INSTRUCTIONS

FRUIT COCKTAIL PIE

	9 in	Utensils: pie pan
	med	mixing bowl
	32	vanilla wafers
	2 C	commercial sour cream
	½ C	sugar
	1 tsp	vanilla extract
	1 can	fruit cocktail, 1-lb. 14-oz can

Line the pie pan with vanilla wafers. In the mixing bowl, combine sour cream, sugar, and vanilla extract. Drain the fruit cocktail and fold fruit into mixture. Pour fruit mixture into pie pan over vanilla wafers. Bake at 350° for 25 minutes. Chill before serving.

LIMA BEAN CASSEROLE

FOR 4	FOR 6	INGREDIENTS
1 qt	1 qt	Utensils: saucepan
12 in	12 in	skillet
2 qt	3 qt	baking dish
1 C	1 C	water
¼ tsp	¼ tsp	salt
1 pkg	1 pkg	frozen lima beans
3 tbl	3 tbl	olive oil
1 C	1½ C	chopped onions
½ C	¾ C	chopped green peppers
1	2	minced garlic cloves
1 lb	1½ lb	ground beef
¾ tsp	1 tsp	salt
7 oz	8¾ oz	canned whole-kernel corn
6 oz	6 oz	canned tomato paste
¼ C	⅓ C	dry sherry wine
3 tbl	¼ C	dry bread crumbs
2 tsp	3 tsp	grated Parmesan cheese

In a saucepan, bring water to a vigorous boil. Add salt and lima beans. Cover and bring back to a boil quickly. Reduce heat and cook covered for 10 to 12 minutes. Drain. Heat the olive oil in a skillet, add chopped onions, chopped green peppers, and minced garlic cloves. Sauté for 5 minutes. Add ground beef and cook until browned. Drain off excess grease. Add salt, drained corn, tomato paste, sherry wine, and lima beans. Mix together well and place mixture in baking dish. Sprinkle with dry bread crumbs and grated Parmesan cheese. / / Bake for 30 minutes in preheated 350° oven.

TOSSED SALAD

FOR 4	FOR 6	INGREDIENTS
med	lrg	Utensil: salad bowl
1 med hd	1 lrg hd	lettuce
2 slices	3 slices	red onion slices
½	1	avocado (if available)

Wash and drain lettuce and break into salad bowl. Add onion slices, cover, and refrigerate until ready to serve. / / Just before serving peel and slice avocado into salad, add dressing, and toss.

FOR 4	FOR 6	INGREDIENTS
½ pt	½ pt	Utensil: glass jar
3 tbl	5 tbl	olive oil
1½ tbl	2 tbl	wine vinegar
¾ tsp	1 tsp	salt
⅛ tsp	¼ tsp	pepper
2 tbl	3 tbl	grated Romano cheese
	med	Utensils: mixing bowl
	sm, lrg	muffin tins
	2 C	flour
	3 tsp	baking powder
	1 C	chopped apples
	1 C	sugar
	1	egg
	3 tbl	melted butter or margarine
	⅓ tsp	salt
	¾ C	milk
	⅓ C	chopped nuts
	⅓ C	brown sugar, firmly packed
	1 tsp	cinnamon

INSTRUCTIONS

Dressing

In a glass jar, combine the olive oil, wine vinegar, salt, and pepper. Refrigerate. / / Just before serving, shake dressing in jar vigorously, add to salad, sprinkle grated Romano cheese on salad, and toss.

APPLE MUFFINS

In a mixing bowl, mix the flour and baking powder. Peel and chop apples. Add peeled, chopped apples, plus sugar, egg, butter, salt, and milk. Mix together until barely mixed. Place in greased muffin tins and top with combined nuts, brown sugar, and cinnamon. Bake at 400° for 15 minutes. Makes 18 muffins.

menu 8

Cabernet†
Liver and Onions
Green Bean Casserole
Perfect Potatoes
Caramel-Coconut Squares

TIMETABLE

*6:00 pm	Prepare and bake Caramel-Coconut Squares
*6:45	Prepare Green Bean Casserole and cover
7:00	Prepare Liver and Onions
7:40	Bake Green Bean Casserole at 350°
7:40	Prepare potatoes
7:55	Reheat liver
8:00	Dinner is served

† A dry Claret wine; serve at cool room temperature (65°)

* May be prepared in the morning or the night before and refrigerated

FOR 4	FOR 6	INGREDIENTS
10 in	12 in	Utensil: skillet
1½ lb	2 lb	calves liver
1 lrg	2 med	onion
1½ tbl	2 tbl	butter or margarine
1 tsp	1 tsp	salt
¼ tsp	¼ tsp	pepper
¼ C	⅓ C	dry white wine
2 tbl	3 tbl	minced parsley

INSTRUCTIONS

LIVER AND ONIONS

Wash and remove membranes from liver. Cut into thin slices and then into strips. Peel and slice onion into thin slices. Melt the butter in skillet, add onions, cover, and cook over low heat for 15 minutes. Add liver and cook for 3 to 4 minutes over medium heat. Add salt and pepper, stir in white wine, and bring liquids to a boil. Turn off heat, sprinkle with parsley, and cover until ready to serve.

GREEN BEAN CASSEROLE

FOR 4	INGREDIENTS	INSTRUCTIONS
2 qt	Utensil: baking dish	Drain green beans and carrots and place in casserole baking dish. Drain and slice water chestnuts into casserole. Mix the cream of mushroom soup into the vegetables. / / Top the casserole with chow mein noodles and bake, uncovered, at 350° for 20 minutes.
2 cans	whole-cut green beans, 15½-oz can	
1 can	sliced carrots, 8½-oz can	
1 can	sliced water chestnuts, 5-oz can	
1 can	cream of mushroom soup	
1 can	chow mein noodles, 3-oz can	

PERFECT POTATOES

FOR 4	FOR 6	INGREDIENTS	INSTRUCTIONS
2 qt	2 qt	Utensils: saucepan	Bring water, butter, and salt to a boil in large saucepan. Remove from heat, add milk, and stir in potato flakes with a fork until moistened. Let stand until liquid is absorbed (about ½ minute). In a small saucepan, heat sour cream. Then add mustard, salt, and sugar. Stir the sour cream mixture into potatoes. Add onions and stir thoroughly. Sprinkle with paprika and keep covered until ready to serve.
1 qt	1 qt	saucepan	
1¼ C	1¾ C	water	
2 tbl	3 tbl	butter or margarine	
½ tsp	¾ tsp	salt	
⅓ C	½ C	milk	
1½ C	2 C	instant mashed potato flakes	
½ C	¾ C	commercial sour cream	
2 tsp	1 tbl	prepared mustard	
½ tsp	¾ tsp	salt	
½ tsp	¾ tsp	sugar	
2 tbl	3 tbl	chopped green onions	
¼ tsp	⅓ tsp	paprika	

23

CARAMEL-COCONUT SQUARES

FOR 4	INGREDIENTS
9 × 13 in	Utensil: baking pan
½ C	butter or margarine
1 C	graham cracker crumbs
1 C	flaked coconut
6 oz	butterscotch chips
6 oz	chocolate chips
1 C	chopped pecans
1 can	sweetened condensed milk, 15-oz can

Place butter in baking pan and heat on stove until melted. Remove pan from heat and place the remaining ingredients (in layers) into baking pan, without stirring. Bake in preheated oven at 350° for 30 to 40 minutes. Cut into squares while still warm.

---

menu 9

Grenache Rosé†
Liver in Tomato Sauce
Steamed Rice
Zucchini and Cheese
Grapefruit-Avocado Salad
Mocha Raisin Nut Bars

TIMETABLE

*2:30 pm	Chill wine
*2:30	Prepare Grapefruit-Avocado Salad
*6:00	Prepare Mocha Raisin Nut Bars
7:00	Scrub and slice zucchini squash
7:10	Prepare Liver in Tomato Sauce
7:35	Cook rice
7:40	Cook zucchini
7:55	Remove Grapefruit-Avocado Salad from mold
8:00	Dinner is served

† A light, dry rosé wine; serve chilled (45°)   * May be prepared in the morning or the night before and refrigerated

LIVER IN TOMATO SAUCE

FOR 4	FOR 6	INGREDIENTS
10 in	12 in	Utensil: frying pan or skillet
1 lb	1½ lb	beef liver
1 med	1 lrg	chopped onion
2	3	minced garlic cloves
3 tbl	4 tbl	cooking oil
1 lb	1 lb 12 oz	canned tomatoes
1 tsp	1½ tsp	sugar
½ tsp	1 tsp	salt
½ tsp	1 tsp	pepper

Rinse liver under running water, remove membranes, and dry with paper towel. Slice liver into ½ inch strips and set aside. In a frying pan or skillet, sauté the onion and garlic in oil until lightly browned. Slide the onion-garlic mixture to one side and add the liver strips to the pan. Cook for 5 minutes, turning everything over once. Place the onion-garlic mixture on top of liver; add tomatoes, sugar, salt, and pepper; Simmer for 20 minutes, covered. Serve over rice.

STEAMED RICE

FOR 4	FOR 6	INGREDIENTS
1 qt	2 qt	Utensil: saucepan
2 C	3 C	water
½ tsp	¾ tsp	salt
1 tsp	1½ tsp	shortening
1 C	1½ C	long-grain white rice

Bring water to a boil in a saucepan. Add salt and shortening. Slowly add rice, shaking pan to level rice grains. Turn heat to low, cover tightly, and cook 20 to 25 minutes, or until all liquid is absorbed. Keep covered until ready to serve.

ZUCCHINI AND CHEESE

FOR 4	FOR 6	INGREDIENTS
10 in	12 in	Utensil: covered skillet
¼ C	⅓ C	butter or margarine
2 lb	3 lb	zucchini squash
¼ tsp	½ tsp	garlic salt
¼ tsp	½ tsp	salt
⅛ tsp	¼ tsp	pepper
2 tbl	3 tbl	grated Parmesan cheese

Wash and slice zucchini. Melt butter in skillet, add sliced zucchini, garlic salt, salt, and pepper. Cover and simmer over low heat for 10 minutes. Sprinkle with cheese and simmer 5 minutes longer.

FOR 4	FOR 6	INGREDIENTS	INSTRUCTIONS

GRAPEFRUIT-AVOCADO SALAD

FOR 4	FOR 6	INGREDIENTS	
1 qt	2 qt	Utensil: gelatine mold	
1 pkg	2 pkg	lime gelatine	
1 C	2 C	boiling water	
8 oz	1 lb	canned grapefruit	
½	1	avocado	

Empty gelatine into a mold, add boiling water, and stir until the gelatine is completely dissolved. Combine juice drained from the can of grapefruit and enough cold water to total 1 cup (to serve four) or 2 cups (to serve six). Stir the mixture well. Peel the avocado and slice it into the gelatine mixture. Add the grapefruit and chill until firmly set.

MOCHA RAISIN NUT BARS

	med	Utensils: mixing bowl	
	9 × 13 in	baking pan	
	2 C	white cake mix	
	½ C	cold coffee	
	1	egg	
	½ C	chopped raisins	
	½ C	chopped nuts	

Combine cake mix, cold coffee, and egg in a mixing bowl. Mix as directed on the cake mix package. (Beating procedure varies with each brand.) Stir in the chopped raisins and nuts. Pour batter into a greased baking dish or pan. Bake as directed on cake mix package. While cake is still warm, spread the glaze over the top. Let cool. / / Just before serving, cut the cake into about 30 bars.

Coffee Glaze

	sm	Utensil: mixing bowl	
	1½ C	powdered sugar	
	1 tbl	melted butter or margarine	
	⅛ C	cold coffee	
	1 tsp	vanilla extract	

Measure the powdered sugar into mixing bowl. Gradually add the melted butter, cold coffee, and vanilla extract, beating until smooth.

menu 10

Barbera†
Meat Loaf
Buttered Baked Potatoes
Orange Glazed Carrots
Pineapple and Cottage Cheese Salad
Ice Cream Cake

TIMETABLE
*5:00 pm   Prepare Ice Cream Cake, except for strawberries
*6:30   Prepare meat loaf
*6:55   Scrub potatoes
7:00   Place meat loaf and potatoes in oven at 350°
7:00   Prepare carrots
7:45   Prepare salad
8:00   Dinner is served

† A dry Burgundy wine; serve at cool room temperature (65°)

* May be prepared in the morning or the night before and refrigerated

FOR 4	FOR 6	INGREDIENTS
lrg	lrg	Utensils: mixing bowl
10 × 5 × 3	10 × 5 × 3	loaf pan
1	1	egg
4 slices	5 slices	bread
1 lb	1½ lb	lean ground beef
1 sm	1 med	chopped onion
1 tsp	1½ tsp	salt
½ tsp	¾ tsp	pepper
1 tsp	1½ tsp	Worcestershire sauce
½ tsp	½ tsp	oregano
1 can	1 can	cream of mushroom soup
sm	sm	Utensil: mixing bowl
½ C	½ C	catsup
2 tbl	2 tbl	sugar
2 tbl	2 tbl	cider vinegar

INSTRUCTIONS

MEAT LOAF

In a mixing bowl, whip the egg slightly with a fork. Break the bread slices into small chunks into the mixing bowl. Add the remainder of the ingredients and mix well until blended. Place mixture into loaf pan, patting it down evenly.

Sauce

Combine catsup, sugar, and vinegar in a mixing bowl and pour the mixture over the meat loaf. Refrigerate until ready to bake. / / Bake in preheated 350° oven for 1 hour.

27

BUTTERED BAKED POTATOES

FOR 4	FOR 6	INGREDIENTS
4	6	medium baking potatoes

Scrub potatoes well. / / Place on a sheet of aluminum foil in oven. Bake at 350° for 1 hour. Serve with butter, salt, and pepper.

ORANGE GLAZED CARROTS

FOR 4	FOR 6	INGREDIENTS
2 qt	3 qt	Utensil: saucepan
6 lrg	8 lrg	carrots
¾ C	1 C	water
¾ tsp	1 tsp	salt
3 tbl	¼ C	sugar
¼ tsp	½ tsp	salt
1½ tsp	2 tsp	flour
1 tsp	1½ tsp	grated orange peel
⅓ C	½ C	orange juice
1 tbl	1½ tbl	butter or margarine

Clean and slice carrots as desired. Bring water to a boil in the saucepan. Add salt and carrots. Cover tightly and bring back to a boil. Reduce heat at once and simmer for 10 to 15 minutes, or until carrots are tender. Drain. Remove carrots from pan temporarily. Mix the sugar, salt, flour, and orange peel in the saucepan, add the orange juice and cook over medium heat until mixture thickens. Add butter and cooked carrots. Stir well and keep covered until ready to serve.

PINEAPPLE AND COTTAGE CHEESE SALAD

FOR 4	FOR 6	INGREDIENTS
4	6	canned pineapple slices
4	6	lettuce leaves
4 tbl	6 tbl	cottage cheese
4	6	maraschino cherries

Using individual serving plates, place a slice of pineapple on a lettuce leaf for each serving. Add a tablespoon of cottage cheese in the center of each pineapple slice and top with a maraschino cherry.

FOR 4	FOR 6	INGREDIENTS	INSTRUCTIONS

ICE CREAM CAKE

FOR 4	FOR 6	INGREDIENTS
2 8-in		Utensils: cake pans
	med	mixing bowl
2 sm		mixing bowls
2 C		white cake mix
⅔ C		water
1		egg
1 pt		vanilla ice cream
½ pt		heavy cream
1 box		strawberries

Preheat oven to 350°. Generously grease and flour one cake pan. In the medium mixing bowl, combine cake mix, water, and egg. Mix and bake as directed on the package. Fill the other cake pan with ice cream, placing it in the freezer. When cake is baked, let cool, then slice cake into two thin layers. Place one thin layer on a serving plate, remove the ice cream layer from its pan and place the frozen ice cream layer on top of the thin cake layer. Cover the ice cream with the second thin layer of cake and return to the freezer. Whip the cream in one small mixing bowl, remove cake from freezer, frost the cake with whipped cream, and return cake to freezer. Clean the strawberries into the other small mixing bowl and refrigerate until ready to serve the dessert. / / Decorate the top of the cake with strawberries just before serving.

---

menu II

Cabernet†
Meatballs and Rice
Green Peas
Broiled Tomatoes
Stuffed Pear Salad
Crunchy Caramel Treats

TIMETABLE

*6:15 pm	Prepare Crunchy Caramel Treats
6:45	Prepare Stuffed Pear Salad
7:00	Prepare tomatoes for broiling
*7:15	Prepare Meatballs and Rice
7:40	Preheat broiler
7:50	Broil tomatoes
7:50	Cook green peas
8:00	Dinner is served

† A dry Claret wine; serve at cool room temperature (65°)

* May be prepared in the morning or the night before and refrigerated

MEATBALLS AND RICE

FOR 4	FOR 6	INGREDIENTS
med	med	Utensils: mixing bowl
10 in	12 in	skillet
1	1	egg
1 lb	1½ lb	ground beef
¾ C	1 C	bread crumbs
½ C	¾ C	milk
¾ C	1 C	chopped onion
2 tsp	1 tbl	salt
2 tbl	3 tbl	butter or margarine
1 C	1½ C	pineapple tidbits
1 C	1½ C	pineapple syrup
1 C	1½ C	precooked rice
¾ C	1 C	chopped green pepper
¼ C	⅓ C	catsup

In a mixing bowl, beat egg slightly, combine with ground beef, bread crumbs, milk, one-half of the chopped onion, and one-half of the salt. Mix well and form into 2-inch meatballs. / / In skillet, brown meatballs in butter. Drain pineapple tidbits, reserving required syrup (add water to total required amount, if necessary). Add the pineapple and syrup to the skillet. Add the remaining onion and salt, plus the rice, chopped green pepper, and catsup. Bring to a boil, then reduce heat, cover, and simmer for 10 minutes.

STUFFED PEAR SALAD

FOR 4	FOR 6	INGREDIENTS
sm	sm	Utensil: mixing bowl
4	6	lettuce leaves
2	3	pears
¾ C	1 C	cottage cheese
⅓ C	½ C	chopped dates
3 tbl	¼ C	chopped pecans

Rinse and drain lettuce leaves and arrange on serving plates. Peel pears, cut in half lengthwise, and core the halves. Arrange pears on lettuce leaves. In mixing bowl, combine cottage cheese, chopped dates, and chopped nuts. Spoon the mixture onto pear halves. Cover and refrigerate until ready to serve.

FOR 4	FOR 6	INGREDIENTS	

GREEN PEAS

FOR 4	FOR 6	INGREDIENTS
1 qt	2 qt	Utensil: saucepan
½ C	¾ C	water
1 pkg	2 pkg	frozen peas, 10-oz pkg
½ tsp	1 tsp	salt
1 tsp	2 tsp	sugar
1 tbl	2 tbl	butter or margarine
¼ tsp	½ tsp	salt
⅛ tsp	¼ tsp	pepper

Bring water to a boil in saucepan, add frozen peas, salt, and sugar. Bring back to a boil, cover, and cook gently over reduced heat for 4 to 6 minutes, or until tender. Drain, stir in butter, salt, and pepper. Keep covered until ready to serve.

BROILED TOMATOES

FOR 4	FOR 6	INGREDIENTS
sm	med	Utensil: cookie sheet
2	3	tomatoes
¼ tsp	⅓ tsp	salt
⅛ tsp	⅛ tsp	pepper
⅛ tsp	⅛ tsp	oregano
⅛ tsp	⅛ tsp	thyme
¼ C	⅓ C	shredded jack cheese

Wash and cut tomatoes in half. Set the halves on a cookie sheet, sprinkle with salt, pepper, oregano, thyme, and shredded Jack cheese. Broil for 10 minutes in preheated broiler.

CRUNCHY CARAMEL TREATS

	INGREDIENTS
2 qt	Utensil: double boiler
6 oz	chocolate chips
6 oz	butterscotch chips
1 C	peanuts
1 C	canned chow mein noodles

Place the chocolate chips and butterscotch chips in double boiler and heat until melted. Mix in the peanuts and chow mein noodles. Spoon out about ½ cup of mixture for each serving and let cool on a piece of waxed paper.

menu 12

Zinfandel†
Mexican-Style Chili
Guacamole Salad
Warm Tortillas
Lemon Whip

TIMETABLE
*6:00 pm   Prepare Lemon Whip and refrigerate
 6:30   Prepare Guacamole Salad
*7:00   Prepare chili casserole
 7:30   Bake chili casserole
 7:45   Warm tortillas
 8:00   Dinner is served

† A dry Claret wine; serve at cool room temperature (65°)   * May be prepared in the morning or the night before and refrigerated

FOR 4	FOR 6	INGREDIENTS

INSTRUCTIONS

MEXICAN-STYLE CHILI

FOR 4	FOR 6	INGREDIENTS
1½ qt	1½ qt	Utensil: baking dish
1 lb	1½ lb	lean ground beef
1 med	1 lrg	chopped onion
15 oz	15 oz	canned chili, without beans
1 C	1½ C	commercial sour cream
8¾ oz	8¾ oz	canned whole-kernel corn
7 oz	7 oz	canned green chili sauce
1 C	1½ C	grated Cheddar cheese

Crumble ½ of the ground beef into a baking dish, sprinkle with ½ of the chopped onion, spoon on a layer of ½ of the chili, then a layer of ½ of the sour cream. Drain the corn and sprinkle ½ of the kernels into casserole. Spoon on a layer of ½ of the green chili. Repeat the layer process above with the remainder of the ingredients. Top the final layer with grated Cheddar cheese and refrigerate until ready to serve. / / Bake in preheated 350° oven for 30 minutes.

GUACAMOLE SALAD

FOR 4	FOR 6	INGREDIENTS
med	med	Utensil: mixing bowl
1 lrg	2 med	sliced avocados
2 tbl	3 tbl	commercial sour cream
¾ tsp	1 tsp	lemon juice
1 med	1 lrg	tomato
1 tbl	2 tbl	Spanish onion
½ tsp	¾ tsp	salt
3 drops	4 drops	Tabasco sauce
4	6	lettuce leaves

Clean and slice avocado into mixing bowl, or blender. Add the commercial sour cream, lemon juice, finely diced tomato, finely diced onion, salt, and Tabasco sauce. Beat mixture until smooth. Serve on lettuce leaves on individual serving dishes.

WARM TORTILLAS‡

FOR 4	FOR 6	INGREDIENTS
10 in	10 in	Utensil: skillet
8	12	prepared tortillas
2 tbl	3 tbl	butter
⅛ tsp	⅛ tsp	garlic salt

Warm the prepared tortillas in pan (wrapped in damp cloth towel) until warm and still soft. Spread each lightly with butter, sprinkle with garlic salt, and roll them up tightly. Stack in a warm towel to serve.

‡ If not available locally, replace with hot bakery rolls.

LEMON WHIP

2 qt		Utensils: saucepan
sm, med		mixing bowls
4		eggs
½ C		sugar
1 tbl		grated lemon rind
½ C		lemon juice
6 tbl		Chablis wine
¼ cake		sponge cake

Separate the eggs, placing the whites in a small mixing bowl and the yolks in the saucepan. Beat the egg yolks with the sugar until thick. Stir in the lemon rind, lemon juice, and wine and cook over low heat until mixture starts to bubble. Beat egg whites until stiff and fold them into the saucepan mixture. Cook for 2 minutes, stirring gently. Pour into a medium mixing bowl or serving bowl and refrigerate until ready to serve. / / When ready to serve, cut sponge cake into strips and spoon lemon whip over cake.

---

menu 13

Gamay†
Mushroom Salisbury Steak
Peas
Gingered Carrots and Pineapple
Potato Whip
Mocha Walnut Torte

† A dry Burgundy wine; serve at cool room temperature (65°)

TIMETABLE
*5:00 pm   Prepare Mocha Walnut Torte and refrigerate
6:30   Prepare Mushroom Salisbury Steak and cover
7:10   Cook potatoes for Potato Whip
7:15   Prepare Gingered Carrots and Pineapple
7:40   Cook peas, drain, and cover
7:45   Prepare Potato Whip
7:55   Reheat meat
8:00   Dinner is served

* May be prepared in the morning or the night before and refrigerated

MUSHROOM SALISBURY STEAK 1568761

FOR 4	FOR 6	INGREDIENTS
10 in	12 in	Utensil: covered skillet
1 lb	1½ lb	ground chuck
½ tsp	¾ tsp	salt
¼ tsp	⅓ tsp	ground pepper
¼ lb	⅓ lb	sliced fresh mushrooms
2 tbl	3 tbl	butter or margarine
2 tbl	3 tbl	flour
1 tsp	1½ tsp	curry powder
1 C	1½ C	water
1	2	beef bouillon cubes

Mix meat, salt, and pepper and shape into meat patties. Pan fry the patties in skillet for 2 to 3 minutes on each side, or until done. Remove patties from skillet and drain off grease. Clean and slice the mushrooms. Sauté mushrooms in butter in the skillet for 5 minutes. Remove the mushrooms from the skillet and set aside. Add flour and curry powder to skillet, heat over low flame, and slowly add water, stirring well to keep the mixture smooth. Crush bouillon cubes in the hot liquid, replace meat patties, cover them with the sautéed mushrooms, and simmer for 2 minutes. Cover the skillet and reheat meat just before serving.

POTATO WHIP

FOR 4	FOR 6	INGREDIENTS
3 qt	4 qt	Utensils: saucepan
sm	sm	saucepan
4 med	6 med	potatoes
¼ C	⅓ C	milk
2 tbl	3 tbl	butter or margarine
¾ tsp	1 tsp	salt

Cook peeled potatoes in boiling water until tender (25 to 30 minutes). In a small saucepan, heat milk. When potatoes are done, drain the water and mash the potatoes in the saucepan. Add hot milk, butter, and salt. Beat until fluffy.

PEAS

FOR 4	FOR 6	INGREDIENTS
1 qt	2 qt	Utensil: saucepan
½ C	1 C	water
1 pkg	2 pkg	frozen peas, 10-oz pkg
1 tsp	2 tsp	sugar
½ tsp	1 tsp	salt
1 tbl	2 tbl	butter or margarine

Bring water to a boil in a saucepan and add frozen peas, sugar, and salt. Bring back to a boil, cover, and cook gently on reduced heat for 4 to 6 minutes, or until tender. Drain, stir in the butter, and cover until ready to serve.

GINGERED CARROTS AND PINEAPPLE

FOR 4	FOR 6	INGREDIENTS
2 qt	2 qt	Utensil: saucepan
5 med	7 med	carrots
⅓ C	½ C	pineapple juice
1	1	chicken bouillon cube
1 tbl.	1½ tbl	chopped candied ginger
8½ oz	13½ oz	canned pineapple tidbits

Wash, peel, and slice carrots. Heat the pineapple juice (drained from the canned tidbits) in the saucepan. Add bouillon cube, carrots, and chopped candied ginger. Cover and cook for 20 to 25 minutes. Add pineapple tidbits, stir gently, and cover until ready to serve.

MOCHA WALNUT TORTE

FOR 4	FOR 6	INGREDIENTS
	med	Utensils: mixing bowl
	2 9-in	round cake pans
	1 lb	brownie mix
	2	eggs
	¼ C	water
	½ C	chopped nuts

Preheat oven to 350°. In the medium mixing bowl, mix together the brownie mix, eggs, water, and nuts. Pour mixture into two greased cake pans and bake for 20 minutes at 350°. Let the layers cool before adding the icing.

Icing

FOR 4	FOR 6	INGREDIENTS
	sm	Utensil: mixing bowl
	1½ C	heavy cream
	½ C	brown sugar, firmly packed
	1 tbl	instant coffee

In a small mixing bowl, whip the cream until it begins to thicken. Gradually add the brown sugar and instant coffee, beating until it becomes a good spreading consistency. Ice the cooled layers, one on top of the other. Chill well before serving.

---

menu 14

Pinot Chardonnay†
Orange Pork Chops
Applesauce
Grecian Beans
Honey Muffins
Date Nut Cake

TIMETABLE

*5:00 pm	Refrigerate apple sauce
*5:00	Chill wine
*5:00	Prepare and bake Date Nut Cake
6:30	Prepare Orange Pork Chops
7:00	Cook Pork Chops
7:10	Prepare Honey Muffins
7:20	Preheat oven to 400°
7:30	Bake Honey Muffins
7:30	Prepare Grecian Beans
8:00	Dinner is served

† A dry Chablis wine; serve chilled (45°)

* May be prepared in the morning or the night before and refrigerated

FOR 4	FOR 6	INGREDIENTS	INSTRUCTIONS

ORANGE PORK CHOPS

FOR 4	FOR 6	
10 in	12 in	Utensils: skillet
1 qt	1 qt	saucepan
1 tbl	2 tbl	cooking oil
4	6	large pork chops
1 tbl	1½ tbl	flour
¾ tsp	1 tsp	salt
¼ tsp	⅓ tsp	pepper
2 tbl	3 tbl	sugar
1 tbl	1½ tbl	cornstarch
⅛ tsp	¼ tsp	allspice
1¼ C	2 C	hot water
2 tbl	3 tbl	lemon juice
¼ C	⅓ C	orange juice
¼ C	⅓ C	raisins
8	12	orange segments, peeled

Heat oil in skillet and add pork chops. Sprinkle with flour, salt, and pepper and rub in with fork. Brown the chops on both sides. In a saucepan, combine the sugar, cornstarch, and allspice. Gradually stir in hot water, continue stirring, and cook until thick and smooth. Stir in lemon juice, orange juice, and raisins. Cut the membranes away from orange segments and place 2 segments on each pork chop. Pour sauce over all and cook slowly, uncovered, for 1 hour. To serve, ladle a spoonful of sauce over each chop.

APPLESAUCE

FOR 4	FOR 6	
1 can	2 cans	canned applesauce, 1-lb can

Refrigerate canned applesauce and serve well chilled.

GRECIAN BEANS

FOR 4	FOR 6	INGREDIENTS
8 in	8 in	Utensil: skillet
3 tbl	¼ C	salad oil
½ C	1 C	chopped onion
1 lb	1 lb 12 oz	canned French-style green beans
½ C	¾ C	liquid drained from green beans
½ tsp	¾ tsp	salt
¼ tsp	⅓ tsp	pepper
3 tbl	¼ C	tomato juice

Heat the oil in the skillet, add onions, and brown lightly. Add green beans, measured green-bean liquid, salt, pepper, and tomato juice. Simmer for 20 minutes.

HONEY MUFFINS

med		Utensils: mixing bowl
lrg		muffin tin
1		egg
¼ C		melted butter or margarine
1 C		milk
4 tbl		honey
2 C		flour
2 tsp		baking powder
1 tsp		salt

Beat the egg in a mixing bowl. Add melted butter, milk, and honey. Sift flour onto a piece of waxed paper, measure, and sift into the bowl together with the baking powder and salt. Mix just enough to moisten. Fill greased muffin tins half full and bake in preheated 400° oven for 30 minutes. Makes 12 muffins.

DATE NUT CAKE

FOR 4	FOR 6	INGREDIENTS
1 qt		Utensils: saucepan
lrg		mixing bowl
9 × 13 in		baking pan
1¼ C		water
1 C		dates, finely cut
1 tsp		baking soda
2		eggs
1 C		sugar
¾ C		softened butter or margarine
1½ C		flour, all-purpose
¼ tsp		salt
2 tbl		cocoa
½ C		brown sugar, firmly packed
¾ C		chocolate chips
½ C		chopped nuts

Preheat oven to 350°. Bring water to a boil in saucepan. Add the dates and soda, let cool. In the mixing bowl, mix the eggs slightly with a fork. Add sugar and butter and cream the mixture. Sift flour onto a piece of waxed paper, measure, and sift with the salt and cocoa into the creamed mixture, alternating with the date mixture. Pour batter into a greased baking pan. Sprinkle the brown sugar, chocolate chips, and nuts over the top. Bake at 350° for 30 to 40 minutes.

menu 15

Charbonot†
Peach Spareribs
Baked Potatoes
Lettuce and Cucumber Salad
Creamy Date Dessert

TIMETABLE

*5:30 pm	Prepare Creamy Date Dessert
*5:45	Prepare Peach Spareribs
6:15	Place ribs in oven at 375°
*6:15	Prepare salad and salad dressing and refrigerate
7:00	Bake potatoes
7:45	Add peaches to ribs and continue baking
8:00	Dinner is served

† A dry Burgundy wine; serve at cool room temperature (65°)

* May be prepared in the morning or the night before and refrigerated

OR 4	FOR 6	INGREDIENTS

INSTRUCTIONS

LETTUCE AND CUCUMBER SALAD

...ed	lrg	Utensil: salad bowl
med hd	1 lrg hd	lettuce
sm	1 med	sliced cucumber

Wash and drain lettuce. Tear head of lettuce into salad bowl. Slice the cucumber over the lettuce. Refrigerate until ready to serve. / / Just before serving, toss with dressing.

Dressing

pt	1 pt	Utensil: glass jar
⅓ C	1 C	commercial sour cream
? tsp	1 tbl	lemon juice
drop	1 drop	Tabasco sauce
½ sm	1 sm	diced cucumber
¼ C	¼ C	minced parsley
sm clove	1 lrg clove	minced garlic
½ tsp	2 tsp	salt
¼ tsp	½ tsp	pepper

Mix all ingredients in a blender for about 10 seconds (or in a mixer until well blended). Refrigerate in a glass jar until ready to serve. / / Add to salad just before serving.

PEACH SPARERIBS

FOR 4	FOR 6	INGREDIENTS	
9 × 12	9 × 12	Utensil: baking pan	
3 lb	4 lb	country-style spareribs	

Arrange the spareribs in the baking pan, meaty side up, so that pieces do not overlap. Pour the peach sauce evenly over the meat. / / Bake in preheated 375° oven for 90 minutes, spooning the pan drippings over the meat two or three times after the first hour of cooking. Add the ⅔ cup of reserved peaches to the pan and continue cooking for another 15 minutes.

Peach Sauce

sm	sm	Utensil: mixing bowl	
1 can	1 can	sliced cling peaches, 1-lb 13-oz can	
8 oz	8 oz	canned tomato sauce	
2 tbl	2 tbl	brown sugar, firmly packed	
3 tbl	3 tbl	wine vinegar	
¼ tsp	¼ tsp	ground cloves	
¼ tsp	¼ tsp	ground ginger	
¼ tsp	¼ tsp	pepper	
⅛ tsp	⅛ tsp	nutmeg	
½ tsp	½ tsp	salt	

Drain the liquid from the can of cling peaches, reserving ¼ cup of the liquid. Set aside ⅔ cup of the peaches. Combine the remaining peaches in a blender with the ¼ cup of syrup, tomato sauce, brown sugar, wine vinegar, cloves, ginger, pepper, nutmeg, and salt. Whirl until mixture is smooth (or press peaches through a fine mesh strainer and blend with other ingredients).

BAKED POTATOES

4	6	baking potatoes	

Bake potatoes in oven for 1 hour. When ready to serve, spoon some sauce from meat into each potato, or serve with butter or with sour cream and chives.

CREAMY DATE DESSERT

FOR 4	FOR 6	INGREDIENTS
m	med	Utensil: mixing bowl
¼ lb	1 lb	ricotta cheese
⅓ C	½ C	light cream
½ tbl	2 tbl	instant coffee
½ tbl	2 tbl	brandy
tbl	5 tbl	sugar
	6	pitted dates

Combine all ingredients in a mixing bowl. Beat mixture slowly (on lowest speed of electric mixer) until well blended. Pour into individual sherbert glasses and chill for at least one hour.

---

menu 16

Johannisberger Riesling†
Pork Chops In Mushroom Sauce
Brown Rice
Fresh Green Beans With Bacon
Peppermint Apple Mold
Cherry Pudding Cake

TIMETABLE

*4:00 pm	Chill wine
*4:00	Prepare Peppermint Apple Mold and refrigerate
*6:15	Prepare and bake Cherry Pudding Cake
*6:30	Prepare green beans for cooking
6:55	Brown pork chops
7:15	Cook green beans
7:15	Cook pork chops
7:40	Prepare brown rice
8:00	Dinner is served

† A dry Rhine wine; serve chilled (45°)

* May be prepared in the morning or the night before and refrigerated

43

PORK CHOPS IN MUSHROOM SAUCE

FOR 4	FOR 6	INGREDIENTS	
12 in	12 in	Utensil: skillet	
1 tbl	1 tbl	oil	
6 to 8	10 to 12	pork chops, ½ inch thick	
2 tsp	1 tbl	dry mustard	
¼ tsp	½ tsp	salt	
⅛ tsp	⅛ tsp	pepper	
1 can	2 cans	cream of mushroom soup	

Heat oil in skillet. Sprinkle pork chops with dry mustard, salt, and pepper. Brown the chops in oil and drain off excess grease. Reduce heat and stir in the mushroom soup. Cover and simmer over low heat for 45 minutes, spooning sauce over chops occasionally.

BROWN RICE

FOR 4	FOR 6	INGREDIENTS	
1 qt	2 qt	Utensil: saucepan	
1½ C	2 C	water	
½ tsp	¾ tsp	salt	
1 C	1½ C	brown rice	

Bring water to a rolling boil in a saucepan. Add salt and stir in rice. Reduce heat, cover tightly, and steam for 15 minutes.

FRESH GREEN BEANS WITH BACON

FOR 4	FOR 6	INGREDIENTS	
3 qt	4 qt	Utensil: saucepan	
1 lb	1½ lb	fresh green beans	
3	5	bacon slices	
3 tbl	4 tbl	brown sugar, firmly packed	
¾ tsp	1 tsp	salt	
¼ tsp	½ tsp	pepper	
½ C	½ C	water	

Wash beans, break off ends, remove strings, and cut beans lengthwise (French style). Place in saucepan, together with the bacon cut into chunks, brown sugar, salt, pepper, and water. Cover and simmer for about 45 minutes, or until tender.

PEPPERMINT APPLE MOLD

med		Utensils: mixing bowl
2 qt		gelatine mold
1 pkg		lime gelatine, 3-oz
½ C		boiling water
¼ C		lime juice
1 lb		canned applesauce
⅛ tsp		peppermint extract
½ C		chopped walnuts
6		lettuce leaves

Place gelatine in mixing bowl. Add boiling water and stir until gelatine has dissolved. Add lime juice. Refrigerate until the mixture just starts to jell (about 30 minutes). Fold in the applesauce, peppermint extract, and walnuts, combining well. Turn mixture into a mold and refrigerate until firm. / / Turn mold out onto a bed of lettuce leaves for serving.

CHERRY PUDDING CAKE

med		Utensils: mixing bowl
9 × 13 in		baking pan
sm		saucepan
2 cans		cherry pie filling, 1-lb 5-oz can
½ tsp		cinnamon
¼ tsp		almond extract
1 pkg		one-layer white cake mix, 9½ oz
½ C		butter or margarine
½ C		sliced almonds

In a mixing bowl, combine the cherry pie filling with the cinnamon and almond extract. Pour into a greased baking pan. Sprinkle the cake mix over the top of the pie filling. Melt butter in a small saucepan and drizzle over cake mix. Sprinkle with almonds. Bake in preheated 375° oven for 35 minutes, or until lightly browned.

menu 17

Sylvaner†
Quick Tuna Curry
Steamed Rice
Marinated Green Beans
Orange Sherbet Salad
Chocolate Fudge Cake

TIMETABLE

*3:30 pm	Chill wine
*3:30	Prepare Marinated Green Beans and refrigerate
*4:00	Prepare Orange Sherbet Salad and refrigerate
6:45	Whip cream for cake and refrigerate
6:50	Prepare and bake cake
7:15	Prepare Quick Tuna Curry
7:40	Prepare rice
7:50	Unmold salad onto serving plate
8:00	Dinner is served

† A dry Rhine wine; serve chilled (45°)   * May be prepared in the morning or the night before and refrigerated

---

FOR 4	FOR 6	INGREDIENTS

INSTRUCTIONS

QUICK TUNA CURRY

FOR 4	FOR 6	INGREDIENTS
10 in	12 in	Utensil: skillet
⅓ C	½ C	chopped onion
¼ C	⅓ C	chopped green pepper
1	2	minced garlic cloves
2 tbl	3 tbl	butter or margarine
½ C	¾ C	raisins
1 can	2 cans	drained tuna, 6½-oz can
1 tsp	1½ tsp	curry powder
¼ tsp	¼ tsp	salt
⅛ tsp	⅛ tsp	pepper
1 C	1½ C	commercial sour cream

Chop onion and green pepper and mince garlic cloves. Heat the butter in a skillet and sauté onion, peppers, and garlic until tender but not brown. Stir in the raisins, tuna, curry powder, salt, pepper, and sour cream. Heat slowly, stirring frequently, until thoroughly heated (do not let mixture boil). Keep covered. Serve over hot rice.

46

FOR 4	FOR 6	INGREDIENTS

INSTRUCTIONS

STEAMED RICE

FOR 4	FOR 6	INGREDIENTS
1 qt	2 qt	Utensil: saucepan
2 C	3 C	water
1 tsp	1½ tsp	shortening
½ tsp	¾ tsp	salt
1 C	1½ C	long-grain white rice

Bring water to a boil in saucepan. Add shortening and salt. Slowly add rice, shaking pan to level rice grains. Turn heat to low, cover tightly, and cook 20 to 25 minutes, or until all liquid has been absorbed. Keep covered until ready to serve.

MARINATED GREEN BEANS

FOR 4	FOR 6	INGREDIENTS
med	med	Utensil: mixing bowl
1 lb	1 lb 13 oz	canned cut green beans

Drain the green beans and place in mixing bowl. Pour marinade over green beans, cover and refrigerate for several hours.

Marinade

Combine all marinade ingredients in a glass jar or blender and mix well.

FOR 4	FOR 6	INGREDIENTS
½ pt	1 pt	Utensil: glass jar
⅓ C	½ C	catsup
3 tbl	⅓ C	salad oil
3 tbl	¼ C	drained pickle relish
4 tsp	2 tbl	minced onion
1 tbl	2 tbl	water
2 tsp	1 tbl	Worcestershire sauce
2 drops	3 drops	Tabasco sauce
2 tbl	3 tbl	sugar
⅓ tsp	½ tsp	salt
⅓ tsp	½ tsp	dry mustard
⅓ tsp	½ tsp	garlic powder
1 sm	1 med	bay leaf
2	3	whole cloves

ORANGE SHERBET SALAD

FOR 4	FOR 6	INGREDIENTS
sm	med	Utensils: mixing bowl
		gelatin mold
1 qt	2 qt	
1 pkg	2 pkg	orange-pineapple gelatin, 3 oz
½ C	1 C	boiling water
1 can	2 cans	mandarin oranges, 11-oz can
½ pt	1 pt	orange sherbet
1	2	sliced bananas

Place the gelatin in a mixing bowl, add boiling water, and stir until dissolved. Pour the juice from the mandarin oranges into mixture, and stir in the sherbet until dissolved. Refrigerate until partially set. Peel and slice bananas into gelatin. Mix in the mandarin oranges, pour into mold, and chill until firmly set.

CHOCOLATE FUDGE CAKE

INGREDIENTS	
2 qt	Utensils: saucepan
9 × 13 in	baking pan
sm	mixing bowl
1 pkg	packaged chocolate pudding
2 C	milk
1 pkg	chocolate cake mix, 1 lb 2 oz
½ C	chocolate chips
½ C	chopped nuts
½ pt	heavy cream
½ C	powdered sugar

Preheat oven to 350°. Empty pudding mix into saucepan. Slowly add milk, stirring to keep mixture smooth. Cook, stirring steadily, until the mixture just starts to boil. Blend dry cake mix into the hot pudding. Pour into greased baking pan, sprinkle with the chocolate chips and chopped nuts, and bake for 30 to 35 minutes. Whip the cream in a small mixing bowl and blend in the powdered sugar. Serve the cake warm topped with whipped cream.

menu 18

Grenache Rosé†
Ribs and Beans
Vegetable Wheel
Blueberry Muffins
Peaches Flambé

TIMETABLE

*5:45 pm   Chill wine
*5:45   Prepare Ribs and Beans
*6:25   Bake ribs at 350°
*6:30   Prepare Vegetable Wheel and refrigerate
 6:55   Prepare Blueberry Muffin batter
*7:25   Remove ribs from oven, prepare next step, reset oven to 400°
 7:30   Bake Ribs and Beans; bake Blueberry Muffins
 7:40   Prepare peaches for broiler
 8:00   Dinner is served
             Preheat broiler and finish peaches just before serving the dessert course

† A light, dry rosé wine; serve chilled (45°)   * May be prepared in the morning or the night before and refrigerated

OR 4	FOR 6	INGREDIENTS	INSTRUCTIONS

VEGETABLE WHEEL

OR 4	FOR 6	INGREDIENTS
ned	lrg	Utensil: serving platter
	1	grapefruit
2	18	cherry tomatoes
2	18	stuffed olives
	12	baby Kosher dill pickles
	6	carrots
	6	celery
½	1	green bell pepper
	12	green onions

Wash grapefruit and place on center of platter. Place toothpicks through tomatoes, olives, and baby dill pickles and stick them into the grapefruit. Wash, clean, and slice the carrots, celery stalks, and pepper and wash the green onions. Arrange the vegetables on the platter around the grapefruit to form a wheel with the grapefruit as the hub. Refrigerate until ready to serve.

49

RIBS AND BEANS

FOR 4	FOR 6	INGREDIENTS
sm	sm	Utensils: mixing bowl
9 × 12 in	9 × 12 in	baking pan
3 lb	4½ lb	country-style spareribs, cut in 2-inch pieces
1 tbl	1½ tbl	brown sugar, firmly packed
½ tsp	¾ tsp	salt
¼ tsp	⅓ tsp	ground cloves
¼ tsp	⅓ tsp	ground ginger
1 tbl	1½ tbl	Worcestershire sauce
8¾ oz	13½ oz	canned pineapple tidbits
½ tsp	¾ tsp	onion salt
1 lb 5 oz	1 lb 15 oz	canned baked beans
⅛ tsp	¼ tsp	ground cloves
⅛ tsp	¼ tsp	ground ginger

Arrange the spareribs in a baking pan. In a small mixing bowl, combine the brown sugar, salt, ground cloves, ground ginger, Worcestershire sauce and the syrup drained from the can of pineapple tidbits. Spoon one-half of this mixture over the spareribs, sprinkle with onion salt, and bake ribs, uncovered, in a preheated 350° oven for one hour. After baking, remove ribs from pan, drain off grease from pan, and combine the baked beans, pineapple tidbits, cloves, and ginger in the pan. Arrange ribs on top of bean-and-pineapple mixture and spoon the remaining syrup mixture over the top. / / Bake, uncovered, at 400° for 30 minutes.

BLUEBERRY MUFFINS

	INGREDIENTS
2 sm, 1 lrg	Utensils: mixing bowls
for 12	muffin tin
¼ C	shortening
½ C	sugar
2	eggs
1 can	blueberries, 15-oz can
⅓ C	flour (all-purpose)
4 tsp	baking powder
¾ tsp	salt
1⅔ C	flour (all-purpose)
⅔ C	milk

Cream the shortening and sugar in a large mixing bowl. Add and beat in eggs. Drain the blueberries and mix lightly in a small mixing bowl with ⅓ cup of flour. Mix baking powder, salt, and flour in another small mixing bowl. Add flour mixture to sugar mixture alternately with milk. Add the blueberries and flour mixture to the batter and stir in lightly. Pour into greased muffin tin and bake at 400° for 30 minutes or until evenly browned. Makes 12 muffins. Serve hot.

FOR 4	FOR 6	INGREDIENTS	INSTRUCTIONS

PEACHES FLAMBÉ

FOR 4	FOR 6	INGREDIENTS
1 ½ qt	1 ½ qt	Utensils: rectangular baking dish
sm	sm	saucepan
4	6	canned cling peaches
2 tsp	3 tsp	lemon juice
1 tsp	1 ½ tsp	brown sugar, firmly packed
2 tsp	1 tbl	butter or margarine
¼ C	⅓ C	rum, light or dark
4 scoops	6 scoops	peach ice cream

Drain peaches and place in baking dish with cut side up. Sprinkle with lemon juice and place brown sugar and a dot of butter in the cavity of each peach half. Move broiler rack so that peaches will be 3 inches from flame. Broil for 4 minutes. Warm rum in a saucepan and ignite rum. Pour flaming rum over peaches and serve at once with a scoop of peach ice cream.

---

menu 19

Chianti Wine†
Italian Salad
Garlic Bread
Rigatoni With
Sauce Del Mondo
Anise Coffee

TIMETABLE

*4:30 pm	Prepare sauce
*7:00	Slice, butter, and wrap Garlic Bread
*7:20	Prepare salad and salad dressing
7:30	Boil water for Rigatoni
7:35	Warm Garlic Bread in 200° oven
7:40	Reheat sauce if it was prepared earlier
7:45	Add Rigatoni to boiling water
7:50	Toss salad with salad dressing
7:55	Wash and drain Rigatoni
8:00	Dinner is served

† A dry red wine; serve at cool room temperature (65°)

* May be prepared in the morning or the night before and refrigerated

FOR 4	FOR 6	INGREDIENTS
med	lrg	Utensil: salad bowl
1 sm hd	1 lrg hd	lettuce
1 sm	1 med	tomato
1 pt	1 pt	Utensil: glass jar
3 tbl	5 tbl	olive oil
1½ tbl	2½ tbl	wine vinegar
⅛ tsp	¼ tsp	garlic powder
½ tsp	¾ tsp	sweet basil
½ tsp	¾ tsp	salt
¼ tsp	⅓ tsp	fresh ground black pepper
sm	sm	Utensil: saucepan
4 tbl	6 tbl	butter
½ tsp	¾ tsp	garlic powder
1 sm	1 med	French bread

INSTRUCTIONS

ITALIAN SALAD

Wash and dry lettuce and break leaves into salad bowl. Cut the tomato into small wedges and add to lettuce. Refrigerate until ready to serve. / / Toss salad with dressing just before serving.

Dressing

Mix olive oil, wine vinegar, garlic powder, sweet basil, salt, and fresh ground black pepper in glass jar and refrigerate until ready to serve. / / Shake well before adding to salad.

GARLIC BREAD

Melt butter in saucepan and add garlic powder. Slice the loaf of bread and brush each slice with melted garlic butter. Arrange slices back in loaf form and wrap with aluminum foil. / / Heat at 200° for 25 minutes.

Sauce Del Mondo

1 lb tomato pureé
1 sma. onion
1/8 tsp. garlic powder
1 tsp. salt
1/4 tsp. black pepper

1/4 C water
3 oz mushrooms
1 1/2 tbl olive oil
1/3 lb. ground beef
3 oz. It. sausage

FOR 4	FOR 6	INGREDIENTS

SAUCE DEL MONDO

2 qt	3 qt	Utensils: saucepan
10 in	12 in	skillet
1 lb	1 lb	canned tomato purée
	13 oz	
1 sm	1 med	onion
⅛ tsp	¼ tsp	garlic powder
¾ tsp	1 tsp	salt
⅛ tsp	¼ tsp	black pepper
⅓ tsp	½ tsp	oregano
¼ C	⅓ C	water
⅓ C	½ C	Sauterne wine
3 oz	4 oz	fresh mushrooms
1½ tbl	2 tbl	olive oil
⅓ lb	½ lb	ground beef
3 oz	4 oz	Italian sausage, mild or sweet

Place tomato puree in saucepan and start simmering over the lowest heat. Add peeled onion cut in halves, garlic powder, salt, black pepper, oregano, water, and Sauterne wine to puree. Clean and slice mushrooms and sauté them in the skillet with the olive oil. When mushrooms are tender (about 10 minutes), add them, together with the olive oil remaining in the skillet, to the sauce. Using the same skillet, break the ground beef into small pieces and cook until slightly browned. Drain off grease and add beef to sauce. Cut the Italian sausage into one-inch pieces, brown lightly in the skillet, drain off grease, and add sausage to the sauce. Cover and simmer the sauce for about 3 hours, stirring frequently. If sauce becomes too thick, add a little water and wine.

RIGATONI

4 qt	5 qt	Utensil: saucepan
3 qt	4 qt	water
2 tsp	1 tbl	salt
1 lb	1½ lb	rigatoni

Cook rigatoni according to instructions on the package, or, if purchased in bulk, bring water to a vigorous boil, add salt and rigatoni, and cook until tender (10 to 15 minutes), stirring frequently. When cooked, drain off water, rinse the rigatoni in scalding hot water, drain, and serve with sauce. Any other type of pasta may be substituted for rigatoni.

FOR 4	FOR 6	INGREDIENTS	INSTRUCTIONS

ANISE COFFEE

FOR 4	FOR 6	INGREDIENTS	INSTRUCTIONS
med	med	Utensil: Italian coffee pot (if available)	Brew Italian-style (espresso) coffee or strong black regular coffee and add one tablespoon of Anisette liqueur to each cup.
4 C	6 C	brewed Italian coffee or very strong regular coffee	
4 tbl	6 tbl	Anisette liqueur	

menu 20

Barbera†
Skillet Spanish Rice
Lima Beans
Guacamole Mold
Mocha Lime Sherbet

TIMETABLE

*3:00 pm   Prepare Guacamole Mold
7:00   Prepare Skillet Spanish Rice
7:45   Cook Lima Beans
7:55   Turn Guacamole Mold out onto serving plate
8:00   Dinner is served
After dinner Prepare Mocha Lime Sherbet.

† A dry Burgundy wine; serve at cool room temperature (65°)

* May be prepared in the morning or the night before and refrigerated

---

FOR 4	FOR 6	INGREDIENTS	INSTRUCTIONS

LIMA BEANS

FOR 4	FOR 6	INGREDIENTS	INSTRUCTIONS
1 qt	2 qt	Utensil: saucepan	In saucepan, bring water to a vigorous boil. Add salt and lima beans, cover, and bring back to a boil quickly. Reduce heat and cook, covered, for 10 to 12 minutes. Drain. Add butter, salt, and pepper, and stir gently.
1 pkg	2 pkg	frozen lima beans	
1 C	1½ C	water	
¼ tsp	½ tsp	salt	
2 tbl	4 tbl	butter or margarine	
¼ tsp	½ tsp	salt	
⅛ tsp	¼ tsp	pepper	

54

FOR 4	FOR 6	INGREDIENTS
sm	sm	Utensils: saucepan
10 in	12 in	skillet
C	1½ C	water
C	1½ C	precooked rice
½ tsp	¾ tsp	salt
tsp	1 tbl	butter or margarine
lb	1½ lb	lean ground beef
sm	1 med	onion
½ C	¾ C	chopped green pepper
tsp	1½ tsp	garlic powder
tsp	1½ tsp	salt
½ tsp	¾ tsp	pepper
can	1 can and 1 8-oz can	tomato sauce, 15-oz can
½ C	¾ C	water
slices	5 slices	Cheddar cheese
pt	1½ pt	lime sherbet
2 tbl	3 tbl	coffee-flavored liqueur

INSTRUCTIONS

SKILLET SPANISH RICE

In saucepan, bring water to a boil. Add rice, salt, and butter. Cover and cook over low heat for 5 minutes. Meanwhile, crumble the ground beef and brown in skillet. Chop the onion and green pepper and add to skillet. Add the garlic powder, salt, and pepper. Cook until meat is done and the onions and green peppers are tender. Add tomato sauce and water. Stir the cooked rice into the mixture and simmer until warmed through. Lay the cheese slices on top of the mixture. Place cover on skillet and turn off heat. Keep covered until ready to serve.

MOCHA LIME SHERBET

Scoop sherbet into serving glasses and add ½ tablespoon of liqueur to each serving.

FOR 4	FOR 6	INGREDIENTS
1 qt	1 qt	Utensils: saucepan
med	med	mixing bowl
1 qt	2 qt	gelatin mold
¾ C	1 C	water
2 env	3 env	unflavored gelatin
1 lrg	2 med	tomatoes
1 lrg	2 med	avocados
1½ tbl	2 tbl	lemon juice
3 tbl	¼ C	chopped green pepper
⅓ C	½ C	minced onion
¾ tsp	1 tsp	seasoned salt
⅛ tsp	⅛ tsp	pepper
¾ tsp	1 tsp	chili powder
¾ C	1 C	commercial sour cream
¾ C	1 C	mayonnaise
3	5	parsley sprigs

INSTRUCTIONS

GUACAMOLE MOLD

Place cold water in saucepan and sprinkle the gelatin over the water. Let stand 5 minutes to soften. Place saucepan over low heat, stirring until gelatin has dissolved. Refrigerate until slightly thickened, about 20 minutes. Meanwhile, in mixing bowl, place washed and peeled tomatoes and crush with a potato masher. Peel avocados and slice into tomato mixture. Crush to blend well. Add lemon juice, green pepper, onion, seasoned salt, pepper, chili powder, sour cream, and mayonnaise. Mix to blend well. Turn the slightly thickened gelatin into the avocado mixture and combine well. Turn into lightly oiled mold. Chill until firm. Garnish with parsley sprigs.

menu 21

Chianti†
Supper from Sicily
Italian Bread
Wilted Spinach Salad
Chocolate Ice Cream

† A dry red wine; serve at cool room temperature (65°)

TIMETABLE

*6:30 pm	Prepare Supper from Sicily
7:25	Place casserole in oven at 350°
*7:25	Prepare Italian Bread
7:40	Place bread in oven
7:45	Prepare salad dressing
7:55	Toss salad with salad dressing
8:00	Dinner is served

* May be prepared in the morning or the night before and refrigerated

---

SUPPER FROM SICILY

OR 4	FOR 6	INGREDIENTS	
qt, 3 qt	2 qt, 3 qt	Utensils:	saucepans
0 in	10 in		skillet
1/2 qt	2 qt		covered baking dish
qt	1 qt	water	
/2 tsp	1/2 tsp	salt	
oz	4 oz	medium egg noodles	
lb	1 1/2 lb	lean ground beef	
/3 C	1/2 C	chopped onion	
can	1 can	tomato paste, 6-oz can	
/3 C	3/4 C	water	
tsp	1 1/2 tsp	salt	
/8 tsp	1/4 tsp	pepper	
/2 C	3/4 C	milk	
oz	8 oz	cream cheese, cubed	
/3 C	1/2 C	grated Parmesan cheese	
/3 tsp	1/2 tsp	garlic salt	
/2 C	3/4 C	chopped green pepper	

INSTRUCTIONS

Bring 1 quart of water to boil in 2-quart saucepan. Add salt and noodles and cook, uncovered, for 8 to 10 minutes, or until tender. Drain noodles in colander and rinse gently in hot water. Brown beef in skillet; add chopped onion and cook until tender. Drain off excess grease. Add tomato paste, water, salt, and pepper. Cook over medium heat for 5 minutes. In a 3-quart saucepan, heat milk and cream cheese until smooth. Stir in Parmesan cheese, garlic salt, green pepper, and drained noodles. In a baking dish, arrange alternate layers of noodles and meat sauce. / / Bake, covered, at 350° for 35 minutes.

FOR 4	FOR 6	INGREDIENTS	INSTRUCTIONS

ITALIAN BREAD

¾ loaf	1 loaf	Italian bread	Slice the bread loaf, butter each slice, and arrange slices back into original
4 tbl	6 tbl	butter	loaf form. Wrap in aluminum foil. / / Heat at 350° for 20 minutes.

WILTED SPINACH SALAD

med	lrg	Utensils: salad bowl	Wash the spinach and drain, twice. Tear into bite-size pieces and place
sm	sm	skillet	in salad bowl. Cover and refrigerate until ready to serve. / / Cook bacon
½ lb	¾ lb	fresh spinach	in skillet until crisp. Remove from grease and drain on paper towels. To
3 slices	4 slices	bacon	bacon grease in skillet, add sugar, chopped onion, salt, and vinegar. Bring
1 tsp	1½ tsp	brown sugar, firmly packed	to a boil, pour over spinach, and toss. Top with crumbled bacon. Serve
2 tbl	3 tbl	diced onion	immediately.
¼ tsp	⅓ tsp	salt	
1 tbl	1½ tbl	vinegar	

CHOCOLATE ICE CREAM

1 qt	Utensils:	double boiler
2		ice cube trays
med		mixing bowl
2 squares	baking chocolate	
1 can	sweetened condensed milk, 15-oz can	
¾ C	water	
½ pt	heavy cream	
1 tsp	vanilla extract	

Place the chocolate squares in the top of a double boiler over rapidly boiling water until chocolate is melted. Add condensed milk and cook until very thick, about 15 minutes, stirring constantly. Stir in water gradually, then pour mixture into ice cube trays and freeze until rubbery, about 45 minutes. When the chocolate mixture is ready, whip the cream in a mixing bowl. Fold in the chocolate mixture and vanilla extract. Pour into ice cube trays and return to freezer for at least 5 hours. Stir once during freezing process.

menu 22

TIMETABLE

*3:30 pm	Chill wine
*3:30	Prepare Torte Pie and refrigerate
*6:00	Prepare fruit bowl and refrigerate
6:20	Prepare Bavarian Potatoes
7:10	Clean trout
7:30	Prepare fruit dressing
7:40	Cook trout
8:00	Dinner is served

† A dry Sauterne wine; serve chilled (45°)

* May be prepared in the morning or the night before and refrigerated

---

FOR 4	FOR 6	INGREDIENTS
lrg	lrg	Utensils: mixing bowl
12 in	12 in	skillet
4	6	small fresh trout
3	4	egg yolks
½ C	¾ C	sliced almonds
3 tbl	4 tbl	butter or margarine
2 tbl	3 tbl	cooking oil
¼ tsp	½ tsp	salt
⅛ tsp	⅛ tsp	pepper

INSTRUCTIONS

TROUT WITH ALMONDS

Clean trout. Beat egg yolks slightly in a mixing bowl. Slice the almonds onto a piece of waxed paper. Melt butter with cooking oil in skillet. Salt and pepper the trout, dip into egg yolk mixture, then into almonds, and fry in skillet until firm and brown (5 to 7 minutes each side).

FOR 4	FOR 6	INGREDIENTS

BAVARIAN POTATOES

FOR 4	FOR 6	INGREDIENTS
3 qt	4 qt	Utensils: saucepan
12 in	12 in	skillet
med	lrg	mixing bowl
3 med	5 med	potatoes
1 tsp	1 tsp	salt
1 med	1½ med	chopped onion
1½ tbl	2 tbl	butter or margarine
2 tsp	3 tsp	wine vinegar
1 tsp	1 tsp	salt
⅛ tsp	⅛ tsp	pepper

Peel potatoes, place in boiling salted water (enough to cover potatoes), and cook for 20 to 30 minutes, or until tender. Meanwhile, sauté the chopped onion in skillet with butter until well browned. Drain and cube the potatoes into mixing bowl. Add vinegar and salt and pepper to sautéed onions, mix well, and pour mixture over potatoes.

TORTE PIE

	sm, med	Utensils: mixing bowls
	9 in	pie pan
	3	egg whites
	1 tsp	vanilla extract
	¼ tsp	salt
	1 C	sugar
	1 C	walnuts
	½ C	soda cracker crumbs
	1 tsp	baking powder
	½ pt	heavy cream
	½ C	powdered sugar

Preheat oven to 300°. In a medium mixing bowl, beat together egg whites, vanilla extract, and salt until foamy. Gradually add sugar and beat until stiff peaks are formed. Mix walnuts, cracker crumbs, and baking powder in a small mixing bowl, then fold into egg whites. Spread mixture into a well-greased pie pan. Bake at 300° for 40 minutes. Leave pie in oven with heat off and door open for about 15 minutes. Whip the heavy cream and blend in the powdered sugar. Pour over pie and refrigerate for at least 4 hours before serving.

FOR 4	FOR 6	INGREDIENTS
med	med	Utensil: mixing bowl
½	1	cantaloupe
½ sm	1 sm	fresh pineapple
1 sm	1 med	orange
4	6	lettuce leaves
½ pt	1 pt	cottage cheese
sm	sm	Utensil: mixing bowl
¼ C	½ C	heavy cream
1 tbl	1½ tbl	honey
½ C	¾ C	mayonnaise
1 tbl	1½ tbl	lime juice

INSTRUCTIONS

FRUIT BOWL

Remove skin and rind from cantaloupe and slice bite-size pieces into medium mixing bowl. Clean pineapple and slice into bowl. Peel oranges and cut into thin slices. Add to bowl. Refrigerate until ready to serve. / / On a serving platter, arrange a leaf of lettuce for each serving. Place a large tablespoon of cottage cheese in the center of each leaf and arrange fruit around the mound of cottage cheese. Pour dressing over fruit and cheese just before serving.

Dressing

Whip the heavy cream in a small bowl and blend in the honey, mayonnaise, and lime juice. Pour over fruit and cheese. (Can be prepared no earlier than one hour before serving time.)

menu 23

TIMETABLE

*5:30 pm	Chill wine
*5:30	Prepare tomatoes for broiling and refrigerate
*5:45	Prepare Apple Crisp
*6:25	Bake Apple Crisp at 350°
*6:25	Boil green beans
*6:50	Prepare Tuna Casserole
*7:10	Remove Apple Crisp
7:20	Bake Tuna Casserole at 325°
7:30	Sauté green beans and cover
7:50	Turn oven control to "broil," cover the Tuna Casserole, broil tomatoes
8:00	Dinner is served

† A dry Chablis wine; serve chilled (45°)   * May be prepared in the morning or the night before and refrigerated

---

FOR 4	FOR 6	INGREDIENTS
1½ qt	1½ qt	Utensils: baking dish
sm	sm	mixing bowl
4	6	sliced baking apples
¾ tsp	1 tsp	cinnamon
3 tbl	¼ C	sugar
6 tbl	½ C	water
½ C	¾ C	flour
6 tbl	½ C	sugar
3 tbl	¼ C	butter or margarine

INSTRUCTIONS

APPLE CRISP

Peel, core, and slice apples into greased baking dish. Sprinkle with cinnamon and sugar and add water. In a small mixing bowl, mix flour, sugar, and butter with a pastry blender. Spread flour mixture over apples. Bake at 375° for 40 minutes. This may be served warm or cold, and with ice cream if desired.

FOR 4	FOR 6	INGREDIENTS

TUNA CASSEROLE

FOR 4	FOR 6	INGREDIENTS
4 qt	4 qt	Utensils: saucepan
1½ qt	2 qt	covered baking dish
6 oz	8 oz	noodles
1 tsp	1 tsp	salt
2 cans	3 cans	tuna fish, 6½-oz can
1 sm	1 med	minced onion
1 can	1 can	cream of mushroom soup
⅓ C	½ C	milk
1 tsp	1½ tsp	salt
⅛ tsp	¼ tsp	ground pepper
⅛ tsp	¼ tsp	ground thyme
2 C	3 C	crushed potato chips

INSTRUCTIONS

Bring 2 quarts of water to a boil in saucepan, add salt and noodles, and cook uncovered for 8 to 10 minutes, or until noodles are tender. Drain noodles in colander and place one-half of the noodles into the baking dish. Spread with a layer of drained tuna fish, minced onion, and mushroom soup. Add milk and a layer of remaining noodles. Sprinkle with salt, pepper, and thyme and cover with the crushed potato chips. / / Bake for 30 minutes at 325°.

BROILED TOMATOES

FOR 4	FOR 6	INGREDIENTS
2 med	3 med	tomatoes
1 tsp	1½ tsp	dill seed
2 tsp	1 tbl	packaged bread crumbs
2 tsp	1 tbl	butter or margarine

Wash tomatoes, cut into halves, and place in broiling pan, cut side up. Dot each tomato half with butter, sprinkle with dill seed and bread crumbs. Broil for 10 minutes.

FOR 4	FOR 6	INGREDIENTS	INSTRUCTIONS

FRESH FRENCH GREEN BEANS

FOR 4	FOR 6	INGREDIENTS
4 qt	4 qt	Utensils: saucepan
10 in	12 in	skillet
1 lb	1½ lb	fresh green beans
½ tsp	¾ tsp	salt
2 tbl	3 tbl	butter or margarine
1 tbl	1½ tbl	chopped parsley
½ tsp	¾ tsp	salt
⅛ tsp	¼ tsp	pepper

Wash beans, break off ends, remove strings, and cut lengthwise (French style). Bring 6 cups of water to a boil, add salt and beans, and cook, uncovered, for 25 to 35 minutes, or until tender. Drain beans and sauté them in skillet with butter for 2 to 3 minutes. Sprinkle with chopped parsley, season with salt and pepper. Keep covered until ready to serve.

---

menu 24

White Pinot†
Tuna Cutlets
California Green Salad
Corn on the Cob
Sour Dough Rolls
Strawberry Shortcake

TIMETABLE

*6:00 pm	Chill wine
*6:00	Prepare tuna cutlets and refrigerate
*6:30	Prepare and wrap rolls
*6:40	Prepare salad and salad dressing
7:00	Clean, slice, and sugar strawberries and refrigerate
7:30	Boil water for corn
7:40	Cook tuna cutlets
7:45	Place rolls in the oven
7:50	Cook corn
8:00	Dinner is served

† A dry Chablis wine; serve chilled (45°)

* May be prepared in the morning or the night before and refrigerated

FOR 4	FOR 6	INGREDIENTS
2 qt	2 qt	Utensil: saucepan
2 tbl	3 tbl	shortening
4 tbl	6 tbl	flour
½ C	¾ C	milk
1 tbl	1½ tbl	lemon juice
1	2	eggs
1 tsp	1½ tsp	salt
¼ tsp	⅓ tsp	pepper
1½ C	2 C	soft bread crumbs
2 cans	3 cans	drained tuna, 6½-oz can
sm, med	sm, med	Utensils: mixing bowls
10 in	12 in	skillet
1	2	eggs
¾ C	1 C	soda cracker crumbs
1½ tbl	2 tbl	shortening
sm, med	sm, med	Utensil: mixing bowls
2 boxes	3 boxes	fresh strawberries
⅓ C	½ C	sugar
¾ C	1 C	heavy cream
⅓ C	½ C	powdered sugar
4 slices	6 slices	small angel food or sponge cake

INSTRUCTIONS

TUNA CUTLETS

Melt the shortening in a saucepan and blend in the flour. Add milk and cook until thick. Remove from heat and add lemon juice, beaten eggs, salt, pepper, and bread crumbs. Add tuna, mix well, and form mixture into cutlet shapes. Refrigerate.

For Frying

When ready to fry the cutlets, beat eggs in a small mixing bowl and crush crackers into crumbs in a medium mixing bowl. Dip cutlets into beaten eggs, then dip into cracker crumbs, and fry in the skillet with the shortening until golden brown.

STRAWBERRY SHORTCAKE

Wash, drain, and slice strawberries into a medium mixing bowl. Add sugar, mix gently to coat all berries, cover, and refrigerate. When ready to serve, slice cake onto serving plates. Whip the cream in a small mixing bowl, add and blend in the powdered sugar. Place a mound of strawberries on each cake slice and top with the whipped cream. Top the whipped cream with one or two whole strawberries.

CALIFORNIA GREEN SALAD

FOR 4	FOR 6	INGREDIENTS
med	lrg	Utensil: salad bowl
½ hd	1 hd	iceberg lettuce
½ hd	½ hd	romaine lettuce
⅓ C	½ C	sliced salami
1 jar	1 jar	marinated artichoke hearts, 6-oz jar
½	1	Bermuda onion

Wash and drain lettuce and break into salad bowl. Chop salami and add to salad. Add the marinated artichoke hearts and onion rings sliced from the Bermuda onion. Cover and refrigerate until ready to serve. / / Toss with salad dressing just before serving.

Dressing

FOR 4	FOR 6	INGREDIENTS
1 pt	1 pt	Utensil: glass jar
⅓ C	½ C	olive oil
3 tbl	4 tbl	wine vinegar
⅓ C	½ C	catsup
1 tsp	1½ tsp	salt
½ tsp	¾ tsp	coarsely ground black pepper
1 tbl	1½ tbl	grated Parmesan cheese
⅛ tsp	⅛ tsp	paprika
3 drops	4 drops	Worcestershire sauce
1 sm	2 sm	crushed garlic cloves

In a glass jar, combine the olive oil, wine vinegar, catsup, salt, black pepper, grated Parmesan cheese, paprika, Worcestershire sauce, and crushed garlic cloves. Shake vigorously and refrigerate until ready to serve. / / Shake well, add to salad, and toss the salad just before serving.

CORN ON THE COB

FOR 4	FOR 6	INGREDIENTS
lrg	lrg	Utensil: steamer or kettle
3 qt	3½ qt	water
4	6	corn on the cob

Bring water to a boil in large steamer or kettle, add the ears of corn, and cook for 5 to 8 minutes. Remove corn from water and serve immediately with salt and butter.

FOR 4	FOR 6	INGREDIENTS	INSTRUCTIONS

SOUR DOUGH ROLLS

FOR 4	FOR 6	INGREDIENTS	
sm	sm	Utensil: saucepan	
4	6	sour dough rolls	
2 tbl	3 tbl	butter	
4 tsp	6 tsp	grated Parmesan cheese	

Melt butter in saucepan. Slice sour dough rolls in half and butter the inside. Sprinkle each roll with 1 teaspoon grated Parmesan cheese and wrap the rolls in aluminum foil. / / Bake for 15 minutes in preheated 400° oven.

---

menu 25

Gamay Rosé†
Tuna and Nut Casserole
Marinated Avocados
Spicy Orange Muffins
Cherry-Topped Cake

TIMETABLE

*4:00 pm	Chill wine
*4:00	Prepare Cherry Topped Cake
*6:30	Prepare Tuna and Nut Casserole
7:15	Bake tuna casserole at 350°
7:15	Prepare Spicy Orange Muffins
7:35	Bake muffins at 350°
7:40	Prepare Marinated Avocados
8:00	Dinner is served

† A light, dry rosé wine; serve chilled (45°)   * May be prepared in the morning or the night before and refrigerated

MARINATED AVOCADOS

FOR 4	FOR 6	INGREDIENTS
med	med	Utensil: serving bowl
1	1½	avocados
½ tsp	¾ tsp	salt
⅛ tsp	¼ tsp	pepper
1 tbl	1½ tbl	vinegar
2 tbl	3 tbl	olive oil
½ tsp	¾ tsp	oregano

Peel and slice avocado into shallow serving bowl. Sprinkle with salt, pepper, vinegar, and olive oil. Gently turn slices in marinade to cover well. Sprinkle with oregano.

SPICY ORANGE MUFFINS

FOR 6	INGREDIENTS
sm, med	Utensils: mixing bowls
lrg	muffin tin
sm	saucepan
1 can	mandarin oranges, 11-oz can
1½ C	flour
2 tsp	baking powder
½ tsp	salt
½ tsp	nutmeg
¼ tsp	allspice
½ C	sugar
⅓ C	butter or margarine
1	egg
¼ C	milk
¼ C	melted butter or margarine
¼ C	sugar
½ tsp	cinnamon

Drain the mandarin oranges and spread out on paper towels. In a medium mixing bowl, sift flour, measure, then sift again with the baking powder, salt, nutmeg, allspice, and sugar. Cut in the butter until it is in fine particles. In a small mixing bowl, beat the egg slightly with a fork, stir in the milk, then add to dry ingredients. Mix just enough to moisten the flour. Add drained orange segments and mix lightly until evenly distributed. Spoon into large, greased muffin tin, ¾ full. Bake at 350° for 20 to 25 minutes.

While muffins are baking, melt the butter in a small saucepan. In a small mixing bowl, combine the sugar and cinnamon. When muffins are done, remove from tins while still hot. Dip the top of each muffin into melted butter, then into the cinnamon mixture, rolling to coat well.

TUNA AND NUT CASSEROLE

FOR 4	FOR 6	INGREDIENTS
2 qt	3 qt	Utensils: saucepan
1½ qt	2 qt	covered baking dish
½ C	½ C	water
½ pkg	1 pkg	frozen peas, 10-oz pkg
½ tsp	1 tsp	salt
½ C	¾ C	chopped onion
1 C	1½ C	chopped celery
1 can	2 cans	tuna fish, 6½-oz can
1 can	1 can	chow mein noodles, 3-oz can
1 can	2 cans	cream of mushroom soup
¼ C	¼ C	water
1 can	2 cans	water chestnuts, 6-oz can
½ tsp	1 tsp	salt
¼ tsp	½ tsp	pepper
¼ lb	¼ lb	cashew nuts

Bring water to a boil in saucepan, add frozen peas, salt, onion, and celery. Bring back to a boil, cover, and cook gently over low heat for 4 to 6 minutes. Add drained tuna fish, chow mein noodles, mushroom soup, water, water chestnuts (sliced), salt, and pepper. Combine all ingredients and transfer the mixture to baking dish. Top with cashew nuts, cover. / / Bake in preheated 350° oven for 45 minutes.

CHERRY-TOPPED CAKE

lrg	Utensils: mixing bowl	
2	cake pans, 9 inch	
1 pkg	white cake mix, 1-lb 2-oz	
1⅓ C	water	
2	eggs	

Preheat oven to 350°. In the mixing bowl, combine the cake mix, water, and eggs. Blend until smooth, then beat for 2 minutes. Pour into greased cake pans and bake for 25 to 30 minutes. Let cool.

Topping

2 sm	Utensil: mixing bowls
1½ C	heavy cream
½ C	powdered sugar
1 tsp	vanilla extract
1 can	cherry pie filling, 1-lb 6-oz can
4 drops	red food coloring
2 tbl	grated orange rind

In a mixing bowl, whip the cream, blending in the powdered sugar and vanilla extract. In another mixing bowl, mix the pie filling with red food coloring and grated orange rind; reserve ⅓ cup of the liquid part of the pie filling. Spread 1 cup of whipped cream on bottom layer of cake, spoon reserved ⅓ cup of juice on top of the whipped cream. Add top layer of cake and frost the whole cake with the remaining whipped cream. Spoon the pie-filling mixture over the top of cake, allowing it to drip over sides. Chill.

CHAPTER TWO

Menus for Entertaining

menu 26

Chenin Blanc†
Baked Sole in White Wine
Glazed Carrots
Dilled Lettuce **and** *Tomato Salad*
Bakery Rolls
Peach Almond Pudding

TIMETABLE

Morning	If frozen fish are used, set out to thaw
*4:30 pm	Chill wine
*5:00	Prepare pudding and refrigerate
*6:00	Whip cream and complete preparation of dessert
*6:45	Prepare fish casserole
*7:15	Prepare salad and salad dressing
7:20	Bake fish at 375°
7:30	Prepare and cook carrots
7:40	Place rolls in oven
7:50	Toss salad with salad dressing
7:55	Glaze carrots
8:00	Dinner is served

† A dry Chablis wine; serve chilled (45°)

* May be prepared in the morning or the night before and refrigerated

FOR 4	FOR 6	INGREDIENTS
2 qt	3 qt	Utensil: saucepan
1 C	1½ C	water
¾ tsp	1 tsp	salt
12 sm	16 sm	carrots
1 tbl	1½ tbl	butter or margarine
1 tbl	4 tsp	sugar
1 tsp	1 tsp	chopped parsley

INSTRUCTIONS

GLAZED CARROTS

Peel the carrots. Bring water to a boil in saucepan, add salt and carrots, and cook, covered, until just tender (about 10 minutes). Drain off liquid. Add butter and sugar and tip pan back and forth gently until all carrots are glazed. Sprinkle with chopped parsley.

BAKED SOLE IN WHITE WINE

FOR 4	FOR 6	INGREDIENTS
qt	2 qt	Utensils: saucepan
½ qt	2½ qt	baking dish
med	3 med	potatoes
C	4 C	water
¼ lb	⅓ lb	fresh, sliced mushrooms
tbl	1½ tbl	butter or margarine
¼ tsp	1 tsp	salt
¼ tsp	⅓ tsp	ground black pepper
⅓ C	½ C	white wine
½ C	¾ C	commercial sour cream
lb	1½ lb	fillets of sole (fresh or frozen)
½ tsp	¾ tsp	paprika
½ tsp	2 tsp	chopped fresh parsley

Boil peeled potatoes in water until done (25 to 30 minutes). While the potatoes are cooking, wash and slice the mushrooms and lightly butter the baking dish. Slice the cooked potatoes and lay them in the baking dish. Add a layer of mushrooms, dot with butter, and sprinkle with one-half of the salt and pepper. Pour the wine over the casserole, and spread on one-half of the sour cream. Lay the fish fillets on top of the sour cream, sprinkle with the remaining salt and pepper, sprinkle with paprika, and top with the remaining sour cream. // Bake in a preheated 375° oven for 40 minutes. Before serving, sprinkle with chopped parsley and, if desired, a little lemon juice.

PEACH ALMOND PUDDING

	FOR 6	INGREDIENTS
	2 qt	Utensils: saucepan
	sm	mixing bowl
	1 pkg	vanilla pudding mix, 3¼-oz
	1½ C	milk
	¼ tsp	almond extract
	¾ C	diced cling peaches
	½ C	heavy cream

Prepare pudding mix according to directions on package, using 1½ cup of milk as the liquid. (Empty contents of package into saucepan, slowly add milk, stirring constantly to keep the mixture smooth. Cook over medium heat, stirring steadily, until pudding just starts to boil.) Stir in almond extract. Place waxed paper or transparent wrap directly on pudding and chill for one hour. Whip the cream in a small mixing bowl and fold the whipped cream and diced cling peaches into the pudding. // Spoon into serving dishes and refrigerate until ready to serve.

FOR 4	FOR 6	INGREDIENTS	INSTRUCTIONS

DILLED LETTUCE AND TOMATO SALAD

FOR 4	FOR 6	INGREDIENTS	
med	lrg	Utensil: salad bowl	Wash lettuce and drain well. Cut the tomato into small wedges. Break the lettuce into the salad bowl, add tomato wedges, and sprinkle with dill seed. Cover and refrigerate until ready to serve. / / Toss the salad with the salad dressing just before serving.
1 med hd	1 lrg hd	lettuce	
1 med	1 lrg	tomato	
½ tsp	¾ tsp	dill seed	

Dressing

½ pt	½ pt	Utensil: glass jar	Mix the salad oil, wine vinegar, garlic cloves, salt, and pepper in a glass jar and refrigerate until ready to serve.
3 tbl	5 tbl	salad oil	
1½ tbl	2 tbl	wine vinegar	
1 sm	1 lrg	crushed garlic cloves	
¼ tsp	⅓ tsp	salt	
½ tsp	¾ tsp	black pepper	

BAKERY ROLLS

8	12	bakery rolls	Wrap rolls in aluminum foil and heat at 375° for 20 minutes.

menu 27

Zinfandel†
Barbecued Beef Roast
Foiled Potatoes and Onions
Tossed Bean Salad
French Bread
Cantaloupe with Strawberries

† A dry Claret wine; serve at cool room temperature (65°)

TIMETABLE

*5:00 pm	Marinate beef roast
*5:15	Slice, butter, and wrap French Bread
*5:30	Prepare salad and salad dressing and refrigerate
*6:00	Prepare dessert and refrigerate
6:20	Tenderize beef roast
6:30	Prepare Foiled Potatoes and Onions packages
7:00	Place the potato and onion packages on the grill
7:20	Place beef roast on the grill (for well-done)
7:30	Place beef roast on the grill (for medium-rare)
7:50	Place bread on the grill
8:00	Dinner is served

* May be prepared in the morning or the night before and refrigerated

FOR 4	FOR 6	INGREDIENTS
		INSTRUCTIONS

BARBECUED BEEF ROAST

10 × 10 in	12 × 14 in	Utensil: baking dish or pan
4 lb	6 lb	seven-bone or chuck roast
2 tsp	3 tsp	unseasoned meat tenderizer
		Marinade:
¼ C	⅓ C	Worcestershire sauce
¼ C	⅓ C	olive oil
2 tbl	3 tbl	lemon juice
	2	crushed garlic cloves

Combine the marinade ingredients in a baking dish or pan, add the roast, and spoon the marinade over meat. Turn the roast over occasionally. About one hour before cooking meat, sprinkle the tenderizer evenly on all sides, piercing the roast generously and deeply with a fork. Let stand at room temperature for one hour before cooking. Barbecue the roast over hot coals for 15 to 20 minutes each side.

77

FOILED POTATOES AND ONIONS

FOR 4	FOR 6	INGREDIENTS	
10 in	10 in	Utensil: skillet	Cook bacon strips in skillet until crisp. Place bacon on paper towel to remove grease. Pare the potatoes and slice them onto two 12-inch pieces of heavy aluminum foil, dividing them equally. Sprinkle with salt and pepper. Slice the onion and cut the cheese into small cubes. Add the onion slices and cheese cubes to the foil packages. Crumble bacon on top. Slice the butter equally into the packages and mix well. Bring the edges of the foil up on each package, leaving space for the steam to expand, and seal the packages well. Place on grill over hot coals and cook for one hour, turning packages often.
4	6	bacon strips	
4 med	6 med	baking potatoes	
1 tsp	1½ tsp	salt	
¼ tsp	⅓ tsp	pepper	
1 med	1 lrg	onion	
1 C	1½ C	sharp Cheddar cheese	
6 tbl	8 tbl	butter or margarine	

TOSSED BEAN SALAD

FOR 4	FOR 6	INGREDIENTS	
med	lrg	Utensil: salad bowl	Drain the sliced carrots, garbanzo beans, cut green beans, and red kidney beans. Place the drained ingredients in the bottom of a salad bowl. Break the lettuce into the bowl and top with onion slices. Refrigerate until ready to serve. / / Toss the salad with the salad dresing just before serving.
½ can	1 can	sliced carrots, 8¼-oz can	
½ can	1 can	garbanzo beans, 8½-oz can	
½ can	1 can	cut green beans, 8-oz can	
½ can	1 can	red kidney beans, 8½-oz can	
¾ med	1 med hd	lettuce	
4 slices	6 slices	red onion	

| FOR 4 | FOR 6 | INGREDIENTS | | INSTRUCTIONS |

FOR 4	FOR 6	INGREDIENTS

Dressing

Combine all ingredients in a glass jar and refrigerate until ready to serve salad. / / Shake well before adding to salad.

FOR 4	FOR 6	INGREDIENTS
pt	1 pt	Utensil: glass jar
tbl	6 tbl	olive oil
tbl	3 tbl	lemon juice
½ tsp	¾ tsp	oregano
	1	crushed garlic clove
¼ tsp	1 tsp	salt
½ tsp	½ tsp	pepper

FRENCH BREAD

Slice bread loaf, melt butter in a saucepan, and butter each slice. Arrange slices back into original loaf form, wrap with heavy aluminum foil, and refrigerate until ready to warm. / / Place loaf on barbecue grill about 10 minutes before ready to serve.

FOR 4	FOR 6	INGREDIENTS
sm	sm	Utensil: saucepan
½ loaf	¾ loaf	French bread
tbl	6 tbl	butter

CANTALOUPE WITH STRAWBERRIES

Cut the cantaloupe in halves and remove the seeds from the center of each half. Divide the fresh strawberries into the centers of the cantaloupe halves, dribble the Kirsch over the strawberries, and sprinkle powdered sugar on top. Chill well before serving.

FOR 4	FOR 6	INGREDIENTS
	3	small cantaloupes
½ box	1 box	strawberries
tsp	6 tsp	Kirsch
tbl	1½ tbl	powdered sugar

menu 28

Pinot Chardonnay†
Barbecued Pork Chops
Apple-Spice Pilaff
Marinated Bean Salad
Ricotta Apple Pudding

TIMETABLE
Night
before   Marinate Bean Salad and refrigerate
*5:00 pm   Marinate pork chops and chill wine
*5:10   Prepare Ricotta Apple Pudding and refrigerate
7:00   Prepare Apple-Spice Pilaff
7:30   Barbecue pork chops on grill
8:00   Dinner is served

† A dry Chablis wine; serve chilled (45°)

* May be prepared in the morning or the night before and refrigerated

---

FOR 4	FOR 6	INGREDIENTS	INSTRUCTIONS

BARBECUED PORK CHOPS

4–6	6–8	large pork chops, 1-inch thick	Add pork chops to the marinade (below) and spoon liquid over the chops. Turn chops occasionally while marinating. / / Barbecue the chops over glowing charcoals (not too hot) for 15 minutes on each side, basting frequently with the marinade.

Marinade

Combine the marinade ingredients together in a baking dish or pan and mix well.

10 × 10 in	12 × 14 in	Utensil: baking dish or pan
¼ C	⅓ C	soy sauce
¼ C	⅓ C	dry sherry wine
¼ C	⅓ C	water
2 tbl	3 tbl	brown sugar, firmly packed
1	2	crushed garlic cloves

OR 4	FOR 6	INGREDIENTS	INSTRUCTIONS

APPLE-SPICE PILAFF

qt, 2 qt	1 qt, 2 qt	Utensils: saucepans
C	1½ C	long-grain white rice
tbl	½ C	butter or margarine
tsp	1½ tsp	salt
⁄8 tsp	¼ tsp	pepper
tsp	1½ tsp	grated orange peel
⁄3 C	½ C	chopped onion
⁄2 C	¾ C	chopped celery
⁄4 C	⅓ C	chopped parsley
⁄8 tsp	¼ tsp	dried rosemary
C	3 C	apple cider or juice

Brown rice in the butter in the large saucepan, stirring well. Add salt, pepper, grated orange peel, chopped onion, and chopped celery. Sauté the mixture for about 5 minutes, stirring well. Add parsley and rosemary and set mixture aside. In the small saucepan, bring the cider to a boil and stir it into the rice mixture with a fork. Cover rice tightly and cook over low heat for 35 minutes, or until all the liquid is absorbed. Keep covered until ready to serve.

MARINATED BEAN SALAD

can	2 cans	cut green beans, 8-oz can
can	2 cans	cut wax beans, 8-oz can
can	2 cans	red kidney beans, 8-oz can
⁄4 C	½ C	finely chopped onion
⁄4 C	½ C	chopped green pepper

Drain the liquid from the cans of beans and add beans to marinade mixture (below). Chop the onion and green pepper, add to mixture, and stir to coat all beans with the marinade. Cover and refrigerate for 24 hours.

Marinade

ed	lrg	Utensil: salad bowl
⁄4 C	⅓ C	salad oil
⁄2 C	¾ C	sugar
⁄2 C	⅔ C	cider vinegar
⁄4 tsp	1 tsp	salt
⁄4 tsp	1 tsp	pepper

Combine all marinade ingredients in bowl and mix well.

FOR 4	FOR 6	INGREDIENTS

INSTRUCTIONS

RICOTTA APPLE PUDDING

	med	Utensil: mixing bowl
	1 lb	ricotta cheese
	½ tsp	cinnamon
	2 C	applesauce
	3 tbl	sugar

Combine all ingredients in a mixing bowl and blend well. Pour into serving dish and refrigerate until ready to serve.

---

menu 29

Barbera†
California Chili
Green Salad
French Bread
Chocolate Angel Cake

† A dry Burgundy wine; serve at cool room temperature (65°)

TIMETABLE

Night before	Prepare Chocolate Angel Cake; place beans in water
*5:15 pm	Prepare California Chili
*6:30	Slice, butter, and wrap French Bread
7:45	Place French Bread in oven at 300°
7:45	Prepare salad and salad dressing
8:00	Dinner is served

* May be prepared in the morning or the night before and refrigerated

FOR 4	FOR 6	INGREDIENTS	INSTRUCTIONS

CALIFORNIA CHILI

FOR 4	FOR 6	INGREDIENTS
5 qt	6 qt	Utensils: saucepan
10 in	12 in	skillet
¼ lb	⅓ lb	pinto beans
1 lb 12 oz	1 lb 12 oz and 1 lb	canned tomatoes
¼ C	⅓ C	butter or margarine
1½ C	2 C	chopped green peppers
5 C	7 C	chopped onion
¼ C	⅓ C	chopped parsley
1	2	chopped garlic clove
1 lb	1½ lb	lean ground beef
½ lb	¾ lb	lean ground pork
¼ C	⅓ C	chili powder
1 tbl	1½ tbl	salt
½ tsp	¾ tsp	pepper
1 tsp	1½ tsp	cuminseed
1 tsp	1½ tsp	MSG

Place beans in saucepan, cover with cold water, and let soak overnight. Drain water from beans, add tomatoes, and simmer for 5 minutes. Melt butter in skillet; sauté green peppers, onion, parsley, and garlic for 10 minutes. Add mixture to saucepan. Brown the beef and pork in the skillet for 5 minutes. Drain off the grease and add the beef and pork to the saucepan. Add the chili powder, salt, pepper, cuminseed, and monosodium glutamate (MSG). Cover and simmer for 1 hour. Remove cover and simmer for another 30 minutes.

FRENCH BREAD

FOR 4	FOR 6	INGREDIENTS
sm	sm	Utensil: saucepan
½ loaf	¾ loaf	French bread
3 tbl	¼ C	butter

Slice the loaf of bread. Melt butter in saucepan and brush each slice with melted butter. Arrange slices back into loaf form and wrap with aluminum foil. / / Heat in 300° oven for 15 minutes.

FOR 4	FOR 6	INGREDIENTS	INSTRUCTIONS

GREEN SALAD

med	lrg	Utensil: salad bowl	Wash and dry lettuce and break leaves into salad bowl. Toss with dressing just before serving.
1 sm hd	1 med hd	lettuce	

Dressing

Mix all ingredients in glass jar. Shake well before adding to the salad.

FOR 4	FOR 6	INGREDIENTS
1 pt	1 pt	Utensil: glass jar
3 tbl	5 tbl	olive oil
1½ tbl	2½ tbl	wine vinegar
⅛ tsp	⅛ tsp	garlic powder
½ tsp	¾ tsp	sweet basil
½ tsp	¾ tsp	salt
¼ tsp	⅓ tsp	freshly ground black pepper

CHOCOLATE ANGEL CAKE

FOR 4	FOR 6	INGREDIENTS
	sm	Utensils: double boiler
	2 sm,	mixing bowls
	1 med	
	8 × 8 in	baking dish
	1 pkg	chocolate chips, 6-oz pkg
	1 tbl	sugar
	2	eggs
	½ pt	heavy cream
	5 oz	angle food cake

In the top of double boiler, melt chocolate chips and sugar. Separate eggs. In a medium mixing bowl, beat egg yolks. Remove chocolate mixture from double boiler and stir into beaten egg yolks. Let mixture cool 5 minutes. In a small mixing bowl, beat egg whites until stiff; in another small mixing bowl, beat cream until stiff. Fold egg whites and whipped cream into chocolate mixture. Break the angel food cake into bite-size pieces. Arrange a layer of cake pieces in bottom of buttered baking dish (use about one-half of the cake for the bottom layer). Cover the cake with a layer of chocolate mixture. Add a layer of the remaining cake pieces and cover with the remaining chocolate mixture. Chill overnight.

<h1>menu 30</h1>

Pinot Chardonnay†
Chicken and Rice Pilaff
Pepper Tomatoes
Fluffy Cranberry Mold
Bakery Rolls
Chocolate Refrigerator Cake

TIMETABLE

Night before	Prepare Chocolate Refrigerator Cake
*4:00 pm	Chill wine
*4:00	Prepare Fluffy Cranberry Mold
*6:30	Prepare Chiken and Rice Pilaff
6:45	Place Chicken Casserole in oven at 375°
*7:15	Prepare rolls
*7:20	Prepare Pepper Tomatoes
7:40	Place rolls in oven
7:40	Place tomatoes in oven
7:45	Unmold salad onto serving plate
8:00	Dinner is served

† A dry Chablis wine; serve chilled (45°)

* May be prepared in the morning or the night before and refrigerated

FOR 4	FOR 6	INGREDIENTS
8 × 8 in	9 × 9 in	Utensil: shallow baking dish
3	4	large tomatoes
1 sm	1 med	green peppers
1½ tsp	2 tsp	sugar
¾ tsp	1 tsp	salt
⅛ tsp	⅛ tsp	pepper
1½ tbl	2 tbl	prepared mustard
2 tbl	3 tbl	soda cracker crumbs
4 tsp	6 tsp	butter or margarine

INSTRUCTIONS

PEPPER TOMATOES

Wash tomatoes and cut out cores. Cut tomatoes into halves horizontally and place in baking dish. Chop the green peppers into fine pieces. Sprinkle the tomato surfaces with salt, pepper, and sugar. Spread a thin layer of mustard on each tomato and sprinkle with chopped green pepper and cracker crumbs. Dot with butter. / / Bake at 375° for 10 to 20 minutes.

CHICKEN AND RICE PILAFF

FOR 4	FOR 6	INGREDIENTS	
2 qt	3 qt	Utensil: shallow, covered baking dish	
7 oz pkg	14 oz pkg	precooked rice	
½ pkg	1 pkg	dry onion soup mix	
1 can	2 cans	cream of mushroom soup	
1⅓ C	2⅔ C	boiling water	
⅓ C	⅔ C	dry sherry wine	
2 tbl	4 tbl	chopped pimientos	
4	6	chicken breasts	
2 tbl	4 tbl	melted butter or margarine	
1 tsp	2 tsp	salt	
⅛ tsp	¼ tsp	pepper	
⅛ tsp	¼ tsp	paprika	

In the baking dish, combine rice, onion soup mix, cream of mushroom soup, boiling water, sherry wine, and chopped pimientos. Place chicken breasts on top of rice mixture. Brush the chicken breasts with melted butter and then season with salt, pepper, and paprika. Cover. / / Bake in preheated 375° oven for 1 hour and 15 minutes.

FLUFFY CRANBERRY MOLD

		INGREDIENTS	
	med	Utensils: mixing bowl	
	2 qt	gelatin mold	
	1 pkg	lemon gelatin	
	1 C	boiling water	
	½ C	mayonnaise	
	⅓ C	cottage cheese	
	1 tbl	lemon juice	
	¼ tsp	salt	
	1 lb	canned whole cranberry sauce	
	½ C	chopped celery	
	2	bananas	

In a mixing bowl, dissolve the gelatin in boiling water. Add the mayonnaise, cottage cheese, lemon juice, and salt. Beat the mixture and put into refrigerator until almost set. Beat until fluffy. Fold in the cranberries, celery, and sliced bananas. Refrigerate in a gelatin mold until ready to serve.

BAKERY ROLLS

	12	bakery rolls

Wrap rolls in aluminum foil. / / Heat for 20 minutes at 375°.

CHOCOLATE REFRIGERATOR CAKE

4 qt		Utensils: saucepan
2 sm		mixing bowls
1½ qt		loaf pan
6 oz		sweet chocolate
6 tsp		water
2		eggs
2 tbl		powdered sugar
½ C		chopped walnuts
1 C		heavy cream
1 pkg		lady fingers
6		maraschino cherries with stems

Heat chocolate and water in saucepan until chocolate has melted. Remove from heat. Separate eggs. Add egg yolks to saucepan and beat until blended. Add the sugar and nuts. In a small mixing bowl, beat the egg whites and fold into the chocolate mixture. In a small mixing bowl, whip the cream and fold into the chocolate mixture. Line the loaf pan with waxed paper and cover the bottom with lady fingers. Pour the chocolate mixture into the pan and chill for 12 hours. / / Unmold the cake when ready to serve and top each serving with a maraschino cherry.

menu 31

TIMETABLE
*Morning	Bake Meringue Pie
*3:00 pm	Chill wine
*3:00	Prepare Chicken and Wild Rice
4:00	Place Chicken Casserole in oven at 300°
*4:00	Prepare Lime-Avocado Salad
7:25	Cook cauliflower
7:50	Prepare crumbs for cauliflower
8:00	Dinner is served

† A dry Chablis wine; serve chilled (45°)

* May be prepared in the morning or the night before and refrigerated

---

FOR 4	FOR 6	INGREDIENTS	INSTRUCTIONS

CHICKEN AND WILD RICE

FOR 4	FOR 6	INGREDIENTS
12 in	12 in	Utensils: skillet
2½ qt	3 qt	covered baking dish
3 lb	5 lb	chicken fryer parts
⅓ C	½ C	olive oil
1 tsp	1¼ tsp	salt
⅛ tsp	⅛ tsp	pepper
½ C	¾ C	flour
¼ C	⅓ C	chopped onion
½ tsp	¾ tsp	garlic powder
¾ tsp	1 tsp	dried rosemary
4 oz	6 oz	canned mushrooms
½ C	¾ C	Sauterne wine
¾ C	1 C	uncooked wild rice
½ tsp	¾ tsp	salt
⅛ tsp	⅛ tsp	pepper

Wash chicken parts and drain on paper towels. Heat olive oil in skillet. Sprinkle chicken parts with salt, pepper, and flour. Brown parts in skillet and set aside. Clean and chop onion. Add onions, together with the garlic powder, rosemary, mushrooms (with their juice), and Sauterne wine, to the remaining olive oil in skillet. Bring to a boil and transfer into baking dish. Add the wild rice, salt, and pepper. Place chicken parts on top of other ingredients in baking dish. / / Add enough hot water to almost cover the chicken, cover, and bake in preheated 300° oven for 3½ to 4 hours.

CAULIFLOWER WITH CRUMBS

FOR 4	FOR 6	INGREDIENTS
sm, 2 qt	sm, 3 qt	Utensils: saucepans
med hd	lrg hd	cauliflower
¾ tsp	1 tsp	salt
½ C	¾ C	bread crumbs
4 tbl	6 tbl	butter or margarine
⅛ tsp	⅛ tsp	paprika

Place cauliflower in a saucepan, add salt and boiling water to cover. Cook, uncovered, 20 to 30 minutes, or until tender. Drain. In a small saucepan, brown the bread crumbs in butter. Sprinkle with paprika. Place cauliflower in serving bowl and sprinkle the crumb mixture over top.

LIME-AVOCADO SALAD

	INGREDIENTS
med	Utensils: mixing bowl
1 qt	gelatin mold
1 pkg	lime gelatin
¾ tsp	salt
1½ C	hot water
2 tbl	lemon juice
1 tbl	grated onion
1 C	mashed avocado
5	lettuce leaves
¼ C	mayonnaise

Place the gelatin and salt in mixing bowl. Add hot water and stir until gelatin has dissolved. Add lemon juice and grated onion. Chill until slightly thickened. Beat until light and fluffy. Fold in the mashed avocado and pour into lightly oiled gelatin mold. Chill until firm. / / Unmold onto serving plate lined with lettuce leaves and top with mayonnaise.

FOR 4	FOR 6	INGREDIENTS	INSTRUCTIONS

MERINGUE PIE

FOR 4	FOR 6	INGREDIENTS
	2 sm	Utensils: mixing bowls
	10 in	pie plate
	1 qt	saucepan
	4	eggs
	¼ tsp	cream of tartar
	1½ C	sugar
	1½ tbl	lemon juice
	½ C	heavy cream

Preheat oven to 250°. Separate eggs. In a mixing bowl, beat egg whites until stiff. Add cream of tartar and one cup of sugar and blend in. Pour mixture into pie plate and bake for 1 hour at 250°. Let cool. / /

In a saucepan, beat the egg yolks, then beat in one-half cup of sugar and lemon juice. Cook over low heat until thick, stirring constantly. Cool. In a small bowl, whip the cream. When egg yolk mixture has cooled, pour into pie shell and top with whipped cream. Refrigerate until ready to serve.

menu 32

Pinot Chardonnay†
Chicken Bird
Corn Custard
Orange-Cranberry Salad
Buttermilk Biscuits
Honey Prune Bread
Lemon Sherbet

TIMETABLE

*4:00 pm	Chill wine
*4:00	Prepare Orange-Cranberry Salad and refrigerate
*4:30	Prepare Honey Prune Bread
*6:30	Prepare chicken stuffing
6:55	Prepare chicken halves and place in oven at 375°
7:10	Prepare Corn Custard
7:20	Place corn in oven
7:25	Stuff chicken cavities, baste, and return to oven
7:35	Unmold salad onto serving plates
7:45	Place biscuits in baking pan; set oven at 450°
7:50	Remove chicken and corn from oven
7:50	Place biscuits in oven
8:00	Dinner is served

† A dry Chablis wine; serve chilled (45°)

* May be prepared in the morning or the night before and refrigerated

FOR 4	FOR 6	INGREDIENTS
6 in, 12 in	6 in, 12 in	Utensils: skillets
med	lrg	cookie sheet
3 tbl	5 tbl	butter or margarine
2 tbl	3 tbl	chopped onion
3 tbl	4 tbl	chopped green pepper
2 tbl	3 tbl	chopped celery
1	2	minced garlic cloves
3 tbl	4 tbl	chopped parsley
8-oz can	2 6-oz cans	canned oysters
1 tsp	1½ tsp	salt
¼ tsp	⅓ tsp	ground black pepper
¼ tsp	⅓ tsp	cayenne pepper
1 C	1½ C	bread crumbs
⅓ C	½ C	oyster juice
2	3	broiler chickens split in halves
1 tbl	1½ tbl	melted butter or margarine
½ C	¾ C	water
1 tbl	1½ tbl	melted butter or margarine

INSTRUCTIONS

CHICKEN BIRD

Melt butter in skillet. Chop the onion, green bell pepper, and celery and add to skillet. Mince the garlic cloves and chop the parsley and add to skillet. Drain and reserve the oyster juice from the canned oysters, chop the oysters, and add to skillet with the salt, ground black pepper, and cayenne pepper. Sauté the mixture for 10 minutes, stirring well. Add the bread crumbs and oyster juice and mix well. / / Place chicken halves on cookie sheet with the skin side up. Brush with melted butter, add water to cookie sheet, and bake at 375° for 25 minutes. After the required baking time, remove sheet from oven, turn chickens over, and fill cavities with the stuffing. Baste with the remaining melted butter and bake for 20 minutes more.

CORN CUSTARD

FOR 4	FOR 6	INGREDIENTS
1 qt	1½ qt	Utensil: baking dish
2	3	eggs
¼ C	½ C	milk
1 tbl	2 tbl	melted butter or margarine
2 tsp	4 tsp	sugar
½ tsp	1 tsp	salt
⅛ tsp	¼ tsp	pepper
1 lb can	2 lb can	canned whole-kernel corn
⅛ tsp	⅛ tsp	paprika

Whip the eggs in a buttered baking dish, using a fork. Add milk, butter, sugar, salt, pepper, and corn (including the liquid in the can). Bake at 375° for 30 minutes, or until mixture has set. Sprinkle with paprika before serving.

ORANGE-CRANBERRY SALAD

	INGREDIENTS
med	Utensils: mixing bowl
2 qt	gelatine mold
1 pkg	orange gelatin
1½ C	boiling water
1 lb	canned cranberry sauce
1 sm	chopped apple unpeeled
1 C	chopped celery
¼ hd	lettuce

Place gelatin in mixing bowl. Add boiling water and stir until gelatin has dissolved. Blend in the cranberry sauce and refrigerate until the mixture just starts to jell. Fold in the chopped apple and chopped celery. Turn mixture into a gelatin mold and refrigerate until firm. Wash and dry lettuce and shred onto a serving plate. Turn mold out on top of a bed of shredded lettuce.

BUTTERMILK BISCUITS

FOR 4	FOR 6	INGREDIENTS	INSTRUCTIONS
1 8 in	2 8 in	Utensil: cake pan	Preheat oven to 450°. Separate and place biscuits in cake pan with the
1 pkg	2 pkg	prepared refrigerator buttermilk biscuits	sides touching. Bake for 8 to 10 minutes.

HONEY PRUNE BREAD

FOR 4	FOR 6	INGREDIENTS	INSTRUCTIONS
	med	Utensils: mixing bowl	Preheat oven to 325°. In a mixing bowl, beat the egg, then add the
	1	loaf pan	vanilla extract, baking soda, prunes, and water. Mix and let stand for 15
	1	egg	minutes. Add the honey. Sift the flour and sugar together and mix into
	1½ tsp	vanilla extract	the prune mixture. Fold in the chopped walnuts. Pour mixture into a
	1 tsp	baking soda	greased and floured loaf pan and bake for 1 hour. Let bread cool for 20
	1¾ C	chopped, pitted prunes	minutes before removing from pan.
	1 C	boiling water	
	½ C	honey	
	2 C	flour	
	⅔ C	sugar	
	1½ C	chopped walnuts	

LEMON SHERBET

FOR 4	FOR 6	INGREDIENTS	INSTRUCTIONS
1 pt	1½ pt	lemon sherbet	Spoon sherbet into serving dishes and serve with Honey Prune Bread.

menu 33

Grenache Rosé†
Chicken Cacciatora
White Rice
Sicilian Artichokes
Soufflé Salad
Cherry Sundae

TIMETABLE

*4:00 pm	Chill wine
*4:00	Prepare Soufflé Salad
*5:00	Prepare Sicilian Artichokes
*6:00	Prepare Chicken Cacciatora and cover
7:30	Place artichokes in oven at 325°
7:30	Prepare rice
7:40	Unmold salad onto serving plate
8:00	Dinner is served

After dinner Prepare Cherry Sundae just before serving

† A light, dry rosé wine; serve chilled (45°)   * May be prepared in the morning or the night before and refrigerated

---

FOR 4	FOR 6	INGREDIENTS
med		Utensils: mixing bowl
		gelatin mold
2 qt		
1 pkg		lime gelatin
1 C		boiling water
3 tbl		lemon juice
⅛ tsp		salt
⅓ C		mayonnaise
8½ oz		canned crushed pineapple
½ C		seedless grapes halved
2		bananas
5		lettuce leaves

INSTRUCTIONS

SOUFFLÉ SALAD

In mixing bowl, add gelatin and boiling water and stir until gelatin has dissolved. Mix in the lemon juice, salt, mayonnaise, and juice from the pineapple. Refrigerate until it just starts to set. Beat until creamy, then add the pineapple, grapes, and sliced bananas. Pour into lightly oiled gelatin mold. Chill until firm. / / Place lettuce leaves on serving plate and turn mold out onto lettuce-leaf bed.

94

SICILIAN ARTICHOKES

FOR 4	FOR 6	INGREDIENTS
4 qt	5 qt	Utensils: saucepan
sm	sm	mixing bowl
9 × 9 in	9 × 12 in	baking pan
4	6	artichokes
1 tsp	1½ tsp	salt
¼ C	⅓ C	chopped onion
1	2	chopped garlic clove
1 tbl	1½ tbl	chopped fresh parsley
2 tbl	3 tbl	grated Romano cheese
1 C	1½ C	bread crumbs
½ tsp	¾ tsp	salt
½ tsp	¾ tsp	pepper
¼ C	⅓ C	olive oil
2 tbl	3 tbl	water
2 tbl	3 tbl	olive oil

In a saucepan, cover the artichokes with boiling water. Add salt and cook uncovered for 20 to 30 minutes, or until a leaf will pull out. Drain. Cut off stalks and tips of artichokes, press open centers, and remove chokes. Spread remaining leaves open. In a small mixing bowl, mix onion, garlic, parsley, cheese, bread crumbs, salt, and pepper. Moisten mixture with olive oil and water and fill each leaf with a small amount of the mixture. Fill the centers with the mixture also. / /

Place artichokes in baking pan, sprinkle with remaining olive oil, and pour a little water in the bottom of the pan. Bake for 25 to 30 minutes at 325°.

WHITE RICE

FOR 4	FOR 6	INGREDIENTS
1 qt	2 qt	Utensil: saucepan
1 C	1½ C	long-grain white rice
2 C	3 C	water
1 tsp	1½ tsp	shortening
½ tsp	¾ tsp	salt

Bring water to a boil in a saucepan. Add shortening and salt. Slowly add rice, shaking pan to level rice grains. Turn heat to low, cover tightly, and cook 20 to 25 minutes, or until all liquid is absorbed. Keep covered until ready to serve.

FOR 4	FOR 6	INGREDIENTS	INSTRUCTIONS

CHICKEN CACCIATORA

FOR 4	FOR 6	INGREDIENTS
12 in	12 in	Utensil: skillet
1 lrg	2 med	chicken fryer
¼ C	⅓ C	flour
½ tsp	¾ tsp	paprika
½ tsp	¾ tsp	salt
3 tbl	4 tbl	olive oil
1	2	chopped garlic clove
1 tbl	1½ tbl	minced parsley
1 can	2 cans	mushrooms, 4-oz can
15-oz can	15-oz and 8-oz cans	canned tomato sauce
½ C	¾ C	dry white wine
⅛ tsp	¼ tsp	MSG
½ tsp	¾ tsp	salt
⅛ tsp	¼ tsp	pepper

Wash and dry chicken and cut into pieces. Place the flour, paprika, and salt into a paper bag. Add a few pieces of chicken at a time and shake to coat with flour. Heat the olive oil in the skillet, and sauté the chicken pieces until lightly browned all over. While sautéing, sprinkle with chopped garlic and minced parsley. After all pieces of chicken are browned, add the mushrooms with their juice, tomato sauce, wine, monosodium glutamate (MSG), salt, and pepper. Cover and simmer about 30 minutes, stirring occasionally. Serve with rice.

CHERRY SUNDAE

2 qt	Utensil: saucepan
1 lb 5 oz	canned cherry pie filling
½ C	port wine
½ C	orange marmalade
1 qt	vanilla ice cream

Empty pie filling into saucepan. Stir in the wine and marmalade. Heat thoroughly. Spoon hot sauce over individual ice cream servings.

menu 34

Grenache Rosé†
Chicken Paprikash
Spicy Spinach
Pear and Raspberry Salad
Bakery Onion Bread
Sherry Cream

TIMETABLE

*4:00 pm	Chill wine
*4:00	Prepare Sherry Cream
*5:00	Defrost raspberries
*5:30	Prepare chicken
7:00	Place chicken casserole in oven at 325°
*7:00	Prepare Spicy Spinach
7:20	Place spinach in oven
*7:20	Prepare bread
7:40	Place bread in oven
7:45	Prepare Pear and Raspberry Salad
8:00	Dinner is served

† A light, dry rosé wine; serve chilled (45°)

* May be prepared in the morning or the night before and refrigerated

| FOR 4 | FOR 6 | INGREDIENTS | INSTRUCTIONS |

SHERRY CREAM

3 sm		Utensils: mixing bowls
1 qt		saucepan
1½ qt		shallow baking dish
1½ C		milk
1 env		unflavored gelatin
5 tbl		cold water
2		eggs
⅓ C		sugar
⅓ C		Sherry wine
½ C		heavy cream
12		split lady fingers

Scald milk in saucepan. In a small mixing bowl, soften the gelatin in cold water and add to the scalded milk. Separate eggs. Beat egg yolks slightly and add to milk mixture together with sugar and wine. Beat egg whites until stiff and whip the cream in separate bowls. Fold the egg whites into whipped cream, then add to the gelatin mixture. Line serving dish with lady fingers, add gelatin mixture, and top with more lady fingers. Refrigerate until ready to serve.

FOR 4	FOR 6	INGREDIENTS
12 in	12 in	Utensils: skillet
4 qt	6 qt	saucepan
9 × 12 in	10 × 14 in	baking pan
3½ lb	5 lb	fryer chickens or parts
3 tbl	4 tbl	butter or margarine
⅓ C	⅔ C	chopped onion
6 oz	12 oz	noodles
2 qt	3 qt	water
1 tsp	1½ tsp	salt
3 tbl	6 tbl	flour
1½ tbl	2 tbl	paprika
1½ tsp	2 tsp	salt
¼ tsp	½ tsp	pepper
1 can	2 cans	canned chicken broth
¾ pt	1 pt	commercial sour cream
¾ tbl	1 tbl	Worcestershire sauce

INSTRUCTIONS

CHICKEN PAPRIKASH

Cut chicken into pieces. Wash and drain on paper towels. Melt butter in a large skillet and brown chicken. While chicken is browning, chop the onions and start water boiling for noodles. As soon as water has come to a rapid boil, add noodles and salt, and cook uncovered for 7 minutes. Drain noodles into colander and rinse gently with hot water. Remove the chicken from the skillet when browned. Blend into the pan drippings the flour, paprika, salt, and pepper. Add onions and slowly add chicken broth, stirring mixture as you pour. Cook until mixture thickens, stirring constantly. Mix in the sour cream and Worcestershire sauce. Place all of the noodles into a baking pan, add one-half of the sauce, and mix well. Arrange the chicken parts on top of the noodle layer. Pour the remaining sauce over the top. / / Bake for one hour in preheated 325° oven.

SPICY SPINACH

FOR 4	FOR 6	INGREDIENTS
10 in	12 in	Utensils: skillet
1½ qt	2 qt	baking dish
2 lb	3 lb	fresh spinach
4	6	bacon strips
⅓ C	½ C	chopped onion
⅓ tsp	½ tsp	cinnamon
1½ tbl	2 tbl	red wine vinegar
¾ tsp	1 tsp	salt
⅓ tsp	½ tsp	pepper

Wash spinach and cut leaves crosswise into ½-inch strips. Cut bacon strips into 1-inch pieces and cook in skillet until crisp. Remove bacon and dry on paper towel. Sauté onion in bacon grease until lightly browned. Remove from heat, add cinnamon, vinegar, salt, and pepper. Combine with spinach and place in greased baking dish. Crumble bacon pieces on top and cover. / / Bake at 325° for 40 minutes.

PEAR AND RASPBERRY SALAD

FOR 4	FOR 6	INGREDIENTS
4 halves	6 halves	canned pears, 1-lb 13-oz can
4 tbl	6 tbl	frozen raspberries, 10-oz pkg
4	6	lettuce leaves

Defrost raspberries. Arrange pear halves on lettuce leaves. Place about 1 tablespoon of raspberries into center of each pear half.

BAKERY ONION BREAD

FOR 4	FOR 6	INGREDIENTS
½ loaf	1 loaf	onion bread
2 tbl	4 tbl	butter

Butter each slice of bread and place slices back into loaf form. Wrap with aluminum foil. / / Heat for 20 minutes at 325°.

menu 35

Grey Riesling†
Foil Chicken (Coq Au Vin)
White and Wild Rice
Avocado and Tomato Salad
French Bread
Cheery Cherry Torte

TIMETABLE

*5:00 pm	Chill wine
*5:00	Prepare dessert and refrigerate
*6:00	Prepare chicken
*6:50	Wrap bread in aluminum foil
*7:00	Prepare salad and salad dressing
7:00	Bake chicken in 350° oven
7:15	Heat water for rice
7:25	Cook rice
7:30	Place bread in oven to warm
7:50	Toss salad with salad dressing
8:00	Dinner is served

† A dry Rhine wine; serve chilled (45°)

* May be prepared in the morning or the night before and refrigerated

FOR 4	FOR 6	INGREDIENTS	INSTRUCTIONS

CHEERY CHERRY TORTE

FOR 4	FOR 6	INGREDIENTS
lrg		Utensils: mixing bowl
1½ qt		baking dish
3		egg whites
½ tsp		cream of tartar
1 C		sugar
1 tsp		vanilla extract
1 C		crumbled soda crackers
½ C		chopped nuts
1 box		whipped topping mix
1 can		cherry pie filling

Preheat oven to 350°. In a large mixing bowl, beat the egg whites and cream of tartar until stiff. Blend in the sugar, vanilla extract, crumbled soda crackers, and nuts. Place mixture in a greased baking dish and bake for 25 minutes. Let cool. Beat the whipped topping mix according to the instructions on the package and spread the topping on the cooled meringue. Top with the cherry pie filling and refrigerate until ready to serve.

FOR 4	FOR 6	INGREDIENTS
12 in	12 in	Utensils: skillet
sm	sm	mixing bowl
med	lrg	cookie sheet
1 lrg	2 med	chicken fryer
¼ C	⅓ C	butter or margarine
8 sm	12 sm	White onions
½ lb	¾ lb	fresh mushrooms
1	2	minced garlic cloves
¾ tsp	1 tsp	salt
¼ tsp	½ tsp	thyme
¼ C	⅓ C	minced parsley
⅛ tsp	¼ tsp	ground rosemary
¼ tsp	⅓ tsp	ground pepper
1 C	1½ C	dry red wine
sm	sm	Utensil: saucepan
4 tbl	6 tbl	butter
½ loaf	¾ loaf	French bread

FOIL CHICKEN

Wash and dry chicken parts and brown the chicken in a large skillet with the margarine. Lay out a 12-inch long piece of aluminum foil (heavy) for each serving. Divide chicken pieces evenly and lay on the pieces of foil. Add the onions to the margarine still in the skillet and brown for about 10 minutes. Then add the mushrooms and cook about 3 minutes longer. Divide the onion-and-mushroom mixture evenly and add to the chicken on the foil pieces. Turn up the edges of the foil. In a small mixing bowl, combine the minced garlic cloves, salt, thyme, minced parsley, rosemary, pepper, and wine. Pour the mixed spices over the chicken in the foil and seal the foil packages well. / / Place the packages on a cookie sheet and bake in preheated 350° oven for 1 hour. Serve the individual packages and let the guests unwrap their own packages on their plates.

FRENCH BREAD

Soften the butter in a saucepan over low heat. Slice the loaf of French bread, butter each slice, and arrange the loaf slices in original shape. Wrap the loaf in aluminum foil. / / Heat at 350° for 30 minutes.

WHITE AND WILD RICE

FOR 4	FOR 6	INGREDIENTS
2 qt		Utensil: saucepan
2 C		water
2 tbl		butter or margarine
1 pkg		white and wild rice mix, 6-oz pkg

To water in a saucepan, add butter and the contents of the spice envelope included in the package of white and wild rice mix. Bring to a boil over high heat. Add rice, stir well, and bring back to a boil. Lower heat, cover pan, and simmer for 15 minutes. Leave covered and stir well just before serving.

AVOCADO AND TOMATO SALAD

FOR 4	FOR 6	INGREDIENTS
med	lrg	Utensil: salad bowl
1 sm hd	1 lrg hd	lettuce
½ bnch	1 bnch	watercress
1 med	2 sm	tomatoes
½	1	avocado
2 tsp	3 tsp	lemon juice

Wash and dry lettuce and watercress. Tear into salad bowl. Cut tomatoes into small wedges and add to lettuce and watercress. / / Cut avocado into slices just before serving and squeeze lemon juice over each slice. Toss with salad dressing.

Dressing

FOR 4	FOR 6	INGREDIENTS
1 pt	1 pt	Utensil: glass jar
⅓ C	½ C	salad oil
3 tbl	4 tbl	wine vinegar
⅓ tsp	½ tsp	catsup
1 sm	1 med	crushed garlic clove
¼ tsp	⅓ tsp	salt
⅛ tsp	¼ tsp	freshly ground black pepper
¼ tsp	⅓ tsp	paprika

In a glass jar combine the salad oil, wine vinegar, catsup, crushed garlic clove, salt, pepper, and paprika. Refrigerate until ready to serve. / / Shake vigorously and add to salad.

menu 36

Cabernet Rosé†
Ham Cheese Strata
Baked Bananas
Tomato Caper Salad
Brandied Peach Compote

TIMETABLE
*Morning   Chill wine
*Morning   Prepare Ham Cheese Strata casserole
 7:00 pm   Place Ham Cheese Strata in oven at 325°
*7:05   Prepare salad and salad dressing and refrigerate
 7:25   Prepare and bake bananas
 7:30   Prepare Peach Compote
 8:00   Dinner is served

† A dry rosé wine; serve chilled (45°)   * May be prepared in the morning or the night before and refrigerated

---

FOR 4	FOR 6	INGREDIENTS
1 qt	2 qt	Utensils: saucepan
med	med	mixing bowl
9 × 9 in	10 × 13 in	baking dish
¾ C	1 C	water
1 pkg	2 pkg	frozen broccoli, chopped
½ tsp	1 tsp	salt
8	12	white bread slices
½ lb	¾ lb	diced sharp Cheddar cheese
1½ C	2½ C	diced cooked ham
4	6	eggs
2½ C	4 C	milk
1½ tbl	2½ tbl	minced onion
¼ tsp	¼ tsp	salt
¼ tsp	½ tsp	dry mustard

INSTRUCTIONS

HAM CHEESE STRATA

In the saucepan, bring water to a boil. Add broccoli and salt and cover. Bring water back to a boil, reduce heat, and cook gently for 8 to 10 minutes. Drain. While broccoli is cooking, cut large circles from bread, and from each circle cut a small hole out of the center to form a doughnut shape. Fit the scraps of bread (not the circles or holes) into the bottom of the baking dish. Place the cheese into the casserole to form a layer, then add a layer of broccoli. Add the diced ham as a layer and top with the doughnuts and doughnut holes to form a pattern. In the mixing bowl, beat the eggs, then add milk, minced onion, salt, and dry mustard. Mix well and add mixture to casserole, pouring evenly over the top. Cover and refrigerate for at least 6 hours. / / Bake uncovered in preheated slow (325°) oven for 1 hour.

FOR 4	FOR 6	INGREDIENTS

BAKED BANANAS

FOR 4	FOR 6	INGREDIENTS
8 × 8 in	8 × 8 in	Utensil: baking pan
3	5	firm bananas
3 tbl	5 tbl	butter or margarine
2 tbl	3 tbl	honey
1 tbl	1½ tbl	lime juice

Peel bananas and cut each into 4 chunks. Melt the butter in a small baking pan and add the banana chunks. Drizzle honey and lime juice over bananas and bake at 325° for 30 minutes.

TOMATO CAPER SALAD

FOR 4	FOR 6	INGREDIENTS
sm	med	Utensil: platter
½ hd	¾ hd	lettuce
3 med	4 med	tomatoes

Wash and drain lettuce. Cut into shreds and lay the shreds on a serving platter. Wash and slice tomatoes and arrange the slices on top of the lettuce shreds. Cover and refrigerate until ready to serve. / / Just before serving, spoon the dressing over the tomatoes.

Dressing

FOR 4	FOR 6	INGREDIENTS
½ pt	½ pt	Utensil: glass jar
1 tsp	1½ tsp	lemon juice
½ tsp	¾ tsp	dill seed
1 tsp	1½ tsp	capers
1 tsp	1½ tsp	olive oil
¼ tsp	⅓ tsp	salt
¼ tsp	⅓ tsp	pepper

Combine all of the ingredients in a glass jar and refrigerate until ready to serve. / / Shake well and spoon over tomatoes.

BRANDIED PEACH COMPOTE

FOR 4	FOR 6	INGREDIENTS	INSTRUCTIONS
4 med	6 med	fresh ripe peaches	Peel and slice the peaches. Add the peaches to the syrup below and let them soak for 5 minutes. Remove the peaches place in serving dishes and boil the syrup mixture until it becomes very thick. Stir in the honey and pour the sauce over the peaches.

Syrup

FOR 4	FOR 6	INGREDIENTS	INSTRUCTIONS
1 qt	2 qt	Utensil: saucepan	In a saucepan, bring the brandy, corn syrup, and almond extract to a boil. Boil for 1 minute and remove from heat.
¼ C	⅓ C	brandy	
3 tbl	¼ C	corn syrup	
¼ tsp	⅓ tsp	almond extract	
1 tbl	1½ tbl	honey	

menu 37

Delaware†
Ham with Sherry Maple Glaze
Pineapple Loaf
Broccoli Casserole
Banana Spice Cake

TIMETABLE
*4:30 pm Chill wine
*5:00   Prepare Banana Spice Cake
 6:30   Place ham in oven at 250°
*6:30   Prepare Pineapple Loaf
*6:55   Prepare Broccoli Casserole
 7:30   Turn oven heat to 325°
 7:30   Glaze ham and return to oven
 7:30   Place Pineapple Loaf in oven
 7:30   Place Broccoli Casserole in oven
 8:00   Dinner is served

† A dry white wine; serve chilled (45°)   * May be prepared in the morning or the night before and refrigerated

---

FOR 4	FOR 6	INGREDIENTS	INSTRUCTIONS

HAM WITH SHERRY MAPLE GLAZE

sm	sm	Utensil: roasting pan
2 lb	3 lb	canned ham
½ C	½ C	Sherry wine
½ C	½ C	maple syrup

Place ham in roaster, fat side up, and bake for 1 hour in preheated 250° oven. Remove, baste with wine and syrup, and return to oven for 30 minutes at 325°.

PINEAPPLE LOAF

med	med	Utensils: mixing bowl
1 qt	1½ qt	shallow baking dish
¾ C	1 C	sugar
3 tbl	¼ C	butter or margarine
13½ oz	1 lb 4 oz	canned pineapple chunks
1 sm loaf	⅔ lrg loaf	bread slices

In a mixing bowl, cream together the sugar and butter. Stir in the pineapple chunks and juice from the can. Trim off crusts of the bread slices and break slices into small pieces. Stir into mixture. Pour into buttered baking dish. / / Bake for 30 minutes at 325°.

106

BROCCOLI CASSEROLE

FOR 4	FOR 6	INGREDIENTS
qt	4 qt	Utensils: saucepan
qt	2 qt	baking dish
½ lb	2 lb	fresh broccoli
½ tsp	¾ tsp	salt
can	1 can	cream of mushroom soup
can	1 can	fried onion rings
	(3½ oz)	

Wash and trim broccoli and cut into spears. Place spears in saucepan, cover with water, add salt. Cover and cook for 15 to 20 minutes, or until tender. Drain and place in baking dish. Cover with the mushroom soup and top with onion rings. / / Bake at 325° for 30 minutes.

BANANA SPICE CAKE

	lrg	Utensils: mixing bowl
	2 9-in	round cake pans
	1 pkg	spice cake mix
	⅛ tsp	baking soda
	¾ C	water
	1 C	mashed ripe bananas
	2	eggs

Preheat oven to 350°. In mixing bowl, combine the cake mix, baking soda, water, mashed bananas, and eggs. Beat with mixer for 4 minutes. Pour batter into greased cake pans. Bake at 350° for 25 minutes. Let cool 10 minutes, then remove from pans to cool further.

Frosting

	sm	Utensil: mixing bowl
	1 lb pkg	powdered sugar
	1	ripe banana
	2 tsp	lemon juice
	1 tsp	vanilla extract
	¼ C	butter or margarine
	½ C	chopped walnuts

Blend the powdered sugar, mashed banana, lemon juice, vanilla extract, and butter in mixing bowl. Beat until smooth. If mixture becomes too stiff to spread easily, add a few drops of water. Frost the tops and sides of cake layers, stack the layers, and top cake with chopped walnuts.

menu 38

Cabernet†
Hamburger Stroganoff
Hot Noodles
Fried Green Peppers
Cantaloupe-Grape Mold
Apple-Spice Dessert

TIMETABLE

*4:00 pm	Prepare Cantaloupe-Grape Mold
*5:30	Prepare Apple-Spice Dessert
*6:30	Prepare lemon sauce
*6:55	Prepare Fried Green Peppers
7:15	Place green peppers in oil
7:20	Unmold gelatin salad onto serving plate
7:30	Prepare Hamburger Stroganoff
7:45	Cook noodles
7:50	Fry peppers
8:00	Dinner is served

† A dry Claret wine; serve at cool room temperature (65°)

* May be prepared in the morning or the night before and refrigerated

---

FOR 4	FOR 6	INGREDIENTS	INSTRUCTIONS

HAMBURGER STROGANOFF

FOR 4	FOR 6	INGREDIENTS
10 in	12 in	Utensil: skillet
1 lb	1½ lb	lean ground beef
½ tsp	¾ tsp	salt
¼ tsp	⅓ tsp	pepper
1 can	1 can	cream of mushroom soup
2 oz	4 oz	canned mushrooms
1 C	1½ C	commercial sour cream
1 tbl	1½ tbl	chopped fresh parsley

Form the ground beef into hamburger patties and place in the skillet. Sprinkle with salt and pepper, then brown on both sides. Drain off all but one tablespoon of the drippings. Stir in the mushroom soup and canned mushrooms with liquid from the can. Simmer for 5 minutes. Blend in the sour cream and heat, but do not boil. Top with chopped parsley and serve over noodles.

HOT NOODLES

FOR 4	FOR 6	INGREDIENTS
4 qt	4 qt	Utensil: saucepan
2 qt	2 qt	water
1 tsp	1 tsp	salt
6 oz	8 oz	medium-wide noodles

Bring 2 quarts of water to a boil in saucepan. Add salt and noodles and cook, uncovered, for 8 to 10 minutes, or until noodles are tender. Drain noodles in a colander and rinse with hot water.

FRIED GREEN PEPPERS

FOR 4	FOR 6	INGREDIENTS
1 med,	1 lrg,	Utensils: shallow bowls
2 sm	2 sm	
10 in	12 in	skillet
3	5	large green peppers
2 tbl	3 tbl	olive oil
½ tsp	¾ tsp	salt
½ tsp	¾ tsp	pepper
½ C	¾ C	flour
1	2	eggs
1 C	1½ C	olive oil

Roast peppers in oven at 450° for 10 minutes, or until peppers peel easily. Peel, remove seeds, and cut into thin slices. / / Place sliced peppers into a medium, shallow bowl, add oil, salt, and pepper, and mix to coat slices with oil. Let stand for ½ hour. Drain off oil into skillet. Place flour and slightly beaten egg into two small, shallow bowls. Add olive oil to skillet and heat. Roll pepper slices in flour, dip into egg, and fry in very hot oil until golden brown.

CANTALOUPE-GRAPE MOLD

FOR 4	FOR 6	INGREDIENTS
	sm	Utensils: mixing bowl
	2 qt	gelatin mold
	1 pkg	orange gelatin
	1 C	boiling water
	½ can	frozen orange juice, 6-oz can
	½ C	water
	1 tbl	lemon juice
	1 C	finely diced fresh cantaloupe
	1 C	seedless green grapes, halved
	5	lettuce leaves

Place gelatin in mixing bowl, add boiling water, and stir until the gelatin has dissolved. Stir in the orange juice, water, and lemon juice. Let mixture cool until slightly thickened. Then stir in the cantaloupe and grapes. Pour mixture into a lightly oiled mold and refrigerate until firm / / Unmold the salad onto a bed of lettuce leaves just before serving.

APPLE-SPICE DESSERT

FOR 4	FOR 6	INGREDIENTS
	lrg	Utensils: mixing bowl
	9 × 9 in	baking pan
	1 C	sugar
	¼ C	butter or margarine
	1	egg
	1 C	flour
	1 tsp	baking soda
	1 tsp	cinnamon
	¼ tsp	nutmeg
	2 C	peeled, finely chopped apples
	½ C	finely chopped walnuts
	1 tsp	vanilla extract

Cream sugar with the butter in a mixing bowl until smoothly blended. Beat in the egg. Sift and measure the flour, then sift again with the baking soda, cinnamon, and nutmeg into the creamed mixture. Beat together until well mixed. Add apples, beating vigorously to partially crush some of the apple pieces. Stir in the nuts and vanilla extract. Spread the batter evenly into a buttered and floured baking pan. Bake in preheated 350° oven for 40 minutes, or until cake begins to pull away from edges of pan. Serve in squares topped with lemon sauce, whipped cream, or ice cream.

FOR 4	FOR 6	INGREDIENTS
qt	1 qt	Utensil: saucepan
½ C	¾ C	sugar
tbl	1 ½ tbl	cornstarch
¼ tsp	⅓ tsp	salt
C	1 ½ C	boiling water
tsp	1 ½ tsp	grated lemon rind
tbl	3 tbl	lemon juice
tbl	1 ½ tbl	butter or margarine

INSTRUCTIONS

Lemon Sauce

Mix sugar, cornstarch, and salt in saucepan. Add boiling water and stir until blended. Cook slowly until thickened and clear. Add lemon rind, lemon juice, and butter. Blend. Serve hot over cake squares.

---

menu 39

White Riesling†
Hula Chicken
White Rice
Basil Green Beans
Melon with Roquefort
Ricotta Rum Pudding

TIMETABLE

*5:30 pm	Chill wine
*5:30	Prepare Ricotta Rum Pudding and refrigerate
*5:45	Prepare Melon with Roquefort and refrigerate
*7:00	Prepare Hula Chicken
7:30	Prepare rice
7:45	Prepare green beans
7:50	Slice melon and place on lettuce leaves
8:00	Dinner is served

† A dry Rhine wine; serve chilled (45°)

* May be prepared in the morning or the night before and refrigerated

FOR 4	FOR 6	INGREDIENTS
3 qt sm	4 qt sm	Utensils: saucepan skillet
1 med	1 lrg	green pepper
2	3	minced garlic cloves
2 tbl	3 tbl	salad oil
1 can	2 cans	cream of chicken soup
13½-oz can	2 8¾-oz cans	canned pineapple tidbits
2 C	3 C	cubed, cooked chicken
2 tbl	3 tbl	soy sauce
¼ C	⅓ C	slivered almonds
1 tbl	1½ tbl	butter or margarine

1 qt	2 qt	Utensil: saucepan
2 C	3 C	water
1 tsp	1½ tsp	shortening
½ tsp	¾ tsp	salt
1 C	1½ C	long-grain white rice

INSTRUCTIONS

HULA CHICKEN

In the saucepan, sauté the green pepper with garlic in oil for 10 minutes. Blend in the soup and juice drained from pineapple tidbits. Add the chicken, pineapple tidbits, and soy sauce. Simmer for 10 minutes. / / In a small skillet, brown the almonds in butter and sprinkle on top after mixture has been placed in serving bowl. Leftover ham or turkey can be used in place of chicken.

WHITE RICE

Bring water to a boil in a saucepan. Add shortening and salt. Slowly add rice, shaking pan to level the rice grains. Turn heat to low, cover tightly and cook 20 to 25 minutes, or until all liquid is absorbed. Keep covered until ready to serve.

BASIL GREEN BEANS

qt	2 qt	Utensil: saucepan
¼ C	1 C	water
pkg	2 pkg	frozen green beans, 9-oz pkg
¼ tsp	1 tsp	salt
tbl	2 tbl	butter or margarine
tsp	1½ tsp	sweet basil

Bring water to a boil in a saucepan. Add green beans and salt. Cover and bring back to a boil. Reduce heat and cook for 4 to 7 minutes, or until beans are tender. Drain. Stir in butter and sweet basil. Cover until ready to serve.

MELON WITH ROQUEFORT

n	sm	Utensil: mixing bowl
leaves	6 leaves	lettuce
sm	1 lrg	honeydew melon
sm	2 sm	lime
C	2½ C	small-curd cottage cheese
lb	⅓ lb	Roquefort cheese

Wash and dry lettuce leaves and refrigerate. Peel the melon and cut off one end. Remove seeds. Sprinkle with lime juice. In a mixing bowl, blend the cottage cheese and Roquefort cheese. Fill the melon with the cheese mixture. Chill until ready to serve. / / Slice into 1½-inch thick slices and serve on lettuce leaves.

RICOTTA RUM PUDDING

n	med	Utensil: mixing bowl
lb	1 lb	ricotta cheese
C	½ C	milk
¼ tbl	2½ tbl	sugar
tbl	3 tbl	rum, light or dark
oz	1 oz	sweet chocolate

In a mixing bowl, combine ricotta cheese and milk. Beat until mixture is smooth and creamy. Gradually beat in the sugar and rum. Turn mixture into serving bowls and chill. / / Just before serving, sprinkle lightly with grated sweet chocolate.

menu 40

Charbono†
Meatball Stroganoff
Noodles
Stuffed Tomato Salad
French Bread
Fresh Fruit Delight
Scotch Shortbread

TIMETABLE

*5:55 pm	Prepare Scotch Shortbread
*6:00	Preheat oven to 300°
*6:10	Bake shortbread
*6:10	Stuff tomatoes and refrigerate
*6:40	Remove shortbread from oven
*6:40	Prepare Fresh Fruit Delight and refrigerate
*7:00	Slice, butter, and wrap French Bread
7:15	Prepare Meatball Stroganoff and cover to keep warm
7:30	Start water boiling for noodles
7:40	Cook noodles
7:45	Heat bread in oven at 325°
8:00	Dinner is served

† A dry Burgundy wine; serve at cool room temperature (65°)

* May be prepared in the morning or the night before and refrigerated

---

FOR 4	FOR 6	INGREDIENTS
med	med	Utensils: mixing bowl
10 in	12 in	skillet
1 lb	1½ lb	ground beef
½ C	¾ C	chopped onion
1	2	eggs
1 slice	2 slices	white bread
½ tsp	¾ tsp	salt
¼ tsp	⅓ tsp	pepper
1 can	2 cans	cream of mushroom soup
½ C	¾ C	commercial sour cream

INSTRUCTIONS

MEATBALL STROGANOFF

Mix ground beef, chopped onion, eggs, bread, salt, and pepper in a mixing bowl. Shape into meatballs and brown them in a skillet. Drain off grease. Add the mushroom soup. Cover and simmer for 10 minutes. Blend in the sour cream and cover to keep warm. Serve over noodles.

NOODLES

Bring water to a boil in large saucepan. Add salt and noodles. Cook uncovered for 8 to 10 minutes, or until tender. Drain into colander and rinse gently with hot water. Reheat noodles just before serving by rinsing again with hot water.

FOR 4	FOR 6	INGREDIENTS
5 qt	5 qt	Utensil: saucepan
3 qt	3 qt	water
1 tsp	1 tsp	salt
8 oz	12 oz	wide noodles

STUFFED TOMATO SALAD

Peel tomatoes and scrape out part of the center of each. Sprinkle the inside of each tomato with $\frac{1}{8}$ teaspoon salt. In a small mixing bowl, mix together the chopped celery, minced olives, chopped shrimp, mayonnaise, and salt. Stuff the tomatoes with the mixture and place the tomatoes on lettuce leaves, using individual serving plates. Divide the asparagus spears and place them on the plates with the tomatoes. Refrigerate until ready to serve. These may be served as a first course, if desired.

FOR 4	FOR 6	INGREDIENTS
sm	sm	Utensil: mixing bowl
	6	firm tomatoes
½ tsp	¾ tsp	salt
¾ C	1 C	chopped celery
¼ C	⅓ C	minced olives
½ C	¾ C	chopped shrimp
tbl	3 tbl	mayonnaise
tsp	1½ tsp	salt
	6	lettuce leaves
can	1 can	asparagus spears, 15-oz can

FRENCH BREAD

Soften the butter in a saucepan over low heat. Slice and butter the bread. Arrange the slices back into original loaf form and wrap with heavy aluminum foil. / / Warm at 325° for 15 to 20 minutes.

FOR 4	FOR 6	INGREDIENTS
sm	sm	Utensil: saucepan
tbl	6 tbl	butter
½ loaf	¾ loaf	French bread

FRESH FRUIT DELIGHT

FOR 4	FOR 6	INGREDIENTS
med	med	Utensil: mixing bowl
1½ C	2 C	sliced strawberries
2 med	3 med	sliced oranges
¼ C	⅓ C	Cointreau

Wash and slice strawberries into a mixing bowl. Peel oranges, slice into thin slices, cut each slice in half, and add to mixing bowl. Add Cointreau, mix gently, cover with aluminum foil, and refrigerate until ready to serve. Serve with Scotch Shortbread.

SCOTCH SHORTBREAD

	med	Utensils: mixing bowl
	9 in	pie pan
	½ C	butter
	¼ C	sugar
	1¾ C	sifted flour

Cream the butter and sugar in the mixing bowl. Gradually add flour and mix (mixture will become crumbly). Press the mixture into the pie pan, prick with a fork, and bake in preheated 300° oven for 30 minutes. Let cool, cut into wedges, and refrigerate until ready to serve. Serve with fresh fruit.

menu 41

White Pinot†
Mediterranean Seafood Platter
Parsley Potatoes
Broccoli with Almonds
Carrot and Raisin Salad
Lemon Cream

TIMETABLE

Morning	Defrost sole, if purchased frozen
*4:30 pm	Chill wine
*5:30	Prepare Lemon Cream
*6:15	Prepare Carrot and Raisin Salad
*6:45	Prepare potato balls and cover with water
7:05	Prepare and cook Broccoli with Almonds
7:15	Cook potato balls
7:20	Prepare Mediterranean Seafood Platter
7:50	Finish potatoes
7:55	Finish broccoli
8:00	Dinner is served

† A dry Chablis wine; serve chilled (45°)   * May be prepared in the morning or the night before and refrigerated

---

FOR 4	FOR 6	INGREDIENTS
1 qt	2 qt	Utensils: saucepan
sm	sm	mixing bowl
3	4	eggs
½ C	¾ C	sugar
⅓ tsp	½ tsp	salt
¼ C	6 tbl	lemon juice

INSTRUCTIONS

LEMON CREAM

Separate eggs. Beat egg yolks slightly in saucepan with a fork. Add sugar, salt, and lemon juice. Cook over low heat, stirring constantly, until slightly thickened. Cool partially. In a mixing bowl, beat the egg whites until stiff. Fold egg whites carefully into the cooled lemon mixture. Pour into serving glasses and chill. / / Serve with cookies, if desired.

117

CARROT AND RAISIN SALAD

FOR 4	FOR 6	INGREDIENTS
sm	med	Utensil: mixing bowl
2 C	3 C	grated carrots
½ C	¾ C	raisins
⅓ C	½ C	drained, crushed pineapple
3 tbl	5 tbl	pineapple juice
¼ C	⅓ C	mayonnaise
¼ tsp	¼ tsp	salt
4	6	lettuce leaves

Wash, scrape, and grate carrots. Rinse raisins in hot water, drain, and place into mixing bowl with grated carrots. Drain the pineapple, measure the required amounts of pineapple and juice, and add to mixing bowl. Add mayonnaise and salt. Mix well. Chill. / / Spoon onto lettuce leaves on serving plates.

PARSLEY POTATOES

FOR 4	FOR 6	INGREDIENTS
2 qt	3 qt	Utensil: saucepan
2 C	3 C	raw potato balls
3 C	4 C	water
¼ tsp	⅓ tsp	salt
2 tbl	3 tbl	butter or margarine
1 tbl	1½ tbl	chopped parsley

Pare potatoes and cut into balls using a French vegetable cutter or melon cutter. Cover with cold water in saucepan and let stand at least 15 minutes. / / Remove potatoes from saucepan and drain off water. Add fresh water and bring to a boil. Add salt and potatoes and cook, covered, 12 to 15 minutes, or until tender. Drain, add butter and parsley, and heat while gently tossing potato balls. Cover until ready to serve.

BROCCOLI WITH ALMONDS

FOR 4	FOR 6	INGREDIENTS
3 qt	4 qt	Utensils: saucepan
6 in	6 in	skillet
1½ lb	2 lb	fresh broccoli
4 C	6 C	water
½ tsp	¾ tsp	salt
⅓ C	½ C	butter or margarine
3 tbl	¼ C	slivered almonds

Wash broccoli, cut off tough ends of stalks, and split stems so they will cook as rapidly as the tender top portions. In a saucepan, bring water to a boil, add salt and broccoli, and cook, uncovered, for 20 to 30 minutes, or until tender. Drain and cover. Heat butter in a small skillet and add almonds, stirring until almonds start to brown. Pour over broccoli. Reheat if necessary. Cover until ready to serve.

MEDITERRANEAN SEAFOOD PLATTER

FOR 4	FOR 6	INGREDIENTS	
8 in, 12 in	8 in, 12 in	Utensils:	skillet
2 med	2 med		shallow bowls
1 lb	1½ lb	sole fillets	
¼ C	⅓ C	olive oil	
1 tsp	2 tsp	butter or margarine	
⅓ C	½ C	milk	
½ C	¾ C	flour	
½ tsp	¾ tsp	seasoned salt	
⅛ tsp	⅛ tsp	pepper	
3 tbl	5 tbl	butter or margarine	
1 tbl	1½ tbl	lemon juice	
⅓ C	½ C	canned shrimp, 4½-oz can	
⅓ C	½ C	canned or fresh grapes	
1	1½	lemons	

If sole was purchased frozen, defrost and drain on paper towels. Heat olive oil and butter in large skillet. Pour milk into a small bowl. Combine flour, seasoned salt, and pepper in another bowl. Dip fillets of sole first into milk, then into flour mixture. Fry quickly on both sides over high heat, and place on serving platter. In a small skillet, add the remaining butter, lemon juice, shrimp, and grapes. Heat just to warm through, stirring to blend. Pour mixture over fillets. Top with lemon slices.

menu 42

Pinot Noir†
Oregano Beef
Minted Peas
Italian-Style Rice
Creamy Salad
Mocha Frost

† A dry Burgundy wine; serve at cool room temperature (65°)

TIMETABLE

*Morning	Prepare Creamy Salad and refrigerate
*7:00 pm	Whip cream for Mocha Frost and refrigerate
*7:10	Slice and cut beef
*7:20	Clean and slice mushrooms
7:30	Prepare Oregano Beef
7:35	Cook rice
7:45	Prepare peas
8:00	Dinner is served

* May be prepared in the morning or the night before and refrigerated

---

FOR 4	FOR 6	INGREDIENTS
10 in	12 in	Utensil: skillet
1½ lb	2 lb	thinly sliced round steak
⅓ lb	½ lb	fresh mushrooms
4 tbl	6 tbl	olive oil
¾ tsp	1 tsp	salt
1 tsp	1½ tsp	oregano
⅓ tsp	½ tsp	pepper
¼ tsp	⅓ tsp	garlic powder
¼ C	⅓ C	Sauterne wine

INSTRUCTIONS

OREGANO BEEF

Cut thinly sliced round steak into small bite-size pieces. Clean and slice fresh mushrooms. / / Sauté mushrooms in the skillet with olive oil for about 5 minutes. Add the meat to the skillet and sprinkle with salt, oregano, pepper, and garlic powder. Add wine, cover, and simmer on low heat for 20 to 25 minutes, stirring and mixing frequently.

MINTED PEAS

FOR 4	FOR 6	INGREDIENTS
qt	2 qt	Utensil: saucepan
pkg	2 pkg	frozen peas, 10-oz pkg
C	1 C	water
tsp	2 tsp	sugar
tsp	1 tsp	salt
tbl	4 tbl	butter or margarine
½ tsp	3 tsp	chopped parsley
½ tsp	3 tsp	chopped mint
tsp	¼ tsp	pepper

Bring water to a boil in a saucepan. Add sugar, salt, and frozen peas. Bring back to a boil, lower heat, cover, and cook gently for 4 to 6 minutes. Drain, add butter, chopped parsley, chopped mint, salt (if needed), pepper, and stir. Heat for 3 minutes and keep covered until ready to serve.

ITALIAN-STYLE RICE

	2 qt	Utensil: saucepan
	2½ C	water
	2 tbl	butter or margarine
	1 pkg	Italian-style rice, 7-oz pkg

Combine water, butter, and the spices enclosed in the rice package in the saucepan and bring to a boil. Add rice, stir well, and bring back to a boil. Lower the heat, cover the pan, and simmer for 15 minutes. Keep covered until ready to serve.

CREAMY SALAD

	sm	Utensils: saucepan
	sm	mixing bowl
	1 qt	gelatin mold
	1 pkg	lime or lemon gelatin
	13½ oz	crushed pineapple
	3 oz	cream cheese
	½ pt	heavy cream
	¼ C	chopped nuts

Heat pineapple in saucepan to boiling, pour in gelatin and dissolve. Add cream cheese and mix until cheese has melted. Chill the mixture until slightly set. Whip the cream in a small mixing bowl and fold it into the gelatin mixture. Add nuts, stir gently, pour into a gelatin mold and chill until firm.

FOR 4	FOR 6	INGREDIENTS
sm	sm	Utensil: mixing bowl
¼ C	⅓ C	heavy cream
4 tbl	6 tbl	coffee liqueur
14 oz	21 oz	club soda
1 pt	1½ pt	coffee ice cream
4	6	cinnamon sticks

INSTRUCTIONS

MOCHA FROST

Whip the cream in a small mixing bowl, cover, and refrigerate until ready to serve. / / Place one tablespoon of coffee liqueur in a large wine glass or sherbet dish for each serving. Add one tablespoon of whipped cream to each glass and stir until blended. Pour about 2 tablespoons of soda into each glass and stir until foamy. Add a large scoop of coffee ice cream to each glass and fill with soda. Top with a dollop of whipped cream and insert a cinnamon stick into each glass to serve as a stirrer.

---

menu 43

Cabernet†
Pepper Steak and Rice
Grapefruit Waldorf Salad
Parsley Biscuits
Chocolate Crunch Pie

TIMETABLE

*4:30 pm	Prepare Chocolate Crunch Pie and refrigerate
*5:30	Prepare Grapefruit Waldorf Salad
7:00	Prepare biscuits for baking
7:15	Cook steak and cover
7:30	Preheat oven to 400° and Cook rice
7:40	Bake biscuits
8:00	Dinner is served

† A dry Claret wine; serve at cool room temperature (65°)

* May be prepared in the morning or the night before and refrigerated

FOR 4	FOR 6	INGREDIENTS

PEPPER STEAK AND RICE

FOR 4	FOR 6	INGREDIENTS
10 in	12 in	Utensil: skillet
1½ lb	2 lb	boneless chuck steak
1 tbl	1½ tbl	cooking oil
1 pkg	1½ pkg	dry onion soup mix
2 C	3 C	water
1 lrg	2 med	green peppers
1 tbl	1½ tbl	cornstarch

Trim the fat from steak and cut the steak into strips 2 inches long. Heat oil in skillet and brown the meat strips. Stir in onion soup mix and water. Cover and cook 30 minutes over low heat. Stir in sliced bell peppers and cook 10 minutes longer. Blend cornstarch in a little water and add to mixture. Cook until thick. Serve steak mixture over white rice.

Rice

FOR 4	FOR 6	INGREDIENTS
2 qt	2 qt	Utensil: saucepan
1 C	1½ C	long-grain white rice
2 C	3 C	water
½ tsp	¾ tsp	salt
1 tsp	1½ tsp	shortening

Cook rice according to instructions on the package. (Bring water to a boil in a saucepan. Add salt and shortening. Slowly add rice, shaking the pan to level the rice grains. Turn heat to low, cover tightly, and cook 20 to 25 minutes.) Leave covered until ready to serve.

GRAPEFRUIT WALDORF SALAD

FOR 4	FOR 6	INGREDIENTS
med	lrg	Utensil: mixing bowl
1 lrg	2 med	grapefruit
2 med	3 med	red apples
½ C	¾ C	diced celery
¼ C	⅓ C	chopped walnuts
¼ C	⅓ C	sliced, stuffed olives
¼ tsp	⅓ tsp	curry powder
¼ tsp	⅓ tsp	salt
½ C	¾ C	mayonnaise
4	6	lettuce leaves

Peel, section, and slice grapefruit into mixing bowl. Core, peel, and dice apples. Dice celery, chop walnuts, slice olives. Add to mixing bowl. Mix curry powder, salt, and mayonnaise in a small dish, then mix in with the fruit in the mixing bowl. Refrigerate until ready to serve. / / Serve on individual plates spooned onto lettuce leaves.

PARSLEY BISCUITS

FOR 4	FOR 6	INGREDIENTS	
sm	sm	Utensils: saucepan	
sm	sm	mixing bowl	
1½ qt	1½ qt	round baking dish	
2 pkg	3 pkg	refrigerator biscuits	
¼ C	⅓ C	butter or margarine	
⅛ C	¼ C	chopped fresh parsley	
1	1	egg	

Preheat oven to 400°. In a greased baking dish, arrange a layer of 1 package of biscuits. Melt butter in saucepan and brush some melted butter on top of biscuits. Sprinkle with some chopped parsley. Add more layers of biscuits, repeating the same procedure. Beat an egg in a small mixing bowl and brush the beaten egg on the top layer of biscuits. Bake for 20 minutes at 400°.

CHOCOLATE CRUNCH PIE

Crust

med	Utensils: mixing bowl	
med	cookie sheet	
9 in	pie pan	
½ C	butter	
¼ C	brown sugar, firmly packed	
1 C	sifted flour	
½ C	chopped pecans, walnuts, or packaged, grated coconut	

Mix the butter, brown sugar, sifted flour, and chopped nuts together in a mixing bowl using hands to mix. Spread the mixture on a cookie sheet and bake for 15 minutes at 400°. Remove the mixture from the oven and stir well, breaking mixture up into small pieces. Transfer to a pie pan and press the mixture into the sides and bottom of the pan.

Filling

1 qt	Utensils: saucepan	
med	mixing bowl	
1 pkg	chocolate pudding and pie filling mix, 4-oz pkg	
2 C	milk	
1 C	heavy cream	
¼ C	powdered sugar	

Empty the prepared pudding mix into a saucepan and slowly add milk, stirring to keep mixture smooth. Cook over medium heat, stirring steadily until pudding just starts to boil. Pour into pie crust and let cool. Whip the cream in a small mixing bowl until stiff, blend in powdered sugar, spread on pie, and refrigerate until ready to serve.

menu 44

Traminer†
Pork Chops Florentine
Deviled Carrots
Corn Bread
Cherry Cheese Pie

TIMETABLE

*3:00 pm	Chill wine
*3:00	Remove cream cheese from refrigerator to soften
*4:00	Prepare pie and refrigerate
*6:00	Prepare pork chops
6:45	Prepare and cook carrots
7:15	Bake pork chops in oven at 350°
7:15	Prepare Corn Bread mixture
7:25	Turn oven to 400° and set corn bread pan in oven
7:30	Bake Corn Bread
8:00	Dinner is served

† A dry Rhine wine; serve chilled (45°)

* May be prepared in the morning or the night before and refrigerated

FOR 4	FOR 6	INGREDIENTS
2 qt	2 qt	Utensil: saucepan
6	8	carrots
1 C	1 C	water
1 tsp	1½ tsp	salt
⅓ C	½ C	butter or margarine
1½ tbl	2 tbl	brown sugar, firmly packed
1½ tsp	2 tsp	dry mustard
1 drop	2 drops	Tabasco sauce
¼ tsp	½ tsp	salt
⅛ tsp	⅛ tsp	ground pepper

INSTRUCTIONS

DEVILED CARROTS

Wash, peel, and quarter the carrots lengthwise. Boil 1 cup of water in the saucepan, add salt and carrots, and boil for 10 minutes. Drain, add the butter, and sauté the carrots for 5 minutes. Add the brown sugar, mustard, Tabasco sauce, salt, and pepper and cook 10 minutes, or until tender. Cover to keep warm until ready to serve.

125

PORK CHOPS FLORENTINE

FOR 4	FOR 6	INGREDIENTS
10 in	12 in	Utensils: skillet
2 qt	2 qt	saucepan
1½ qt	2 qt	covered baking dish
¾ tsp	1 tsp	salt
⅛ tsp	¼ tsp	pepper
4	6	pork chops, 1-inch thick
2 tbl	3 tbl	shortening
1 pkg	2 pkg	frozen chopped spinach, 10-oz pkg

Salt and pepper the pork chops and brown them in the skillet with shortening. Prepare the cream sauce (see below). In the saucepan, cook the frozen spinach according to the directions on the package and drain. Add the cream sauce to the spinach and mix well. Pour the spinach-and-cream-sauce mixture into a greased baking dish and lay the pork chops on top of the mixture. Cover. / / Bake at 350° for 45 minutes (if preparing Corn Bread, 400° for the last 30 minutes will not affect the chops).

Cream Sauce

FOR 4	FOR 6	INGREDIENTS
1 qt	1 qt	Utensil: saucepan
2 tbl	3 tbl	butter
2 tbl	3 tbl	flour
¾ C	1 C	light cream
⅓ C	½ C	grated Cheddar cheese

In the saucepan, melt the butter and mix in flour. Then slowly add the light cream, stirring constantly, until mixture just comes to a boil. Add the cheese to the cream sauce and stir until the cheese has melted. Cover the cream sauce and set aside.

| FOR 4 | FOR 6 | INGREDIENTS | INSTRUCTIONS |

CORN BREAD

FOR 4	FOR 6	INGREDIENTS
8 × 8 in		Utensils: baking pan
sm, med		mixing bowls
sm		saucepan
¾ C		flour
3 tsp		baking powder
2 tbl		sugar
¾ tsp		salt
¾ C		yellow cornmeal
1		egg
¾ C		milk
3 tbl		melted butter or margarine

Place baking pan in 400° oven to heat. In a medium mixing bowl, sift together flour, baking powder, sugar, and salt. Add the cornmeal. In the small mixing bowl, beat the egg slightly and add the milk. Add the egg-and-milk mixture to the cornmeal mixture. Melt the butter in a small saucepan and add to the cornmeal mixture. Mix all the ingredients together with just a few strokes. Pour into the hot baking pan and bake at 400° for 25 to 30 minutes.

CHERRY CHEESE PIE

FOR 4	FOR 6	INGREDIENTS
9 in		Utensils: pie pan
med		mixing bowl
½ pkg		pie crust mix
1 can		cherry pie filling, 1-lb 6-oz can
12 oz		cream cheese
2		eggs
½ C		sugar
½ tsp		vanilla
1 C		commercial sour cream
¼ tsp		nutmeg

Preheat oven to 425°. Mix pie crust according to directions on the package and roll out. Place crust in pie pan, pour in pie filling, and bake for 15 minutes at 425°. In the mixing bowl, beat the softened cream cheese, eggs, sugar, and vanilla until smooth. Reduce oven heat to 350°. Spoon cheese mixture over top of cherry mix and bake pie for 30 minutes at 350°. Let cool, then spread sour cream over top of pie. Sprinkle with nutmeg and refrigerate until ready to serve.

menu 45

Delaware†
Roast Ham with Ricotta
Spinach Parmesan
Crunchy Sweet Potato Balls
Bakery Rolls
Pineapple Torte

TIMETABLE
*4:30 pm   Chill wine
*4:30   Prepare Pineapple Torte and refrigerate
*6:45   Prepare ham
 7:00   Place ham in oven at 350° (for 5-pound ham)
 7:15   Place ham in oven at 350° (for 3-pound ham)
*7:15   Wrap rolls in foil
*7:20   Prepare Crunchy Sweet Potato Balls
 7:40   Cook spinach and cover
 7:45   Place rolls in oven
 7:45   Place sweet potato balls in oven
 8:00   Dinner is served

† A dry white wine; serve chilled (45°)   * May be prepared in the morning or the night before and refrigerated

FOR 4	FOR 6	INGREDIENTS	INSTRUCTIONS

ROAST HAM WITH RICOTTA

sm	sm	Utensils: roasting pan	
sm	sm	mixing bowl	
3 lb	5 lb	tenderized ham, fully cooked	
½ lb	¾ lb	ricotta cheese	
¼ C	⅓ C	chopped fresh parsley	
2	3	chopped garlic cloves	

Remove the bone from the ham (or have the butcher do it for you) and remove the skin, leaving most of the fat on the ham. In a small mixing bowl, mix the ricotta cheese, chopped parsley, and chopped garlic. Place the mixture into the cavity of the ham. / / Bake in a covered roaster (or a baking pan covered with aluminum foil) at 350° for 10 to 15 minutes per pound.

SPINACH PARMESAN

FOR 4	FOR 6	INGREDIENTS
1 qt	2 qt	Utensil: saucepan
½ C	½ C	water
2 pkg	3 pkg	frozen chopped spinach
½ tsp	¾ tsp	salt
4 tbl	6 tbl	butter or margarine
½ tsp	¾ tsp	salt
½ tsp	½ tsp	pepper
⅛ tsp	¼ tsp	nutmeg
3 tbl	5 tbl	grated Parmesan cheese

Bring water to a boil in saucepan. Add spinach and salt. Cover and bring back to a boil. Reduce heat and cook gently for 6 to 8 minutes. Drain well and add butter, salt, pepper, nutmeg, and cheese. Heat to warm and cover until ready to serve.

CRUNCHY SWEET POTATO BALLS

FOR 4	FOR 6	INGREDIENTS
med	med	Utensils: mixing bowl
sm	sm	saucepan
sm	med	cookie sheet
1 lb	1 lb 13 oz	canned sweet potatoes (yams)
¼ C	⅓ C	melted butter or margarine
¼ C	⅓ C	orange juice
½ tsp	1 tsp	salt
⅛ tsp	¼ tsp	nutmeg
¼ C	⅓ C	chopped nuts
2 C	3 C	crushed cornflakes

Drain all of the liquid from the canned sweet potatoes and place potatoes in a mixing bowl. Mash until smooth. Add melted butter, orange juice, salt, and nutmeg and mix well. Fold in the chopped nuts. Form mixture into balls and roll in crushed cornflakes. Arrange the balls on a greased cookie sheet. / / Bake for 15 minutes at 350°.

BAKERY ROLLS

FOR 4	FOR 6	INGREDIENTS
8	12	bakery rolls

Wrap rolls in aluminum foil. / / Heat for 15 minutes at 350°.

FOR 4	FOR 6	INGREDIENTS	INSTRUCTIONS

PINEAPPLE TORTE

FOR 4	FOR 6	INGREDIENTS	
sm	med	Utensils: mixing bowl	
1½ qt	2 qt	shallow baking dish	
1 pkg	2 pkg	orange gelatin	
1 C	2 C	boiling water	
1 C	2 C	pineapple juice	
1 can	2 cans	crushed pineapple, 13½-oz can	
½ pt	1 pt	heavy cream	
10	20	graham crackers	

Place gelatin in a mixing bowl and add boiling water, stirring until gelatin has dissolved. Add pineapple juice (drained from the crushed pineapple). Let cool until gelatin begins to set, them mix in the crushed pineapple. Whip the cream until stiff and fold into the gelatin mixture. Line baking dish with one-half of the graham crackers and add one-half of the gelatin mixture. Add a layer of the remaining graham crackers and top with the remaining gelatin mixture. Refrigerate for 2 or 3 hours, or until firmly set.

menu 46

Chateau Sauterne†
Salmon in Almond Sauce
Fluffy White Rice
French Green Beans
Marshmallow Fruit
Pineapple Dessert

TIMETABLE

Night before	Prepare Marshmallow Fruit
*3:30 pm	Chill wine
*3:30	Prepare Pineapple Dessert
*6:45	Prepare French Green Beans
*7:10	Prepare Salmon in Almond Sauce
7:30	Bake salmon at 400°
7:30	Prepare Fluffy White Rice
8:00	Dinner is served

† A dry Sauterne wine; serve chilled (45°)

* May be prepared in the morning or the night before and refrigerated

MARSHMALLOW FRUIT

FOR 4	FOR 6	INGREDIENTS	
med	med	Utensil: mixing bowl	
1½ C	1 pt	commercial sour cream	
13½-oz can	1 lb 4-oz can	pineapple chunks	
1 C	1½ C	miniature marshmallows	
⅓ C	1½ C	coconut	
¾ box or ⅓ C	1 box or ½ C	small strawberries (or halved maraschino cherries)	

Whip the sour cream in a mixing bowl until fluffy. Add well-drained pineapple chunks, marshmallows, and coconut. Gently fold in strawberries. Spoon into a serving bowl and refrigerate overnight.

PINEAPPLE DESSERT

2 sm, 1 med	Utensils: mixing bowls
2 qt	shallow baking dish
1 qt	saucepan
1½ C	crushed vanilla wafers
⅓ C	butter or margarine
1 can	crushed pineapple, 1-lb 4-oz can
1 pkg	lemon gelatin
⅓ C	butter or margarine
½ C	sugar
3	eggs
½ C	nuts
¼ C	sugar

In a small mixing bowl, combine the vanilla wafers and butter. Set aside ½ cup of the mixture, and spread the remainder over the bottom of the baking dish. Drain the juice from the pineapple into the saucepan and heat to a boil. Stir in the lemon gelatin until dissolved and let mixture cool.

In a medium mixing bowl, cream the softened butter and sugar. Separate the eggs. Add the egg yolks to the butter-sugar mixture and mix well. Add the gelatin mixture, pineapple, and nuts. In the small mixing bowl, beat the egg whites with sugar until stiff, then fold into the gelatin mixture. Pour the mixture over the crumbs in the baking dish, sprinkle the remaining ½ cup of crumbs over the top, and refrigerate for several hours before serving.

FRENCH GREEN BEANS

med		Utensils: mixing bowl
sm		skillet
1 can		sliced green beans, 1-lb 12-oz can
1		minced garlic clove
2 tbl		chopped onion
⅛ tsp		salt
2		bacon slices
5		lettuce leaves

In a mixing bowl, combine the drained green beans, minced garlic, chopped onion, and salt. Add the salad dressing (see below). In a small skillet, fry bacon until crisp and drain on paper towel (leftover bacon may be used), then refrigerate salad and bacon strips until ready to serve. / / Just before serving, toss the beans lightly, place on serving plate covered with lettuce leaves, and crumble the bacon strips on top.

Dressing

1 pt		Utensil: glass jar
1 pkg		blue cheese salad dressing mix
¼ C		vinegar
2 tbl		red wine
⅔ C		salad oil

Combine the salad dressing mix, vinegar, wine (instead of the required water), and oil in a small glass jar. Shake well before using. Use one-third cup for green beans, and refrigerate dressing not used for future use as a salad dressing.

FOR 4	FOR 6	INGREDIENTS
in	10 in	Utensils: skillet
½ qt	2 qt	baking dish
C	¾ C	butter or margarine
C	¾ C	slivered almonds
C	⅓ C	flour
½ tsp	¾ tsp	salt
tbl	¼ C	lemon juice
¾ C	2½ C	milk
-lb can	1-lb and 7¾-oz cans	canned red salmon

SALMON IN ALMOND SAUCE

Melt butter in the skillet, add slivered almonds, and stir until brown. Remove almonds. Add flour and salt to skillet and heat until brown. Remove skillet from heat, stir in lemon juice and gradually blend in milk. Cook mixture until thick, stirring constantly. Add one-half of the almonds. Place the salmon in a greased baking dish and pour sauce over the fish. Sprinkle with the remaining almonds. / / Bake in preheated 400° oven for 30 minutes.

FLUFFY WHITE RICE

FOR 4	FOR 6	INGREDIENTS
qt	2 qt	Utensil: saucepan
C	1½ C	long-grain white rice
C	3 C	water
tsp	1½ tsp	shortening
½ tsp	¾ tsp	salt

Bring water to a boil in saucepan. Add shortening and salt. Slowly add rice, shaking pan to level rice grains. Turn heat to low, cover tightly, and cook 20 to 25 minutes, or until all liquid is absorbed. Keep covered until ready to serve.

menu 47

Gamay Beaujolais†
Sauerkraut Pork Roll
Scalloped Rice
Beet Salad
Lemon Freeze

TIMETABLE

*Morning	Prepare Beet Salad and refrigerate
*4:30 pm	Chill wine
*4:30	Prepare Lemon Freeze
*6:30	Prepare Sauerkraut Pork Roll
*7:00	Prepare Scalloped Rice
7:15	Preheat oven to 350°
7:20	Place Pork Roll in oven
7:30	Place rice casserole in oven
7:45	Remove salad from gelatin mold
8:00	Dinner is served

† A light, dry Burgundy wine; serve chilled (45°)   * May be prepared in the morning or the night before and refrigerated

---

FOR 4   FOR 6   INGREDIENTS   INSTRUCTIONS

SAUERKRAUT PORK ROLL

FOR 4	FOR 6	INGREDIENTS
lrg		Utensils: mixing bowl
1½ qt		rectangular baking dish
2		eggs
¾ C		dry bread crumbs
1½ lb		fresh ground pork
1 tsp		salt
¼ tsp		ground pepper
½ tsp		Worcestershire sauce
1 can		sauerkraut, 1-lb can
⅓ C		chopped onion
6 slices		bacon

Beat the eggs in a mixing bowl and add the dry bread crumbs, ground pork, salt, ground pepper, and Worcestershire sauce. Mix together well with hands. Arrange the mixture on a piece of waxed paper into an 8 inch by 10 inch rectangle, using hands to pat mixture into shape. Drain the sauerkraut and chop the onion. Spread the drained sauerkraut and chopped onion evenly over the pork mixture. Roll up like a jelly roll and place the roll in a baking dish. Arrange the uncooked bacon slices across the top of the meat. / / Bake in preheated 350° oven for 40 minutes. Drain grease from dish before serving.

FOR 4	FOR 6	INGREDIENTS

SCALLOPED RICE

FOR 4	FOR 6	INGREDIENTS
2 qt	2 qt	Utensils: saucepan
1½ qt	1½ qt	baking dish
1½ C	2 C	water
½ tsp	¾ tsp	salt
¾ tsp	1 tsp	shortening
¾ C	1 C	rice
½ C	¾ C	sliced green onions
⅓ C	½ C	chopped parsley
3 tbl	4 tbl	flour
¾ tsp	1 tsp	salt
1¾ C	2½ C	light cream

Bring water to a boil in saucepan. Add salt and shortening. Slowly add rice, shaking the pan to keep the rice grains even. Turn heat to low, cover tightly, and cook 20 minutes. While the rice is cooking, clean and slice the green onions and chop the parsley. When rice is done, add the sliced onions, chopped parsley, flour, and salt and mix well. Spoon the rice mixture into greased baking dish and pour cream over the mixture. / / Bake uncovered for 30 minutes at 350°.

BEET SALAD

	sm	Utensils: saucepan
	1 qt	gelatin mold
	1 pkg	lemon gelatin
	8¼ oz	canned diced beets
	15¼ oz	crushed pineapple
	¼ C	sugar
	⅛ tsp	salt
	½ C	pecans

Drain the liquid from the beets and pineapple into saucepan, making 1½ cups of liquid. Heat the juices and dissolve the gelatin into it. Add the sugar and salt, pour into a gelatin mold, and chill until almost set. Mix in the pineapple, beets, and nuts. Refrigerate until ready to serve.

FOR 4	FOR 6	INGREDIENTS

INSTRUCTIONS

LEMON FREEZE

sm		Utensils: saucepan
8 in		pie pan
sm, med		mixing bowls
¼ C		melted butter or margarine
¾ C		cornflake crumbs
2 tbl		sugar
2		eggs
15 oz		canned sweetened condensed milk
⅓ C		lemon juice
½ tsp		grated lemon peel
3 tbl		sugar

Melt butter in saucepan and combine with cornflake crumbs and sugar in the pie pan. Press mixture firmly into the sides and bottom of the pan. Separate eggs. Beat egg yolks in the medium mixing bowl until thick and add the condensed milk, lemon juice, and grated lemon peel. In the small bowl, beat the egg whites until stiff and add the sugar to the beaten whites. Fold the egg-white mixture into the lemon mixture. Pour filling into the crumb crust. Freeze until firm. Cut into wedges to serve.

Sauvignon Blanc†
Savory Veal Chops
Hot Buttered Biscuits
Orange Salad with Honey Dressing
Crunchy Creamed Spinach
Peach Pudding Cake

menu 48

TIMETABLE

*6:15 pm	Chill wine
*6:15	Prepare Orange Salad and Honey Dressing and refrigerate
*6:30	Prepare Peach Pudding Cake
6:45	Prepare Veal Chops
7:20	Cook Veal Chops
7:20	Prepare Spinach, cover
7:40	Turn oven to 450°
7:45	Whip cream for cake
7:50	Place biscuits in oven
7:55	Pour dressing over salad
8:00	Dinner is served

† A dry Sauterne wine; serve chilled (45°)

* May be prepared in the morning or the night before and refrigerated

136

FOR 4	FOR 6	INGREDIENTS	INSTRUCTIONS

SAVORY VEAL CHOPS

FOR 4	FOR 6	INGREDIENTS
12 in	12 in	Utensils: skillet
2 sm	2 sm	bowls
4	6	veal chops
2 tbl	3 tbl	flour
2 tbl	2 tbl	cooking oil
1/3 C	1/2 C	grated Parmesan cheese
1/2 tsp	3/4 tsp	salt
1/4 tsp	1/3 tsp	pepper
4 med	6 med	potatoes
2 med	3 med	onions
3	5	beef bouillon cubes
3/4 C	1 C	hot water
1 tbl	1 1/2 tbl	lemon juice

Coat the veal chops with flour and brown slowly in hot oil in a skillet. In a small mixing bowl, combine the Parmesan cheese, salt, and pepper. When both sides of the veal chops are browned, sprinkle about 2 tablespoons of the cheese mixture over the chops. Cover with slices of peeled potatoes and sprinkle with 2 more tablespoons of cheese mixture. Add the onion slices and sprinkle with the remaining cheese mixture. In a small mixing bowl, dissolve the bouillon cubes in hot water. Add lemon juice and pour liquid over the meat. Cover and simmer over low heat for 40 minutes, or until done.

HOT BUTTERED BISCUITS

FOR 4	FOR 6	INGREDIENTS
1	2	Utensil: 8-inch cake pan
1 pkg	2 pkg	prepared refrigerator biscuits

Preheat oven to 450°. Separate and place the biscuits in cake pan (or pans) with sides touching. Bake at 450° for 8 to 10 minutes. If two pans of biscuits are being prepared, bake only one pan before dinner and place the other pan in the oven as the first batch is removed.

FOR 4	FOR 6	INGREDIENTS	INSTRUCTIONS

ORANGE SALAD WITH HONEY DRESSING

FOR 4	FOR 6	INGREDIENTS	
med	lrg	Utensil: salad bowl	Break lettuce into salad bowl. Drain the mandarin oranges and place on top of lettuce. Cut onion into thin slices and add to salad. Refrigerate until ready to serve. / / Pour dressing over all before serving.
1 med hd	1 lrg hd	lettuce	
1 can	2 cans	mandarin oranges, 11-oz can	
1 sm	1 med	red onion	

Dressing

sm	sm	Utensil: mixing bowl	Combine all ingredients except salad oil in mixing bowl or blender. Thoroughly mix, or blend, while slowly adding the salad oil. Beat until smooth and refrigerate until ready to serve.
3 tbl	¼ C	sugar	
⅓ tsp	½ tsp	dry mustard	
⅓ tsp	½ tsp	paprika	
⅓ tsp	½ tsp	salt	
⅓ tsp	½ tsp	celery seed	
3 tbl	¼ C	honey	
3 tbl	¼ C	vinegar	
⅓ C	½ C	salad oil	

CRUNCHY CREAMED SPINACH

FOR 4	FOR 6	INGREDIENTS
qt	2 qt	Utensils: saucepan
in	6 in	skillet
½ C	¾ C	water
pkg	2 pkg	frozen chopped spinach, 10-oz pkg
½ tsp	¾ tsp	salt
slices	3 slices	bacon
tbl	3 tbl	finely chopped onion
tbl	1½ tbl	bacon fat
tbl	1½ tbl	flour
½ tsp	¾ tsp	seasoned salt
⅛ tsp	¼ tsp	pepper
¼ tsp	⅓ tsp	nutmeg
½ C	¾ C	commercial sour cream

Bring water to a boil in saucepan. Add the spinach and salt. Cover and bring back to a boil. Reduce heat and cook 8 to 10 minutes. Drain well. In a small skillet, cook the bacon slices until crisp. Drain on paper towels. In the bacon fat, sauté the chopped onion and add to spinach together with flour, seasoned salt, pepper, and nutmeg. Heat, stirring occasionally, until well heated. Add the sour cream and heat for a few more minutes. Do not let mixture boil. Serve with crumbled bacon on top.

PEACH PUDDING CAKE

	9 × 12 in	Utensils: baking pan
	6 in	skillet
	sm	mixing bowl
	1 can	sliced peaches, 1-lb 13-oz can
	1 pkg	white or yellow cake mix
	½ C	butter or margarine
	½ C	chopped nuts
	½ pt	heavy cream
	½ C	powdered sugar

Preheat oven to 350°. Into a greased baking pan, place the peaches and juices. Springle the dry cake mix over the peaches. Melt butter in a saucepan and drizzle over the cake mix. Sprinkle nuts over all. Bake 40 to 45 minutes. / / Just before serving, whip the cream and blend in the powdered sugar just after cream has whipped. Top cake with whipped cream for serving.

menu 49

TIMETABLE

*5:00 pm	Chill wine
*5:00	If shrimp are purchased uncooked, cook, clean, and refrigerate
*6:00	Prepare Pecan and Carrot Salad and refrigerate
*6:30	Prepare baked honey apples
*6:45	Prepare baked peas
7:00	Prepare shrimp curry
7:15	Bake foiled apples in 350° oven
7:30	Cook rice
7:50	Reheat curry
8:00	Dinner is served

† A dry Rhine wine; serve chilled (45°)   * May be prepared in the morning or the night before and refrigerated

---

FOR 4	FOR 6	INGREDIENTS	INSTRUCTIONS

PECAN AND CARROT SALAD

sm	med	Utensil: mixing bowl	Wash, peel, and grate carrots and mix them in a bowl with the raisins and chopped nuts. Add mayonnaise and mix well. Cover and refrigerate until ready to serve. / / Spoon salad onto lettuce leaves on individual plates.
4	6	carrots	
¾ C	1 C	raisins	
¼ C	⅓ C	chopped pecans	
½ C	¾ C	mayonnaise	
4	6	lettuce leaves	

140

FOIL BAKED HONEY APPLES

OR 4	FOR 6	INGREDIENTS
m	sm	Utensils: mixing bowl
ed	med	cookie sheet
lrg	3 lrg	apples
⁄4 C	⅓ C	honey
⁄4 C	⅓ C	chopped pecans
tsp	1½ tsp	lemon juice
⁄2 pt	1 pt	vanilla ice cream

Core and peel apples, then cut them into halves. Cut a 10-inch square piece of heavy aluminum foil for each half and place the apple halves on the sheets of foil. Mix the honey, chopped pecans, and lemon juice in a small bowl and pour evenly over the apples. Fold the foil over the apples and seal the packets well. / / Place on a cookie sheet and bake at 350° for 45 minutes. Serve on a dish with the foil peeled back and topped with a scoop of vanilla ice cream.

BAKED PEAS

OR 4	FOR 6	INGREDIENTS
½ qt	1½ qt	Utensil: covered baking dish
pkg	2 pkg	frozen peas, 10-oz pkg
⁄2 can	1 can	sliced water chestnuts, 5-oz can
⁄2 tsp	1 tsp	salt
⁄8 tsp	¼ tsp	pepper
⁄8 tsp	¼ tsp	sugar
tbl	2 tbl	butter or margarine

Place the frozen peas in a buttered baking dish. Drain and slice the water chestnuts and spread them over the peas. Sprinkle with salt, pepper, and sugar. Then dot the top with butter. / / Cover and bake for 30 minutes at 350°.

FOR 4	FOR 6	INGREDIENTS	INSTRUCTIONS

SHRIMP CURRY AND RICE

FOR 4	FOR 6	INGREDIENTS
2 qt	3 qt	Utensils: saucepan
10 in	12 in	skillet
3 C	4 C	cooked, clean shrimp
(2 lb)	(3 lb)	(uncooked shrimp)
(2 qt)	(3 qt)	(water)
(1 tsp)	(1 tsp)	(salt)
3 tbl	⅓ C	butter or margarine
1 sm	1 med	chopped onion
1 med	1 lrg	minced garlic clove
½ tsp	¾ tsp	salt
2 tsp	1 tbl	curry powder
2 tsp	1 tbl	flour
1	2	chicken bouillon cubes
1 C	2 C	yogurt

If the shrimp are purchased uncooked, bring water to a boil in a larg saucepan, add 1 teaspoon of salt and uncooked shrimp, and boil for 1! minutes. Drain the shrimp, cool by washing in cold water, remove shell and veins. / / Heat butter in the skillet and sauté the chopped onion an minced garlic until lightly browned. Stir into skillet mixture the salt curry powder, flour, and chicken bouillon cubes and cook for 3 minutes stirring constantly. Add the yogurt and shrimp, stirring until heated al the way through. Cover until ready to serve.

White Rice

FOR 4	FOR 6	INGREDIENTS
1 qt	2 qt	Utensil: saucepan
2 C	3 C	water
½ tsp	¾ tsp	salt
1 tsp	1½ tsp	shortening
1 C	1½ C	long-grain white rice

Bring water to a boil in a saucepan and add salt and shortening. Slowl add rice, shaking the pan to level rice grains. Turn heat to low, cove tightly, and cook 20 to 25 minutes. Keep covered until ready to serve.

Traminer†
Sweet and Sour Pork Chops
Fried Cabbage and Beans
Marinated Onions and Tomatoes
Sour Cream Peach Pie

menu 50

TIMETABLE

*4:30 pm	Chill wine
*5:30	Prepare Marinated Onions and Tomatoes
*6:00	Prepare Sour Cream Peach Pie
6:45	Prepare Sweet and Sour Pork Chops
7:15	Prepare Fried Cabbage and Beans
7:45	Complete Sweet and Sour Pork Chops
8:00	Dinner is served

† A dry Rhine wine; serve chilled (45°)   * May be prepared in the morning or the night before and refrigerated

---

OR 4	FOR 6	INGREDIENTS
		INSTRUCTIONS

SWEET AND SOUR PORK CHOPS

qt	1 qt	Utensils: saucepan
0 in	12 in	skillet
m	sm	mixing bowl
C	3 C	water
½ tsp	¾ tsp	salt
tsp	1½ tsp	shortening
C	1½ C	long-grain white rice
tbl	2 tbl	cooking oil
	6	pork chops, 1-inch thick
¼ tsp	1 tsp	salt
¼ tsp	⅓ tsp	pepper
tbl	1½ tbl	flour
¼ C	6 tbl	brown sugar, firmly packed
½ C	¾ C	vinegar
½ C	¾ C	catsup

Bring water to a boil in saucepan. Add salt and shortening. Slowly add rice, shaking pan to level rice grains. Turn heat to low, cover tightly, and cook 20 to 25 minutes. Meanwhile, heat oil in skillet and add pork chops. Sprinkle with salt, pepper, and flour and rub into chops with a fork. Brown chops on both sides. Sprinkle 1 tablespoon of brown sugar on each chop and heat until sugar melts. In a mixing bowl, stir **vinegar** and catsup together and pour over chops. Cover skillet and cook for 30 minutes over low heat. Then pile 1/2 cup of cooked rice onto each chop, spoon sauce in skillet over rice, and continue cooking for 10 minutes.

FRIED CABBAGE AND BEANS

8 in	8 in	Utensil: skillet	
3 slices	5 slices	bacon	
⅓ sm hd	½ sm hd	cabbage	
1 lb	1 lb 12 oz	canned sliced green beans	
⅓ C	½ C	chopped nuts	
⅓ C	½ C	halved maraschino cherries	

In skillet, fry bacon until crisp. Remove and drain on paper towels. Shred cabbage and cook in the bacon grease, uncovered, for 20 minutes or until tender. Drain green beans and stir beans into the cabbage. Heat to warm through, place in serving bowl, and crumble bacon on top together with chopped nuts and maraschino cherries.

MARINATED ONIONS AND TOMATOES

⅓ C	½ C	Burgundy wine
3 tbl	¼ C	vinegar
½ C	¾ C	salad oil
1 tbl	1½ tbl	sugar
¾ tsp	1 tsp	salt
⅓ tsp	½ tsp	dry mustard
1	1	crushed garlic clove
3	4	tomatoes
1 med	1 lrg	red onion

In a shallow serving bowl, combine the wine, vinegar, salad oil, sugar, salt, dry mustard, and garlic. Wash and slice the tomatoes and onion into the bowl. Gently move the slices around occasionally to give an even distribution of the marinade. Refrigerate and let the slices marinate for at least 2 hours.

SOUR CREAM PEACH PIE

Crust

med	Utensils: mixing bowl	
9 in	pie plate	
½ C	butter or margarine	
3 oz	cream cheese	
¼ tsp	salt	
1 C	sifted flour	
1 tsp	butter or margarine	

Cream softened butter and cream cheese together in mixing bowl. Add salt and flour and slice into butter mixture with a fork until well blended. Form into a ball and roll out on floured board to measure one inch larger than pie plate. Pat firmly into pie plate, then spread lightly with butter.

Filling

sm	Utensil: mixing bowl
1 can	peaches, 1-lb 13-oz can
1	egg
½ pt	commercial sour cream
¼ C	powdered sugar
1 tsp	vanilla extract
1 tsp	cinnamon

Preheat oven to 425°. Drain liquid from peaches and drain peach slices on paper towels, blotting on both sides. Arrange slices in pie plate forming a circular overlapping pattern. In a mixing bowl, beat the egg slightly, then combine with sour cream, sugar, and vanilla. Spoon the mixture over peaches and sprinkle with cinnamon. Bake at 425° for 12 minutes. Reduce heat to 350° and bake 15 to 20 minutes longer. Serve either warm or chilled.

menu 51

TIMETABLE

*2:30 pm	Prepare Sweet and Sour Tongue
*6:00	Prepare Raspberry Parfaits
*7:00	Prepare Scalloped Cabbage
7:30	Cook cabbage
*7:30	Prepare Tomatoes and Cucumbers
7:40	Preheat oven to 450°
7:50	Place Buttermilk Biscuits in oven
7:50	Warm sauce for Sweet and Sour Tongue
8:00	Dinner is served

† A dry Claret wine; serve at cool room temperature (65°)

* May be prepared in the morning or the night before and refrigerate

---

FOR 4　　FOR 6　　INGREDIENTS

INSTRUCTIONS

SWEET AND SOUR TONGUE

FOR 4	FOR 6	INGREDIENTS
med		Utensil: deep kettle
3 lb		beef tongue
2		onions
2		bay leaves
12		whole black peppers (peppercorns)
1 tbl		salt

Place the tongue in a deep kettle. Quarter the onions and add them, alon with the bay leaves, peppers, and salt. Cover the tongue with cold wate Bring water to a boil, then reduce heat and simmer until tender (abo 4 hours). Remove tongue from water, let cool, then cut off bones a gristle at the thick end of the tongue. Slit the skin from the thick e toward the tip on the underside. Use a paring knife to loosen the sk at the thick end. Peel the skin off by pulling from the thick end towa the tip. Cut into slices. Serve with hot sauce.

146

FOR 4	FOR 6	INGREDIENTS	INSTRUCTIONS

Sauce

FOR 4	FOR 6	INGREDIENTS
	1 qt	Utensil: saucepan
	1½ C	brown sugar, firmly packed
	1 C	cider vinegar
	¾ C	water
	½ C	seedless bleached raisins
	½ C	ginger snaps, crumbled
	6 slices	thin lemon slices
	1 sm	onion
	1	bay leaf
	½ tsp	salt

Combine all ingredients for the sauce in the saucepan. Bring to a boil and simmer for 10 minutes. Remove the bay leaf and simmer 10 minutes longer. Serve hot over beef tongue slices.

SCALLOPED CABBAGE

FOR 4	FOR 6	INGREDIENTS
qt	5 qt	Utensils: saucepan
qt	2 qt	flameproof shallow baking dish
C	1½ C	water
½ tsp	¾ tsp	salt
C	6 C	shredded cabbage
¼ C	1 C	canned tomatoes
½ tsp	¾ tsp	salt
⅛ tsp	¼ tsp	pepper
C	1½ C	fluffy fresh bread crumbs
C	1½ C	grated sharp Cheddar cheese
tbl	3 tbl	melted butter or margarine

Bring water to a boil in saucepan. Add the salt and shredded cabbage. Cook, uncovered, about 5 minutes, or until tender but crisp. Drain. Into the baking dish, place one-half of the shredded cabbage and one-half of the tomatoes; sprinkle with salt and pepper. Add one-half of the crumbs and one-half of the cheese. Repeat process with remaining ingredients. Drizzle butter over the top. / / Cover and cook over low heat for 30 minutes, or until cheese melts.

TOMATOES AND CUCUMBERS

FOR 4	FOR 6	INGREDIENTS
sm	med	Utensils: serving platter
sm	sm	mixing bowl
3	5	tomatoes
1	2	cucumbers
½ pt	¾ pt	commercial sour cream
2 tbl	3 tbl	wine vinegar
½ tsp	¾ tsp	sugar
1 tsp	1½ tsp	salt
⅛ tsp	¼ tsp	freshly ground pepper

Wash and slice tomatoes. Peel and slice cucumber. Arrange the slices on a platter and chill. In a small mixing bowl, combine the sour cream, vinegar, sugar, salt, and pepper and stir well. / / Spoon the sour cream mixture over the tomato and cucumber slices and let marinate in refrigerator until ready to serve. Do not marinate more than 30 minutes before serving.

BUTTERMILK BISCUITS

FOR 4	FOR 6	INGREDIENTS
1 8 in	2 8 in	Utensil: cake pan
1 pkg	2 pkg	prepared refrigerator buttermilk biscuits

Preheat oven to 450°. Separate biscuits and place them in cake pan with sides touching. Bake at 450° for 8 to 10 minutes. If preparing two batches, bake one batch at a time so the second batch will be hot when ready to serve.

RASPBERRY PARFAITS

FOR 4	FOR 6	INGREDIENTS
	sm	Utensils: deep mixed bowl
	sm	mixing bowl
	2 pkg	frozen raspberries, 10-oz pkg
	1 C	orange juice
	1 pkg	lemon-flavored whipped dessert mix
	½ tsp	grated orange peel
	½ C	heavy cream

Defrost raspberries. In the deep mixing bowl, blend 1/2 cup of orange juice with the whipped dessert mix. Whip mixture at high speed for a minute. Blend in the other ½ cup of orange juice and whip for another 2 minutes. Stir in the orange peel. In the other mixing bowl, whip the cream until stiff, then fold the cream quickly into the dessert mix. Divide mixture evenly into dessert parfait glasses in layers alternating with bands of raspberries. Chill for at least 1 hour before serving.

CHAPTER THREE

Semiformal Menus

menu 52

TIMETABLE

*Morning	Bake lemon cake
4:15 pm	Prepare and cook roast
*6:15	Marinate oranges and prepare lettuce for salad
*6:45	Prepare Swiss Cheese and Onion Pie
7:20	Preheat oven to 375°
7:30	Place Swiss Cheese and Onion Pie in oven
7:45	Prepare Gingersnap Gravy
7:55	Toss Salad
8:00	Dinner is served

† A light, dry Burgundy wine; serve chilled (45°)

* May be prepared in the morning or the night before and refrigerated

FOR 4	FOR 6	INGREDIENTS	INSTRUCTIONS

AMERICAN SAUERBRATEN

FOR 4	FOR 6	INGREDIENTS
5 qt	5 qt	Utensil: Dutch oven (or large heavy deep skillet)
4 lb	6 lb	rump roast
¼ C	⅓ C	salad oil
½ C	⅔ C	chopped onion
2 tsp	3 tsp	salt
2 tbl	2½ tbl	pickling spices
¾ C	1 C	red wine vinegar
2½ C	3 C	water
⅓ C	½ C	brown sugar, firmly packed

Brown the roast in the oil in a Dutch oven or heavy, deep skillet. When roast is browned, pour off excess grease. Add the chopped onion, salt, pickling spices, vinegar, water, and brown sugar. Cover and simmer over low heat for 3½ hours, or until meat is tender.

INSTRUCTIONS

Gingersnap Gravy

FOR 4	FOR 6	INGREDIENTS
qt	2 qt	Utensil: saucepan
C	3 C	meat juices
)	15	gingersnaps

After meat is cooked, remove amount of meat juices listed in ingredient list. Heat the required amount of meat juices in a saucepan, add the crumbled gingersnaps, and cook until smooth. Serve the gingersnap gravy over the meat slices.

SWISS CHEESE AND ONION PIE

Crust

FOR 4	FOR 6	INGREDIENTS
a	sm	Utensils: mixing bowl
	2	pie pan, 8 inch
	2	packaged pie crust sticks
tbl	4 tbl	boiling water

Crumble pastry sticks into mixing bowl. Add boiling water and blend with fork until dough loses stickiness. Stir until dough forms a ball and completely cleans the bowl. Shape into a flattened round and roll out on floured surface until it becomes one inch larger than pie pan. Press into pie pan.

Filling

FOR 4	FOR 6	INGREDIENTS
) in	10 in	Utensils: skillet
a	sm	mixing bowl
med	2 med	onions
tbl	2 tbl	butter or margarine
	3	eggs
C	1 C	milk
oz	14½ oz	canned milk
tsp	¼ tsp	salt
tsp	¼ tsp	nutmeg
lb	½ lb	grated Swiss cheese

Preheat oven to 375°. Slice onions and simmer with butter in a skillet until soft, but not brown. In the mixing bowl, beat the eggs lightly. Add milk and canned milk, salt and nutmeg. Grate the Swiss cheese and sprinkle ½ the total amount onto the pastry-lined pie pan (or pans). Add onions to the pie pan (or pans) and sprinkle with remaining Swiss cheese. / / Before baking, pour in the milk mixture and bake at 375° for 30 minutes, or until pastry browns and pie filling sets, forming a light crust. Pie can be baked in advance and reheated at serving time, if desired.

FOR 4	FOR 6	INGREDIENTS	INSTRUCTIONS

ORANGE AND GREEN SALAD

FOR 4	FOR 6	INGREDIENTS
med	med	Utensils: mixing bowl
med	lrg	salad bowl
3 tbl	4 tbl	oil
1½ tbl	2 tbl	vinegar
¾ tsp	1 tsp	sugar
2 tbl	3 tbl	orange juice
¾ tsp	1 tsp	lemon juice
⅛ tsp	⅛ tsp	ground ginger
⅛ tsp	⅛ tsp	salt
3 sm	4 sm	sliced oranges
1 med	1 lrg	head lettuce
⅓ bunch	½ bunch	watercress

Combine oil, vinegar, sugar, orange juice, lemon juice, ginger, and salt in the large mixing bowl. Peel and slice oranges into the mixture. Marinate the oranges in the mixture (refrigerated) for at least 8 hours. Clean and dry lettuce and watercress. Tear watercress and lettuce into salad bowl and refrigerate until ready to serve. / / Just before serving, add the marinated oranges and dressing to the salad and toss.

TART LEMON CAKE

	INGREDIENTS
lrg	Utensils: mixing bowl
9 × 12 in	baking pan
1 pkg	lemon cake mix
¾ C	salad oil
4	eggs
1 pkg	lemon gelatin
¾ C	water

Preheat oven to 350°. Combine the lemon cake mix, oil, eggs, lemon gelatin, and water in a mixing bowl. Beat with electric mixer for minutes. Turn the batter into a greased and floured baking pan and bake for 45 minutes at 350°. Remove from oven, poke holes all over top with a fork, and add frosting. Refrigerate until ready to serve. Cake actually better after 24 to 48 hours.

Frosting

	INGREDIENTS
sm	Utensil: mixing bowl
2 C	powdered sugar
3 med	squeezed lemons

Combine powdered sugar and lemon juice in bowl and mix until well blended.

Johannisberger Riesling†
Barbecued Lamb
Asparagus in Curry Sauce
Sliced Tomatoes and Cucumbers
Hot French Bread
Apricot-Pineapple Bars

menu 53

TIMETABLE

*4:00 pm	Chill wine
*5:00	Prepare Apricot-Pineapple Bars
5:40	Prepare lamb for spit
6:00	Place lamb on spit to roast
*6:30	Prepare Mint Sauce
6:45	Prepare Tomatoes and Cucumbers
*7:00	Prepare French bread
*7:15	Prepare Asparagus in Curry Sauce
7:35	Preheat oven to 425°
7:50	Place asparagus and bread in oven
8:00	Dinner is served

† A dry Rhine wine; serve chilled (45°)   * May be prepared in the morning or the night before and refrigerated

---

FOR 4   FOR 6   INGREDIENTS   INSTRUCTIONS

APRICOT-PINEAPPLE BARS

lrg		Utensils: mixing bowl
	9 × 12 in	baking pan
¾ C		butter or margarine
1 C		brown sugar, firmly packed
1¾ C		sifted flour
1 tsp		salt
½ tsp		baking soda
1½ C		rolled oats
1 can		apricot-pineapple pie filling, 1-lb 6-oz can

Preheat oven to 400°. In mixing bowl, combine butter and brown sugar. Sift the flour, salt, and soda together and add to sugar mixture. Stir in the rolled oats. Mix until crumbly. Press one-half of the crumb mixture into the bottom of a greased baking pan. Spread the pie filling over all. Cover with the remaining crumbs, patting lightly. Bake at 400° for 25 minutes. Cool and cut into bars.

BARBECUED LAMB

4 to 5 lb	boned leg of lamb
2	fresh mint sprigs
2	garlic cloves
3 tbl	olive oil
1 tbl	hickory-smoked salt
¾ tsp	seasoned pepper

Have the butcher bone, roll, and tie leg of lamb for roasting on spit. Cut 5 one-inch deep slits in the meat. Place mint into each slit. Slice garlic cloves and place into each slit. Brush the outside of lamb with olive oil. Sprinkle with hickory-smoked salt and seasoned pepper. Place lamb on spit over hot coals and roast until crusty and brown (about 2 hours), or use a meat thermometer and cook until it indicates 170° F. (Or place on low rack in shallow pan, fat side up, and bake in oven, uncovered for about 2 ½ hours at 325°.)

Mint Sauce

sm	Utensils: mixing bowl
1 qt	saucepan
¼ C	finely chopped mint
¼ C	sugar
⅛ tsp	salt
1 C	vinegar

In a mixing bowl, combine mint, sugar, and salt. Heat vinegar in saucepan and stir into mint mixture. Let cool.

SLICED TOMATOES AND CUCUMBERS

FOR 4	FOR 6	INGREDIENTS
2	3	tomatoes
1	1½	cucumbers
½ tsp	¾ tsp	salt
1 tbl	1½ tbl	olive oil
½ tsp	¾ tsp	basil

Wash, peel, and slice cucumbers. Wash and slice tomatoes. Arrange slices on serving platter, sprinkle with salt, olive oil, and basil.

HOT FRENCH BREAD

FOR 4	FOR 6	INGREDIENTS
½ loaf	¾ loaf	French bread
¼ C	6 tbl	butter
3 tbl	¼ C	chopped chives

Slice bread loaf, butter each slice, sprinkle with chopped chives, and arrange slices back into original loaf form. Wrap in heavy aluminum foil. / / Bake at 425° for 10 minutes.

ASPARAGUS IN CURRY SAUCE

FOR 4	FOR 6	INGREDIENTS
4 qt	4 qt	Utensils: saucepan
2 qt	2 qt	shallow baking dish
10 in	10 in	skillet
1½ lb	2½ lb	fresh asparagus
½ tsp	½ tsp	salt
3 tbl	¼ C	margarine
3 sm	3 med	chopped onion
¾ tsp	1 tsp	curry powder
¼ tsp	⅓ tsp	salt
2 tbl	3 tbl	flour
¾ C	1 C	water
⅓ C	½ C	milk
¼ C	5 tbl	heavy cream
⅓ C	½ C	shredded Swiss cheese

Wash and clean asparagus, break off tough ends, and cut lengthwise. Place spears in saucepan, cover with water, add salt, and cook 6 to 8 minutes. Drain and place asparagus in baking dish. Melt margarine in skillet, add chopped onion, curry powder, and salt. Cook for 2 to 3 minutes. Slowly add flour, water, and milk, stirring constantly. Cook until smooth and thick. Add cream and Swiss cheese. Pour mixture over the asparagus in the baking dish. / / Bake in preheated oven at 425° for 10 minutes.

menu 54

TIMETABLE

*4:30 pm	Chill wine
*5:30	Prepare and freeze Watermelon Ice
*6:00	Prepare salad and salad dressing
*6:30	Prepare shrimp for barbecue
7:15	Prepare Pilaff
7:30	Bake Pilaff at 350°.
7:45	Prepare lemon butter for shrimp
7:50	Place shrimp on barbecue
7:55	Toss salad with salad dressing
8:00	Place shrimp in lemon butter
8:00	Dinner is served

† A dry Cablis wine; serve chilled (45°)   * May be prepared in the morning or the night before and refrigerated

FOR 4	FOR 6	INGREDIENTS

INSTRUCTIONS

WATERMELON ICE

sm	med	Utensils: mixing bowl
1	2	ice cube tray
2 C	3 C	blended watermelon
1 tbl	1½ tbl	lemon juice
¼ C	⅓ C	sugar

Remove seeds from watermelon and cut into chunks. Whip in an electric blender, if available, or beat in mixing bowl until liquid. Measure the required amount of blended watermelon and combine with lemon juice and sugar. Pour mixture into ice cube trays and freeze until firm, stirring occasionally.

FOR 4	FOR 6	INGREDIENTS	INSTRUCTIONS

HEARTY GREEN SALAD

FOR 4	FOR 6	INGREDIENTS
8 in	10 in	Utensils: skillet
1 qt	2 qt	saucepan
med	lrg	salad bowl
1 med hd	1 lrg hd	Boston lettuce
6 slices	9 slices	bacon
4	6	eggs

Rinse and drain lettuce and tear into salad bowl. Fry bacon in skillet until crisp, drain on paper towels, and crumble over lettuce. Place eggs in saucepan, cover with water. Bring water to a boil, reduce heat, and simmer 5 to 8 minutes. Let eggs cool, remove shells, then grate into salad bowl. Refrigerate until ready to serve.

Dressing

FOR 4	FOR 6	INGREDIENTS
½ pt	½ pt	Utensil: glass jar
3 tbl	¼ C	salad oil
¼ C	⅓ C	lemon juice
¼ tsp	⅓ tsp	sweet basil
1 tsp	1½ tsp	dried parsley
½ tsp	¾ tsp	salt
¼ tsp	⅓ tsp	pepper
½ tsp	¾ tsp	grated onion
1	1	minced garlic cloves
¼ C	⅓ C	grated Parmesan cheese

In a glass jar, combine all of the dressing ingredients and shake well. Refrigerate until ready to serve. Prepare at least 2 hours in advance.

BARBECUED SHRIMP

FOR 4	FOR 6	INGREDIENTS	
lrg	lrg	Utensils: shallow bowl	
med	med	serving skillet	
2 lb	3 lb	large shrimp (prawns)	
4 oz	5 oz	soy sauce	
½ C	¾ C	butter	
3 tbl	¼ C	lemon juice	
1 tbl	1½ tbl	dried parsley	

Remove the shells from the shrimp, leaving tails on (hold tail with one hand and peel off the shell with the other). Remove the vein from the backs of the shrimp, rinse in cold water, and dry with paper towels. / / Place shrimp in bowl, cover with soy sauce, and marinate for 10 minutes each side. (Do not leave in soy sauce for more than 10 minutes each side.) Place shrimp on barbecue, over hot coals, and cook about 5 minutes each side. Melt butter in a serving skillet or flameproof baking dish. Add lemon juice and parsley. Place barbecued shrimp in bubbling lemon butter and serve at once.

PILAFF

		INGREDIENTS	
	2 qt	Utensil: covered flameproof baking dish	
	½ C	butter	
	1 C	white or brown rice	
	1 coil	vermicelli, coiled	
	1 can	canned chicken consommé	
	⅓ C	water	
	1½	chicken bouillon cubes	

Melt butter in flameproof baking dish. Add rice and crush a coil of vermicelli into dish (with hands). Cook over medium heat until lightly browned, about 10 minutes. Stir in the consommé, water, and bouillon cubes. Cover and bake at 350° for 25 minutes. Remove cover and bake 5 minutes longer. (If a flameproof baking dish is not available, use a skillet to brown the rice and vermicelli and then transfer to a baking dish.)

menu 55

Cabernet Sauvignon†
Beef Rib Roast
Pan-Browned Potatoes
Zucchini Parmesan
Green Pea Salad
Peach Ice Cream Pie

TIMETABLE

*4:30 pm	Prepare Peach Ice Cream Pie
5:30	Place 6-pound roast in oven at 325° (for medium)
6:00	Place 4-pound roast in oven at 325° (for medium)
*6:30	Prepare Zucchini Parmesan
7:05	Prepare and boil potatoes
7:30	Place potatoes in oven around the roast
7:30	Place Zucchini Parmesan in oven
7:35	Prepare Green Pea Salad
8:00	Dinner is served

† A dry Claret wine; serve at cool room temperature (65°)   * May be prepared in the morning or the night before and refrigerated

---

FOR 4	FOR 6	INGREDIENTS
med	med	Utensil: roasting pan
4 lb	6 lb	standing rib roast
½ tsp	¾ tsp	garlic powder

INSTRUCTIONS

BEEF RIB ROAST

Sprinkle the roast with garlic powder. Place roast, fat side up, into open roasting pan (the rib bones will keep the roast off the bottom of the pan). Insert a roast thermometer into the center of the roast. Roast in a 325° oven until thermometer indicates proper degree of doneness. (Approximate cooking time for 4-pound roast is; rare-1 ¾ hours, medium-2 hours, well done-2 hours 20 minutes; for a 6-pound roast: rare-2 hours 15 minutes, medium-2 ½ hours, well done-3 hours 20 minutes.

159

PAN-BROWNED POTATOES

FOR 4	FOR 6	INGREDIENTS
4 qt	5 qt	Utensil: saucepan
1 tsp	1 tsp	salt
4 med	6 med	potatoes
¼ tsp	⅓ tsp	salt
⅛ tsp	¼ tsp	pepper

Bring water to a boil in saucepan (enough water to cover potatoes). Add salt. Pare potatoes and place into boiling water. Cook, covered, for 15 minutes. Drain and place the potatoes into the meat drippings around the roast. Turn the potatoes over in the drippings to coat them all over. Bake potatoes with the roast for the last 30 minutes of cooking time. Salt and pepper lightly before serving.

ZUCCHINI PARMESAN

	INGREDIENTS
2 qt	Utensils: saucepan
1½ qt	shallow baking dish
½ C	water
1½ tsp	salt
1½ lb	zucchini
1 can	pizza sauce, 8-oz can
⅓ C	grated Parmesan cheese
½ lb	mozzarella cheese

Bring water to a boil in saucepan and add salt. Wash zucchini and slice crosswise. Place zucchini into boiling water, lower heat, and cook covered for 20 minutes, or until barely tender. Drain well. Place one-half of the zucchini into bottom of baking dish, forming a layer. Pour on one-half of the pizza sauce and sprinkle with one-half of the Parmesan cheese. Slice the mozzarella cheese into thin slices and place one-half of the slices on top of the Parmesan cheese. Repeat layers ending with the mozzarella cheese. / / Bake at 325° for 30 minutes.

FOR 4	FOR 6	INGREDIENTS
2 qt	3 qt	Utensils: saucepan
med	lrg	mixing bowl
½ C	¾ C	water
1 tsp	1½ tsp	salt
2 pkg	3 pkg	frozen peas, 10-oz pkg
2	3	green onion bulbs
½ C	¾ C	commercial sour cream
½ tsp	¾ tsp	salt
⅛ tsp	⅛ tsp	freshly ground black pepper
5	5	lettuce leaves
5	7	cucumber slices

INSTRUCTIONS

GREEN PEA SALAD

Bring water to a boil in saucepan. And salt and peas. Bring back to a boil, cover, reduce heat, and cook for 2 minutes. Drain. Slice onion bulbs into thin slices and combine in the mixing bowl with the peas, sour cream, salt, and pepper. Mix together gently. Wash lettuce leaves. Wash and slice cucumber (unpeeled). Arrange the lettuce leaves on a serving plate or in a salad bowl, spoon the pea mixture onto lettuce leaves, and garnish with unpeeled cucumber slices. Serve within one hour.

PEACH ICE CREAM PIE

Crumb Crust

FOR 4	INGREDIENTS
med	Utensils: mixing bowl
9 in	pie pan or plate
2 tbl	sugar
½ C	butter
1 C	unsifted flour

Combine sugar and butter in mixing bowl but do not cream. Add flour and mix just enough for dough to form. Turn dough into pie pan and pat evenly into sides and bottom. Prick well with a fork and bake in oven at 375° for 12 to 15 minutes, or until lightly browned. Let cool for 30 minutes before adding pie filling.

Pie Filling

FOR 4	INGREDIENTS
2 qt	Utensil: saucepan
1¼ C	water
1 pkg	lemon gelatin
½ C	chopped fresh peach slices
1 pt	peach ice cream
½ C	chopped nuts

Heat water to boiling in saucepan and remove from heat. Add the lemon gelatin and stir until dissolved. Stir in the chopped peaches. Add ice cream, cut into pieces, to hot liquid. Stir immediately until melted. Chill until mixture just starts to set (15 to 25 minutes). Fold in chopped nuts. Turn into pie shell and chill until firm. May be served with whipped cream or fresh peach slices.

menu 56

TIMETABLE

*2:30 pm	Chill wine
*2:30	Prepare Strawberry Cream Pie
*4:00	Prepare Chicken and Broccoli
*7:15	Prepare Green Salad (not the dressing)
7:25	Place Chicken and Broccoli in oven at 375°
7:25	Prepare salad dressing
7:40	Prepare Crescent Rolls
7:50	Bake rolls
7:55	Toss salad with warmed dressing
8:00	Dinner is served

† A dry Rhine wine; serve chilled (45°)   * May be prepared in the morning or the night before and refrigerated

---

FOR 4	FOR 6	INGREDIENTS	INSTRUCTIONS

CRESCENT ROLLS

FOR 4	FOR 6	INGREDIENTS
med	lrg	Utensil: cookie sheet
1 tube	2 tubes	packaged refrigerator crescent dinner rolls

Preheat oven to 375°. Unroll dough. Separate into 8 triangles per tube of dough. Roll up each triangle (start at wide end of triangle and roll to opposite point). Place rolls, point-side down, on an ungreased cookie sheet. Curve into crescent shape. Bake at 375° for 10 to 13 minutes.

CHICKEN AND BROCCOLI

FOR 4	FOR 6	INGREDIENTS
2 3-qt,	2 4-qt,	Utensils: saucepans
1 2-qt	1 3-qt	
sm	sm	mixing bowl
2 qt	3 qt	baking dish
4 lrg	6 lrg	chicken breasts, split
4 C	6 C	water
2 tsp	1 tbl	salt
1 med	1 lrg	onion
1 stalk	2 stalks	celery
1½ lb	2 lb	broccoli
4 C	6 C	water
½ tsp	¾ tsp	salt
4 tbl	6 tbl	butter or margarine
6 tbl	9 tbl	flour
1 tsp	1½ tsp	seasoned stock base, chicken
½ tsp	1 tsp	seasoned salt
⅛ tsp	¼ tsp	pepper
3 C	4 C	chicken stock
¾ C	1 C	heavy cream
¼ C	⅓ C	sherry wine
⅓ C	½ C	grated Parmesan cheese

Clean the chicken breasts. Bring water to a boil in saucepan. Add salt, onion (halved), celery (cut into chunks), and chicken. Cook, covered, over low heat for about 1 ½ hours, or until the meat starts to pull away from the bones. Remove the bones and skin from the breasts.

While chicken is cooking, trim off the woody part of broccoli stalks and wash the broccoli. Cut into spears. Bring water to a boil in saucepan. Add salt and broccoli spears, with the stalks down. Cook, uncovered, for 20 to 30 minutes, or until tender. Drain. In another saucepan, melt the butter and stir in the flour. Heat butter and flour until it bubbles, stirring constantly. Add the bottled chicken stock base, seasoned salt, and pepper. Strain and measure the stock from the chicken into saucepan, adding gradually and stirring constantly. Bring to a boil and simmer for 10 minutes, stirring occasionally. Cool. Whip the cream in a small bowl and add the whipped cream and sherry to the mixture.

In the casserole, place the broccoli spears, one-half of the sauce, the chicken breasts, and top with the other half of the sauce. Sprinkle grated Parmesan cheese over all. / / Bake at 375° for 30 minutes. Place under broiler for a few minutes to brown, if desired.

WILTED GREEN SALAD

FOR 4	FOR 6	INGREDIENTS	
med	lrg	Utensil: salad bowl	
1 med hd	1 lrg hd	lettuce	
1 stalk	2 stalks	celery	
4 slices	6 slices	sliced red onion	

Break lettuce into salad bowl. Add chopped celery and sliced red onion. / / Toss with dressing just before serving.

Dressing

FOR 4	FOR 6	INGREDIENTS	
6 in	8 in	Utensil: skillet	
2 slices	3 slices	bacon	
2 tsp	1 tbl	flour	
1/3 C	1/2 C	vinegar	
1/3 C	1/2 C	water	
3/4 tsp	1 tsp	dry mustard	
1/3 C	1/2 C	sugar	
3/4 tsp	1 tsp	salt	

Cook finely chopped bacon in skillet until browned. Mix in flour, then add vinegar, water, dry mustard, sugar, and salt. Cook over low heat until mixture thickens. Add to salad while dressing is still warm.

STRAWBERRY CREAM PIE

Crumb Crust

med		Utensils: mixing bowl
9 in		pie pan or plate
2 tbl		sugar
½ C		butter or margarine
1 C		unsifted flour

Combine sugar and butter in mixing bowl, but do not cream. Add flour and mix just enough for dough to form. Turn dough into pie pan and pat evenly into sides and bottom. Prick well with a fork and bake at 375° for 12 to 15 minutes, or until lightly browned. Let cool.

Filling

2 sm		Utensils: mixing bowl
1 qt		saucepan
6 oz		cream cheese
½ C		sugar
1 C		heavy cream
1 qt		whole strawberries
1 tbl		lemon juice
1¼ C		sugar
3 tbl		cornstarch
3 drops		red food coloring

Soften cream cheese and blend with the sugar in a mixing bowl. Whip the cream in another mixing bowl and fold one-half of it into the cream-cheese mixture. Spread the mixture onto the bottom of the cooled pie crust. Press one-half of the whole strawberries into the cream cheese with the tips up. Mash the remaining strawberries in a blender. Place strawberries in a large measuring cup, adding enough water to total 1½ cups. Add lemon juice. Mix sugar and cornstarch together in saucepan. Gradually stir in strawberry liquid and cook at medium heat until thick and clear, stirring constantly. Add red food coloring. Cool, then pour over berry pie. Top with remaining whipped cream. Chill at least 3 hours.

menu 57

Pinot Chardonnay†
Chicken Kiev
Water Chestnut Sauce
Green Sesame Noodles
Orange-Avocado Salad
Fresh Fruit and Cheese

TIMETABLE
*4:30 pm   Chill wine
*5:30   Prepare Orange-Avocado Salad
*6:00   Prepare Chicken Kiev
 7:15   Prepare Water Chestnut Sauce
 7:40   Prepare Green Sesame Noodles
 7:55   Toss salad with salad dressing
 8:00   Dinner is served
After dinner prepare Fresh Fruit and Cheese.

† A dry Chablis wine; serve chilled (45°)   * May be prepared in the morning or the night before and refrigerated

---

FOR 4	FOR 6	INGREDIENTS
6	8	Utensils: skewers
sm	sm	shallow bowl
3 qt	3 qt	wide saucepan
3	4	whole, boned chicken breasts
4 tbl	6 tbl	butter
3 tsp	4 tsp	minced fresh parsley
3 tsp	4 tsp	minced chives
2	3	eggs
¾ C	1 C	flour
½ tsp	¾ tsp	salt
¼ tsp	⅓ tsp	pepper
2-in deep	2-in deep	cooking oil

INSTRUCTIONS

CHICKEN KIEV

Carefully remove skin from boned chicken breasts, cut each breast in half, and pound with wooden mallet until doubled in width. In the center of each half breast place 1 tablespoon butter, ½ teaspoon parsley, and ½ teaspoon chives. Fold in edges and roll up each breast (like a jelly roll); fasten with small skewer. Beat eggs in a small bowl with a fork. Place flour on a paper towel. Heat 2 inches of oil in a heavy saucepan until it indicates 350° on deep-frying thermometer. Dip chicken rolls in egg, then in flour. Add salt and pepper and deep fry, two at a time, for 5 minutes. Drain on paper towels and remove skewers. // Place in 200° oven to keep warm until ready to serve. (May be prepared several days in advance, wrapped in foil, and frozen. To defrost, remove from foil, let stand at room temperature for 1 hour, and bake on rack in shallow pan for 20 to 25 minutes at 450°.)

167

FOR 4	FOR 6	INGREDIENTS

WATER CHESTNUT SAUCE

FOR 4	FOR 6	INGREDIENTS
1 qt, 2 qt	1 qt, 2 qt	Utensil: saucepans
½ C	½ C	water
½ pkg	1 pkg	frozen peas, 10-oz pkg
½ tsp	½ tsp	salt
2 tbl	3 tbl	butter or margarine
2 tbl	3 tbl	flour
¾ C	1¼ C	canned chicken bouillon
¾ C	1 C	evaporated milk
¾ C	1 C	canned water chestnuts
⅓ tsp	½ tsp	salt
⅛ tsp	¼ tsp	pepper

Bring ½ cup water to a boil in 1 quart saucepan. Add frozen peas and ½ teaspoon salt. Bring back to a boil, cover, and cook over reduced heat for 4 to 6 minutes. Drain. Melt butter in 2-quart saucepan and blend in flour. Gradually add the chicken bouillon, milk, and drained peas. Slice the water chestnuts into mixture. Add salt and pepper and stir until thickened. Cover to keep warm. Serve over Chicken Kiev.

GREEN SESAME NOODLES

FOR 4	FOR 6	INGREDIENTS
3 qt, 1 qt	4 qt, 1 qt	Utensil: saucepans
2 qt	3 qt	water
1 tsp	1 tsp	salt
6 oz	8 oz	green (spinach) noodles
2 tbl	3 tbl	butter or margarine
2 tbl	3 tbl	sesame seeds
1 tsp	1½ tsp	lemon juice

Bring water to a boil in large saucepan. Add noodles and 1 teaspoon salt. Cook, uncovered, for 8 to 10 minutes. Drain in colander and rinse gently with hot water. Place noodles in serving bowl. Meanwhile, melt butter in 1 quart saucepan, add sesame seeds, and cook until brown, stirring constantly. Stir in lemon juice. Pour over noodles and toss gently.

ORANGE-AVOCADO SALAD

FOR 4	FOR 6	INGREDIENTS
med	lrg	Utensil: salad bowl
sm hd	med hd	iceberg lettuce
½ med	1 sm	cucumber
½	1	avocado
½	1	green onion
1 can	1 can	mandarin oranges, 11-oz can

Wash and tear lettuce into salad bowl. Peel and slice cucumber, avocado, and onion. Add to salad. Drain and add the mandarin orange sections. Cover and refrigerate until ready to serve.

Dressing

FOR 4	FOR 6	INGREDIENTS
½ pt	1 pt	Utensil: glass jar
3 tbl	¼ C	orange juice
⅓ C	½ C	salad oil
½ tbl	2 tbl	sugar
½ tbl	2 tbl	wine vinegar
2 tsp	1 tbl	lemon juice
¼ tsp	¼ tsp	salt

Combine orange juice, salad oil, sugar, vinegar, lemon juice, and salt in jar. Shake well. Refrigerate until ready to serve.

FRESH FRUIT AND CHEESE

FOR 4	FOR 6	INGREDIENTS
2	3	Delicious apples
2	3	fresh pears
4	6	grape clusters
1 ball	1 ball	Edam cheese

Wash pears and apples. Quarter and core. Wash grapes. Arrange on attractive plate or tray with cheese and knife. Pass individual fruit knives and plates to guests.

menu 58

Chianti†
Chioppino
Italian Salad
French Bread
Zuppa Inglese

TIMETABLE

*3:30 pm	Prepare Zuppa Inglese
*5:00	Prepare salad and salad dressing
*5:30	Prepare Chioppino (only sauce may be prepared in advance)
7:20	Pour sauce over Chioppino and cook
*7:45	Slice and wrap French Bread
7:50	Place bread in oven at 400°
7:50	Toss salad with salad dressing
8:00	Dinner is served

† A light, dry red wine; serve at cool room temperature (65°)

* May be prepared in the morning or the night before and refrigerated

FOR 4	FOR 6	INGREDIENTS
5 qt	6 qt	Utensil: kettle
1 lrg	1 lrg	crab
1 lb	1½ lb	clams
1 lb	1½ lb	prawns
1 lb	1½ lb	sea bass

INSTRUCTIONS

CHIOPPINO

While the sauce is cooking, prepare the fish: remove and shred the crab body meat. Scrub the clams well with a brush. Wash the prawns, leaving them in their shells. Crack the crab legs. Wash and scale the sea bass. Lay the clams in the kettle first, next the prawns, cracked crab legs, and sea bass. Over all this, spread the shredded crab meat.

After the sauce has cooked for 1 hour, pour the sauce over the fish arranged in the kettle. Move fish around gently with a long-handled fork so that the sauce will run to the bottom of the pan. Cover and cook slowly for one-half hour after sauce starts to bubble. Serve in large soup bowls.

FOR 4	FOR 6	INGREDIENTS	INSTRUCTIONS

Sauce

FOR 4	FOR 6	INGREDIENTS
2 qt	3 qt	Utensil: saucepan
⅓ C	½ C	olive oil
1 med	1 lrg	onion
	1	garlic clove
⅓ C	½ C	dry white wine
11½ oz	1 lb	canned solid-pack tomatoes
¼ C	¼ C	canned tomato paste
1 can	2 cans	tomato sauce, 8-oz can
⅓ C	½ C	water
⅓ tsp	½ tsp	thyme
⅓ tsp	½ tsp	marjoram
	1	bay leaf
1 tsp	1 tsp	chopped fresh parsley
1 tsp	1½ tsp	salt
⅛ tsp	⅛ tsp	pepper

Heat olive oil in saucepan. Add chopped onion and minced garlic clove. Cook slowly for 20 minutes. Add wine and cook 10 minutes longer. Add tomatoes, tomato paste, tomato sauce, and water. Stir well. Add thyme, marjoram, bay leaf, parsley, salt, and pepper. Cook slowly for 1 hour, stirring frequently.

FOR 4	FOR 6	INGREDIENTS	INSTRUCTIONS

ITALIAN SALAD

FOR 4	FOR 6	INGREDIENTS	
med	lrg	Utensil: salad bowl	
1 clove	1 clove	garlic	
2	3	tomatoes	
½	¾	cucumber	
4	6	radishes	
¼	⅓	green pepper	
1 sm hd	1 med hd	lettuce	

Rub garlic over sides and bottom of salad bowl. Wash and cut the tomatoes into wedges. Peel and slice cucumber. Wash and slice radishes. Wash green pepper and cut into small pieces. Place all vegetables in salad bowl. Wash and drain lettuce, then shred into salad bowl. Cover and refrigerate until ready to serve.

Dressing

FOR 4	FOR 6	INGREDIENTS
½ pt	½ pt	Utensil: glass jar
¼ C	⅓ C	olive oil
½ tsp	¾ tsp	salt
½ tsp	¾ tsp	pepper
2 tbl	3 tbl	wine vinegar

Combine all ingredients in a glass jar and refrigerate until ready to serve. / / Shake vigorously before adding to salad.

FRENCH BREAD

1 med loaf	1 lrg loaf	French bread

Wrap bread in aluminum foil and heat at 400° for 10 minutes. Dip bread slices into sauce from Chioppino, if desired.

ZUPPA INGLESE

1 qt	Utensils: saucepan
sm	mixing bowl
1 pkg	vanilla pudding mix
(3¼ oz)	
1½ C	milk
1 tsp	grated lemon peel
1 pt	heavy cream
¼ C	sugar
2 tsp	vanilla extract
4 9-in	round sponge cake layers
¼ C	dark rum
¼ C	crème de cacao
1 C	strawberry jam or preserves
	whole strawberries or candied fruit to garnish

Cook vanilla pudding in saucepan according to package instructions, using only 1½ cups of milk. Add lemon peel. Then cool with plastic wrap or waxed paper placed directly on surface of pudding. In a mixing bowl, combine heavy cream and sugar and whip until stiff. Add vanilla extract. Fold one cup of whipped cream into the cooled pudding. Chill the remaining whipped cream. Place a layer of sponge cake on a serving plate. Sprinkle with 1 tablespoon each of rum and crème de cacao. Spread on 2 tablespoons of jam and one-third of the pudding. Repeat process with two more layers of cake, rum, crème de cacao, jam and pudding. Add top layer of cake, sprinkle with remaining rum and crème de cacao, and spread with jam. Frost the sides of the cake with reserved whipped cream. Make a pretty ruffled rim around top edge, but leave jam uncovered. Decorate top with strawberries or candied fruit set in the jam. Refrigerate until ready to serve.

menu 59

Semillon†
Fortune Cookies
Chop Suey
Fried Rice
Peas in Shrimp Sauce
Orange-Pineapple Mold
Chow Mein Noodles
Almond Coconut Ice Cream

† A light dry Sauterne wine; serve chilled (45°)

TIMETABLE

*4:00 pm	Chill wine
*4:00	Prepare Orange-Pineapple Mold
6:15	Place gelatin servings on plates and refrigerate
*6:20	Place noodles and fortune cookies on serving dishes
6:30	Prepare Chop Suey and cover
7:15	Prepare fried rice and cover
7:40	Prepare Peas in Shrimp Sauce and cover
8:00	Dinner is served

* May be prepared in the morning or the night before and refrigerated

---

FOR 4	FOR 6	INGREDIENTS
	1½ oz	canned fortune cookies
12 in	12 in	Utensil: skillet
1½ lb	2 lb	lean pork
⅓ C	½ C	flour
¾ tsp	1 tsp	salt
⅓ tsp	½ tsp	pepper
3 tbl	4 tbl	cooking oil
¾ C	1 C	chopped celery
¾ C	1 C	chopped onions
2 oz	4 oz	canned mushrooms
1 lb	1 lb	canned bean sprouts
2 tbl	3 tbl	soy sauce
¾ tbl	1 tbl	sugar

INSTRUCTIONS

FORTUNE COOKIES

Serve fortune cookies as the first course.

CHOP SUEY

Cut pork into small chunks. Mix flour, salt, and pepper in a small bowl and dredge each chunk of pork in flour mixture. Brown the pork in skillet with cooking oil. Chop the celery and onion and add both to the skillet. Drain the juices from the canned bean sprouts and canned mushrooms into the skillet. Add soy sauce, and sugar. Simmer for 10 minutes stirring occasionally. Add the bean sprouts and mushrooms. Simmer for another 5 minutes. Keep covered until ready to serve.

174

FRIED RICE

FOR 4	FOR 6	INGREDIENTS
12 in	12 in	Utensils: skillet
sm	sm	mixing bowl
1 ½ tbl	2 tbl	cooking oil
⅓ C	½ C	lean pork, finely diced
2 oz	2 oz	canned mushrooms
1 can	2 cans	cooked rice, 12-oz can
	2	green onions
tbl	¼ C	soy sauce
	1	egg
tsp	1 tbl	water

Heat oil in skillet, add the finely diced pork, and cook for 5 minutes. Add drained mushrooms, rice, firely chopped green onions, and soy sauce. Simmer for 10 minutes, stirring occasionally. In a small bowl, whip the egg and water together with a fork. Add egg mixture and cook another 15 minutes. (If canned rice is not available, regular white rice may be substituted, if it is prepared 24 hours in advance and refrigerated.)

PEAS IN SHRIMP SAUCE

FOR 6	INGREDIENTS
2 qt	Utensil: saucepan
2 pkg	packaged frozen peas
1	frozen cream of shrimp soup, 10-oz can

Place peas and soup in saucepan and warm slowly. Stir the mixture occasionally and cook until peas are tender (about 20 minutes).

ORANGE-PINEAPPLE MOLD

FOR 6	INGREDIENTS
1 ½ qt	Utensil: shallow baking dish
1 pkg	orange-pineapple gelatin
1 C	boiling water
1 tsp	seasoned salt
12 oz	canned carrot juice
15 ¼ oz	canned pineapple spears
11 oz	canned mandarin oranges
1	bananas, sliced
6	lettuce leaves

Place gelatin in baking dish, add boiling water, and stir until gelatin has dissolved. Add seasoned salt and one cup of the carrot juice. Refrigerate until mixture just starts to jell. Fold in the drained pineapple spears, drained mandarin oranges, and sliced banana. Refrigerate until firm. / / Cut mold into serving pieces and place on lettuce leaves. (If papaya is available, peel and slice onto serving plates with the gelatin mold.)

FOR 4	FOR 6	INGREDIENTS	INSTRUCTIONS

CHOW MEIN NOODLES

1 can		chow mein noodles, 3-oz can	Serve in bread basket or serving bowl.

ALMOND COCONUT ICE CREAM

1 pt		almond ice cream	Place a large scoop of ice cream in each serving bowl and top with
8 oz		canned coconut syrup	coconut syrup.

---

menu 60

White Riesling†
Tomato Juice Cocktail
Crabmeat Au Gratin
Crescent Rolls
Green Beans
Melon's Secret

TIMETABLE

*Morning	Prepare melon dessert and refrigerate
*4:00 pm	Chill wine
*6:30	Prepare Tomato Juice Cocktail and refrigerate
*6:45	Prepare crabmeat casserole
7:20	Place crabmeat casserole in oven at 350°
7:30	Cook green beans
7:40	Turn oven control to 375°
7:40	Prepare rolls
7:50	Bake rolls at 375°
7:50	Drain green beans and add butter and garlic powder
8:00	Dinner is served

† A dry Rhine wine; serve chilled (45°)   * May be prepared in the morning or the night before and refrigerated

176

TOMATO JUICE COCKTAIL

FOR 4	FOR 6	INGREDIENTS
qt	2 qt	Utensil: juice container
qt	1 qt 14 oz	canned tomato juice
tbl	6 tbl	lemon juice
tsp	3 tsp	Worcestershire sauce

In a juice container, combine tomato juice, lemon juice, and Worcestershire sauce. Mix well and chill until ready to serve. / / Serve in fancy glasses as first course.

CRABMEAT AU GRATIN

FOR 4	FOR 6	INGREDIENTS
qt	4 qt	Utensils: saucepan
½ qt	2 qt	baking dish
0 in	12 in	skillet
tbl	3 tbl	butter or margarine
tsp	1 tbl	flour
tsp	1½ tsp	salt
⅓ C	½ C	milk
C	3 C	chopped celery
½ C	¾ C	chopped green pepper
tsp	1½ tsp	chopped pimientos
tbl	1½ tbl	grated onion
	3	eggs, hard-boiled
can	2 cans	crabmeat, 6½-oz can
½ C	¾ C	grated Cheddar cheese
tbl	3 tbl	butter or margarine
tbl	3 tbl	slivered almonds
C	3 C	bread cubes

Heat butter in saucepan. Add flour and salt and blend well. Remove from heat and gradually stir in milk. Return to heat and cook until the mixture thickens, stirring constantly. Chop the celery, green pepper, pimentos, onion and egg. Drain crabmeat and mix with the celery, green pepper, pimientos, onion, and egg into the saucepan mixture. Turn the mixture out into casserole and sprinkle with grated cheese. Heat butter in skillet and toast almonds, stirring often. Add bread cubes to skillet and toss well to soak up all of the butter. Add bread-and-almond mixture to casserole. / / Bake for 40 minutes at 350°.

FOR 4	FOR 6	INGREDIENTS	INSTRUCTIONS

CRESCENT ROLLS

FOR 4	FOR 6	INGREDIENTS	
med	lrg	Utensil: cookie sheet	
1 tube	2 tubes	packaged refrigerator crescent dinner rolls	

Preheat oven to 375°. Unroll dough and separate into 8 triangles per tube of dough. Roll up (start at wide end of triangle and roll to opposite point). Place rolls, point-side down, on ungreased cookie sheet. Curve into crescent shape. Bake at 375° for 10 to 13 minutes.

GREEN BEANS

FOR 4	FOR 6	INGREDIENTS	
1 qt	2 qt	Utensil: saucepan	
3/4 C	1 C	water	
1 pkg	2 pkg	frozen green beans, 10-oz pkg	
3/4 tsp	1 tsp	salt	
1 tbl	2 tbl	butter or margarine	
18 tsp	1/4 tsp	garlic powder	

Bring water to a boil in saucepan. Add green beans and salt, cover, and bring back to a boil. Reduce heat and cook gently for 4 to 7 minutes, or until beans are tender. Drain. Add butter and garlic powder. Cover until ready to serve.

MELON'S SECRET

FOR 4	FOR 6	INGREDIENTS	
	med, lrg	Utensil: mixing bowls	
	1 pkg	strawberry-banana gelatin	
	1¾ C	boiling water	
	1 med	honeydew melon	
	1 C	sliced strawberries	
	3 pkg	cream cheese, 3-oz pkg	
	3 tbl	milk	

Dissolve the gelatin in boiling water and chill until it begins to set. While gelatin is cooling, peel the melon, leaving it whole. Cut off one end, scoop out the seeds, and drain melon. Clean and slice the strawberries and fold them into the thickened gelatin. Spoon the mixture into the center of the melon. Replace the cut-off end of the melon and hold in place with toothpicks. Chill. Mix the cream cheese and milk, then spread the mixture over the entire melon. Refrigerate until ready to serve. / / Slice into the melon at the table, in the presence of guests.

menu 61

Sauvignon Blanc†
Exotic Cordon Bleu
Lemon Carrots
Cheese and Onion Salad
Herb Rolls
Orange Babas

TIMETABLE
*Morning   Prepare Orange Babas and refrigerate
*5:00 pm   Chill wine
 5:00   Prepare Herb Rolls and let rise
*5:30   Clean, slice, and refrigerate carrots
 5:40   Prepare Cheese and Onion Salad and refrigerate
*6:00   Prepare meat, except for dipping, and refrigerate
 7:30   Preheat oven to 400°
 7:30   Sauté meat
 7:40   Bake rolls
 7:45   Cook carrots
 8:00   Dinner is served

† A dry Sauterne wine; serve chilled (45°)   * May be prepared in the morning or the night before and refrigerated

---

OR 4	FOR 6	INGREDIENTS
	med	Utensils: mixing bowl
) in	12 in	skillet
	12	veal cutlets
	6	boiled ham slices
	6	American cheese slices
C	1½ C	potato flakes
	2	eggs
؛ tsp	¾ tsp	salt
tbl	5 tbl	water
tbl	5 tbl	butter or margarine

INSTRUCTIONS

EXOTIC CORDON BLEU

Pound the veal cutlets with a meat hammer until very thin. Place a slice of ham and a slice of cheese between two veal cutlets and pound the edges together to seal. In the mixing bowl, beat the eggs lightly and mix in the salt and water. / / When ready to sauté the meat, place potato flakes on a sheet of waxed paper. Melt the butter in the skillet. Dip each cutlet into the egg mixture, then into the potato flakes, and sauté them in the skillet until golden brown (about 10 to 11 minutes each side).

179

FOR 4	FOR 6	INGREDIENTS	INSTRUCTIONS

LEMON CARROTS

FOR 4	FOR 6	INGREDIENTS	
2 qt	3 qt	Utensil: saucepan	
6 lrg	8 lrg	carrots	
¾ C	1 C	water	
¾ tsp	¾ tsp	salt	
1 tsp	1½ tsp	brown sugar, firmly packed	
1 tbl	1½ tbl	lemon juice	
1 tbl	1½ tbl	butter or margarine	

Wash, clean, and slice the carrots into rounds. / / Bring water to a boil in the saucepan, add salt and carrots, and cook, covered, for about 15 minutes. Drain. Add butter, brown sugar, and lemon juice. Stir well to coat all carrots. Cover until ready to serve.

CHEESE AND ONION SALAD

FOR 4	FOR 6	INGREDIENTS	
1 qt	2 qt	Utensils: saucepan	
10 in	12 in	skillet	
med	lrg	salad bowl	
½ C	½ C	water	
1 pkg	2 pkg	frozen peas, 10-oz pkg	
1 tsp	2 tsp	sugar	
½ tsp	1 tsp	salt	
3	5	bacon strips	
1 med hd	1 lrg hd	lettuce	
3 tbl	4 tbl	mayonnaise	
1 sm	1 med	sliced Bermuda onion	
1 tbl	1½ tbl	sugar	
6 oz	8 oz	Swiss cheese	

Bring water to a boil in a saucepan. Add frozen peas, sugar, and salt. Bring back to a boil, cover, and cook gently over reduced heat for 4 to 6 minutes, or until tender. Drain and let cool. Cook the bacon strips in a skillet until well done. Remove grease with paper towel. Cover the bottom of the salad bowl with one-half of the lettuce broken into chunks, spread with one-half of the mayonnaise, add a layer of one-half of the onion slices, sprinkle with one-half of the sugar, add a layer of one-half of the cooked peas and a layer of one-half of the Swiss cheese (which has been cut into strips). Repeat the process with the remaining ingredients, crumble the bacon strips on top, and refrigerate until ready to serve.

HERB ROLLS

FOR 4	FOR 6	INGREDIENTS
med		Utensils: mixing bowl
9 in		cake pan
	1 pkg	dry yeast
	¾ C	warm water
	2½ C	biscuit mix
	1 tsp	celery seed
	1 tsp	poultry seasoning

In the mixing bowl, soften the yeast in warm water. Stir in the biscuit mix, celery seed, and poultry seasoning. Knead the dough on a floured surface for 3 minutes, or until smooth. Roll into a 6-inch by 14-inch rectangle and cut lengthwise into three 2-inch strips. Cut each strip into 7 pieces that are 2 inches square. Roll each piece of dough into a ball and place in a greased cake pan. Cover and let rise for 2 hours. Bake at 400° for 15 to 20 minutes.

ORANGE BABAS

FOR 4	FOR 6	INGREDIENTS
med		Utensils: mixing bowl
8		plastic-lined hot drink paper cups (7 ounces)
med		cookie sheet
1 qt		saucepan
	½ pkg	yellow cake mix
	½ C	sugar
	½ C	orange juice
	3 tbl	slivered orange peel
	½ C	water
	½ pt	vanilla ice cream

Prepare the whole package of cake mix and use ½ of the batter for cupcakes and the other half for this recipe, or, if you prefer, use only ½ of the cake mix (2 cups) and prepare the batter according to the directions on the package, using ⅔ cup of water and one egg. Preheat oven to 375°. Grease the hot drink cups and fill one-third full with batter. Bake on a cookie sheet for 25 minutes. While cakes are baking, cook the sugar, orange juice, slivered orange peels, and water in a saucepan for 5 minutes. When cakes are done, let them set for 5 minutes, then turn them out onto a serving dish and drizzle with the hot syrup. Chill well. / / Serve with vanilla ice cream.

menu 62

TIMETABLE

*Morning	Defrost spinach
*4:30 pm	Prepare Walnut Torte and refrigerate
*5:30	Prepare French Crepes
*7:00	Prepare Melon Compote
7:30	Place French Crepes in oven at 350°
7:45	Place rolls in oven
8:00	Dinner is served

† A dry Burgundy wine; serve at cool room temperature (65°)

* May be prepared in the morning or the night before and refrigerated

---

FOR 4	FOR 6	INGREDIENTS
1 qt	1 qt	Utensils: saucepan
10 in	10 in	skillets
½ pkg	1	frozen chopped spinach
⅓ C	½ C	water
¼ tsp	½ tsp	salt
½ lb	1 lb	lean ground beef
¼ lb	½ lb	lean ground pork
1 sm	1 med	onion
1	2	garlic cloves
¾ tsp	1 tsp	salt

INSTRUCTIONS

FRENCH CREPES

Defrost spinach for several hours at room temperature. In the saucepan bring water to a boil. Add spinach and salt. Cover and bring back to a boil. Reduce heat and cook gently for 6 to 8 minutes. Drain well. In the large skillet, brown the beef and pork. Drain off the grease. Chop the onion and add to the meat, together with the minced garlic cloves, spinach, and salt. Cook for 5 minutes, stirring occasionally. Set aside.

182

OR 4	FOR 6	INGREDIENTS
m	sm	Utensils: mixing bowl
5 in	6 in	slcillet
½ qt	3 qt	shallow baking dish
2	3	eggs
¼ tsp	¼ tsp	salt
¼ C	1½ C	milk
½ C	1 C	flour
¼ tsp	¼ tsp	butter or margarine
can	2 cans	tomato sauce, 15-oz can
C	2 C	grated Cheddar cheese
ned	lrg	Utensil: mixing bowl
¾ C	1 C	watermelon balls
¾ C	1 C	honeydew melon balls
¾ C	1 C	cantaloupe balls
1 C	1½ C	blueberries
¼ C	⅓ C	honey
¼ C	⅓ C	orange-flavored liqueur
4	6	small mint leaf sprigs

INSTRUCTIONS

Crepes

In the small mixing bowl, mix the eggs, salt, milk, and flour. Beat with a hand beater (batter will be thin). In a skillet, over low heat, melt the butter. Pour in just enough batter to cover the bottom (about ⅛ cup). Rotate the skillet around until batter fills the bottom of the pan and the mixture becomes dry. Cook a few seconds until bottom of crepe is lightly brown. (Do not cook the top side.) Set the crepe aside and repeat until all batter is used (4 per serving). When all crepes are cooked, fill them by placing cooked side down and adding a large tablespoon of meat mixture to the center of the crepe. Roll up and place in casserole, loose end down. Repeat until all crepes are used and casserole is full. Top the crepes with tomato sauce and sprinkle with grated cheese. / / Bake for 30 minutes at 350°.

MELON COMPOTE

Scoop small balls from each melon into mixing bowl. Add the blueberries, honey, and orange-flavored liqueur and toss well. Place in individual serving bowls, add a sprig of mint, and refrigerate until ready to serve.

FOR 4	FOR 6	INGREDIENTS

MIXED BAKERY ROLLS

FOR 4	FOR 6	INGREDIENTS
8	12	bakery rolls

Wrap rolls in aluminum foil and heat for 15 minutes at 350°.

WALNUT TORTE

	lrg	Utensils: mixing bowl
	2	cookie sheets
	1½ C	sifted flour
	⅓ C	sugar
	⅛ tsp	salt
	½ C	butter or margarine
	1	egg

Preheat oven to 350°. In the large mixing bowl, sift the flour with sugar and salt. Cut in the butter. Stir in the egg and blend batter with hands until it holds together. Divide mixture into three parts and roll into three 10-inch rounds. Place rounds on cookie sheets and bake for 10 minutes.

Walnut Filling

	med	Utensil: mixing bowl
	1 C	commercial sour cream
	1 C	chopped walnuts
	¾ C	powdered sugar
	1 tsp	vanilla extract
	½ C	apricot preserves

In a medium mixing bowl, mix the walnut-filling ingredients. Remove the round from the oven when done and let cool. Place a cooled round on a serving dish, spread with filling, add a second round and spread with filling, then add third round. Top with the apricot preserves. Refrigerate until ready to serve.

menu 63

Pinot Noir†
Chilled Consommé
Lamb Curry
Fluffy Rice
Mixed Green Salad
Minted Pineapple

TIMETABLE

*2:00 pm	Place consommé in refrigerator to chill
*3:30	Prepare salad and salad dressing
*4:00	Prepare Lamb Curry
*7:00	Prepare Minted Pineapple
7:30	Cook rice
7:45	Pour consommé into serving bowls and top with sliced green onions
7:55	Toss salad with dressing
8:00	Dinner is served

† A dry Burgundy wine; serve at cool room temperature (65°)

* May be prepared in the morning or the night before and refrigerated

FOR 4	FOR 6	INGREDIENTS	INSTRUCTIONS

CHILLED CONSOMMÉ

| can | 2 cans 1½ | canned chicken consommé, 10-oz can green onion | Place the canned consommé in the refrigerator at least 6 hours before serving. Pour into chilled serving bowls and top with finely sliced green onion. |

FOR 4	FOR 6	INGREDIENTS
10 in	12 in	Utensils: deep skillet
sm	sm	mixing bowl
1½ lb	2 lb	lean lamb shoulder, cubed
2 tbl	3 tbl	cooking oil
1⅔ C	2½ C	water
1 tsp	1½ tsp	salt
1	1	bay leaf
4	6	peppercorns
1 sm	1 med	sliced onion
¾ tsp	1 tsp	chopped fresh parsley
3 tbl	¼ C	flour
1½ tbl	1 tbl	curry powder
2 tbl	3 tbl	cold water
½ pkg	1 pkg	dry onion soup mix

FOR 4	FOR 6	INGREDIENTS
1 qt	2 qt	Utensil: saucepan
2¼ C	3⅓ C	water
2	3	beef bouillon cubes
1 tsp	1½ tsp	vinegar
½ tsp	¾ tsp	salt
1 C	1½ C	long-grain white rice

INSTRUCTIONS

LAMB CURRY

In a skillet, brown the meat slowly in hot oil. When browned, cover with boiling water. Add salt, bay leaf, peppercorns, onion, and parsley. Cover and cook slowly for 1½ hours, or until meat is tender. Remove meat, leaving 2 cups of stock in the skillet (or 1½ cups if serving 4). Skim off fat, remove peppercorns and bay leaf, then add water if necessary to total correct liquid measurement. In a small mixing bowl, mix the flour and curry powder. Slowly stir in cold water and blend well. Stir in the dry onion soup mix, then stir into the stock remaining in the skillet. Cook, stirring constantly, until the mixture thickens. Add meat and heat through. Serve over fluffy rice. (May be prepared in advance and reheated just before serving.)

Offer small bowls of 3 or more of the following condiments: chutney, chopped hard-cooked eggs, chopped peanuts, sliced green onions, flaked coconut, chopped crisp bacon, or watermelon pickles.

FLUFFY RICE

In a heavy saucepan, bring water to a boil. Add the bouillon cubes, vinegar, and salt, stirring until bouillon cubes are dissolved. Add the rice, stir to level the rice grains, and cover. Reduce heat to very low and cook for 20 to 25 minutes without removing cover. Keep covered until ready to serve.

FOR 4	FOR 6	INGREDIENTS

MIXED GREEN SALAD

FOR 4	FOR 6	INGREDIENTS
med	lrg	Utensil: salad bowl
1 sm hd	1 med hd	lettuce
1 sm hd	1 med hd	romaine lettuce
2	3	green onions
½ C	¾ C	sliced celery
2	3	tomatoes

Wash and dry lettuce and tear into salad bowl. Wash and slice onions and celery into bowl. Cut tomatoes into wedges and add to bowl. Cover and refrigerate until ready to serve. / / Toss with salad dressing just before serving.

FOR 4	FOR 6	INGREDIENTS
m	sm	Utensil: mixing bowl
⅓ C	½ C	commercial sour cream
3 tbl	¼ C	mayonnaise
2 tsp	1 tbl	wine vinegar
¾ tsp	1 tsp	salt
⅛ tsp	¼ tsp	pepper
⅓ tsp	½ tsp	sugar
1½ tsp	2 tsp	lemon juice
¾ tsp	1 tsp	prepared mustard
¾ tsp	1 tsp	catsup
¼ C	⅓ C	chopped onion
	1	chopped garlic clove
2 oz	3 oz	Roquefort cheese

Roquefort Dressing

Combine all ingredients except the Roquefort cheese in a mixing bowl (or blender) and mix until smooth. Crumble the Roquefort cheese into dressing, cover, and refrigerate until ready to serve.

FOR 4	FOR 6	INGREDIENTS

INSTRUCTIONS

MINTED PINEAPPLE

sm	med	Utensil: mixing bowl
½	¾	fresh whole pineapple
2 tbl	3 tbl	crème de menthe

Cut off the outer layer and ends of pineapple. Cut into fourths, lengthwise, and remove tough center core. Cut pineapple into bite-size chunks. / / Place pineapple in mixing bowl, add the crème de menthe, and mix. Serve in individual bowls or glasses.

---

menu 64

Zinfandel†
Lasagne Del Mondo
Green Salad
Garlic Bread
Delightfully Angel

TIMETABLE

*4:00 pm	Prepare sauce for Lasagne
*5:00	Prepare dessert
*6:00	Prepare Lasagne Casserole
*7:00	Slice, butter, and wrap Garlic Bread
*7:15	Prepare salad and salad dressing
7:30	Bake Lasagne Casserole at 350°
7:35	Reheat sauce if it was prepared in advance
7:45	Place Garlic Bread in oven to warm
7:50	Toss salad with dressing
8:00	Dinner is served

† A dry Claret wine; serve at cool room temperature (65°)

* May be prepared in the morning or the night before and refrigerated

FOR 4	FOR 6	INGREDIENTS
2 qt	3 qt	Utensils: saucepan
10 in	12 in	skillet
4 qt	5 qt	kettle
1 qt	1½ qt	baking dish
1 lb	1 lb 13 oz	canned tomato purée
1 sm	1 med	onion
⅛ tsp	¼ tsp	garlic powder
¾ tsp	1 tsp	salt
⅛ tsp	¼ tsp	black pepper
⅓ tsp	½ tsp	oregano
¼ C	⅓ C	water
⅓ C	½ C	Sauterne wine
1½ tbl	2 tbl	olive oil
3 oz	4 oz	fresh mushrooms
⅓ lb	½ lb	ground beef
3 oz	4 oz	Italian sausage, mild or sweet
6 oz	8 oz	lasagne
2 qt	3 qt	water
2 tsp	1 tbl	salt
6 oz	8 oz	ricotta cheese
6 oz	8 oz	mozzarella cheese, sliced thin
2 tbl	3 tbl	grated Romano cheese

INSTRUCTIONS

LASAGNE DEL MONDO

Place tomato purée in saucepan and start simmering over the lowest heat. Add peeled onion cut in halves, garlic powder, salt, black pepper, oregano, water, and Sauterne wine to purée. Clean and slice mushrooms and sauté them in the skillet with the olive oil. When mushrooms are tender (about 10 minutes), add them, together with the olive oil remaining in the skillet, to the sauce. Using the same skillet, break the ground beef into small pieces and cook until slightly browned. Drain off grease and add beef to sauce. Cut the Italian sausage into one-inch pieces, brown lightly in the skillet, drain off grease, and add sausage to the sauce. Cover and simmer the sauce for about 3 hours, stirring frequently. If sauce becomes too thick, add a little water and wine. Some of the sauce may be used in the Lasagne Casserole after cooking about 90 minutes, and the remainder of the sauce should simmer for 3 hours.

Cook the lasagne according to directions on package, or, if purchased in bulk, bring water to a vigorous boil in kettle, add salt and lasagne, and cook until tender (about 15 minutes). Wash in cold water and drain. Arrange layers in casserole as follows: layer of lasagne, thin layer of sauce, layer of lasagne, layer of mozzarella cheese, layer of lasagne, layer of sauce, layer of ricotta cheese, layer of lasagne, layer of sauce, and sprinkle with Romano cheese. / / Bake at 350° for 30 minutes. Serve with sauce.

FOR 4	FOR 6	INGREDIENTS
med	lrg	Utensil: salad bowl
1 med hd	1 lrg hd	lettuce
⅓ sm	½ sm	red onion
⅓ sm	½ sm	green bell pepper
¼ sm	⅓ sm	cucumber
1 pt	1 pt	Utensil: glass jar
3 tbl	5 tbl	olive oil
1½ tbl	2½ tbl	wine vinegar
⅛ tsp	¼ tsp	garlic powder
½ tsp	¾ tsp	sweet basil
½ tsp	¾ tsp	salt
¼ tsp	⅓ tsp	fresh ground black pepper
sm	sm	Utensil: saucepan
4 tbl	6 tbl	butter
½ tsp	¾ tsp	garlic powder
1 sm	1 med	French bread
4 tbl	6 tbl	grated Parmesan cheese

INSTRUCTIONS

GREEN SALAD

Wash and dry lettuce and break leaves into salad bowl. Add the sliced red onion, chopped bell pepper, and sliced cucumber. Refrigerate until ready to serve. / / Toss with salad dressing just before serving.

Dressing

Mix olive oil, wine vinegar, garlic powder, sweet basil, salt, and pepper together in glass jar and refrigerate until ready to serve. / / Shake well before adding to salad.

GARLIC BREAD

Melt butter in saucepan and add garlic powder. Slice the loaf of bread and brush each slice with melted butter. Sprinkle the buttered slices with grated Parmesan cheese, arrange slices back into loaf form, and wrap loaf in aluminum foil. / / Heat at 350° for 15 minutes.

DELIGHTFULLY ANGEL

FOR 4	FOR 6	INGREDIENTS
3 qt		Utensils: saucepan
1½ qt		baking dish
1 sm,		mixing bowls
2 med		
3		eggs
½ env		gelatin
⅓ C		sugar
¼ C		lemon juice
¾ tsp		grated lemon rind
⅓ C		sugar
1 C		heavy cream
10 oz		angel food cake

Separate eggs. Beat egg yolks in small mixing bowl and combine them in the saucepan with the gelatin and sugar. Add lemon juice and lemon rind. Cook over medium heat until the mixture begins to thicken. Cool. In a medium mixing bowl, beat egg whites until stiff, beat in sugar, and fold the egg whites into the mixture in the saucepan. In a medium mixing bowl, beat the whipping cream until stiff and fold into the saucepan mixture.

Break the angel food cake into pieces and lay half of the pieces in the baking dish. Add one-half of the saucepan mixture. Lay the remaining cake pieces in baking dish and top with the remaining saucepan mixture. Refrigerate before serving.

menu 65

Folle Blanche†
Lobster-Crabmeat Casseroles
Marinated Vegetables
Hot Rolls
Lemon Meringue Pie

TIMETABLE

*Morning Prepare Marinated Vegetables, cover, and refrigerate
*5:30 pm Chill wine
*5:30 Prepare Lemon Meringue Pie
*6:30 Prepare Lobster-Crabmeat Casseroles
7:30 Preheat oven to 400°
7:30 Drain Marinated Vegetables and place on serving plate
7:45 Place Lobster-Crabmeat Casseroles in oven
7:50 Place rolls in oven
8:00 Dinner is served

† A dry Chablis wine; serve chilled (45°)   * May be prepared in the morning or the night before and refrigerated

---

FOR 4	FOR 6	INGREDIENTS

INSTRUCTIONS

LOBSTER-CRABMEAT CASSEROLES

FOR 4	FOR 6	INGREDIENTS
2 qt, 4 qt	3 qt, 4 qt	Utensils: saucepans
4	6	individual casseroles
1		cookie sheet
3 qt	3 qt	water
1 tsp	1 tsp	salt
2 8 oz	3 8 oz	frozen rock lobster tails
1 can	2 cans	king crabmeat, 7½-oz can
⅓ C	½ C	butter
⅓ C	½ C	flour
¾ tsp	1 tsp	salt
⅓ tsp	½ tsp	paprika
⅛ tsp	⅛ tsp	pepper
1½ C	2 C	light cream
½ C	¾ C	dry white wine (Chablis)

Bring water to a boil in large saucepan. Add salt and lobster tails. Cook covered for 8 minutes over reduced heat. Drain and rinse with cool water. Drain crabmeat and remove any membranes. Remove meat from lobster tails and cut into small pieces. In the smaller saucepan, melt the butter and stir in the flour, salt, paprika, and pepper. When smooth, stir in the cream and white wine. Cook for 3 or 4 minutes. Stir in the pieces of lobster and crab. Place the individual casserole dishes on a cookie sheet and spoon the mixture into them equally.

FOR 4	FOR 6	INGREDIENTS
2 qt	2 qt	Utensil: saucepan
3 tbl	¼ C	butter
1 C	1½ C	bread crumbs

Crumb Topping

Prepare the crumb topping by melting butter in small saucepan and stirring in the bread crumbs. / / Sprinkle topping on the casseroles and bake at 400° for 15 minutes.

MARINATED VEGETABLES

	2 qt	Utensils: saucepan
	med	mixing bowl
	2 C	water
	1 med	cauliflower
	1 lb	canned whole green beans

Wash cauliflower and cut into small pieces. Bring 2 cups of water to a boil in a saucepan, add cauliflower, and cook covered for 10 minutes. Drain and place into mixing bowl. Drain the green beans and add to mixing bowl.

Marinade

	1 pt	Utensil: glass jar
	1 env	onion salad dressing mix
	⅔ C	salad oil
	⅓ C	wine vinegar
	5	lettuce leaves

Combine the onion dressing mix, salad oil, and wine vinegar and shake well in glass jar. Pour over vegetables, cover the bowl, and marinate for several hours. / / When ready to serve, drain and serve vegetables on lettuce leaves, in serving bowl.

HOT ROLLS

med	lrg	Utensil: cookie sheet	Preheat oven to 400°. Unroll dough and separate into 8 triangles per tube of dough. Roll up (start at wide end of triangle and roll to opposite point). Place rolls, point-side down, on ungreased cookie sheet. Curve into crescent shape. Baker for 10 minutes.
1 tube	2 tubes	packaged refrigerator crescent dinner rolls	

LEMON MERINGUE PIE

Crust

	sm	Utensils: mixing bowl	Preheat oven to 375°. In a small mixing bowl, combine butter and sugar, but do not cream. Add flour and mix just enough for dough to form. Press mixture evenly into bottom and sides of pie pan. Bake for 12 to 15 minutes, or until light golden brown. Remove from oven and chill.
	9 in	pie pan	
	½ C	butter	
	2 tbl	sugar	
	1 C	flour	

Filling

	2 sm	Utensils: mixing bowls	In a small mixing bowl, combine the lemon juice and lemon rind. Gradually stir in the condensed milk. Separate eggs. Add egg yolks to mixing bowl and stir until well blended. Pour into chilled pie crust. In a small bowl, add cream of tartar to egg whites. Beat until almost stiff enough to hold a peak. Add sugar gradually, beating until stiff but not dry. Pile lightly on pie filling. Bake about 15 minutes at 325°, or until lightly browned. Let cool, and chill before serving.
	½ C	lemon juice	
	1 tsp	grated lemon rind	
	1 can	sweetened condensed milk, 15-oz can	
	2	eggs	
	¼ tsp	cream of tartar	
	4 tbl	sugar	

194

menu 66

Pinot Blanc†
Lobster Newburg
Asparagus with Crumb Sauce
Grape and Apple Salad
Crescent Rolls
Rum Balls

TIMETABLE

Day before	Prepare Rum Balls
*4:30 pm	Chill wine
*6:00	Prepare Grape and Apple Salad
6:40	Prepare Crumb Sauce for asparagus
7:10	Prepare Lobster Newburg
7:35	Preheat oven to 375° and prepare Crescent Rolls
7:45	Bake Crescent Rolls
7:45	Cook asparagus
7:50	Reheat Crumb Sauce and lobster
7:55	Place salad in serving bowl
8:00	Dinner is served

† A dry Chablis wine; serve chilled (45°)   * May be prepared in the morning or the night before and refrigerated

---

FOR 4	FOR 6	INGREDIENTS

INSTRUCTIONS

LOBSTER NEWBURG

FOR 4	FOR 6	INGREDIENTS
2 qt	3 qt	Utensils: saucepan
2 sm	2 sm	mixing bowls
2 C	3 C	cooked, cubed lobster
2 tbl	3 tbl	butter or margarine
1 tsp	1½ tsp	salt
¼ tsp	⅓ tsp	pepper
½ tsp	¾ tsp	paprika
2	3	egg yolks
¼ C	⅓ C	sherry wine
1 tbl	1½ tbl	flour
1 C	1½ C	milk
4	6	bread slices

Cut cooked lobster meat into large pieces. Melt butter in saucepan over medium heat. Add salt, pepper, and paprika. Beat egg yolks slightly in small bowl and add to mixture. Add sherry wine. Mix the flour in a small mixing bowl with a little of the milk and add slowly to the sauce with the rest of the milk. Cook over low heat for 10 minutes. Add lobster meat and heat through. Keep covered until ready to serve. Toast bread slices, trim off crusts, and cut each slice into 4 triangles. To serve, pour lobster mixture over pieces of toast.

195

ASPARAGUS WITH CRUMB SAUCE

FOR 4	FOR 6	INGREDIENTS
2 1 qt,	2 1 qt,	Utensils: saucepans
1 4 qt	1 4 qt	
1½ lb	2 lb	fresh asparagus
1	2	eggs
⅓ C	½ C	butter
⅓ C	½ C	soft bread crumbs
1 tbl	1½ tbl	minced fresh parsley
1½ tsp	2¼ tsp	salt
¼ tsp	⅓ tsp	pepper

Wash and clean asparagus, break off tough ends, and cut asparagus lengthwise. Place eggs in saucepan, cover with water, and bring to a boil. Reduce heat and simmer for 5 to 8 minutes. Place eggs in cold water to cool, remove shell, and dice. Melt butter in another small saucepan until it foams. Stir in bread crumbs and heat until crumbs are brown. Stir egg and parsley into crumb mixture. Cover to keep warm. Place asparagus spears in saucepan, cover with water, add ½ tsp salt (for 4) or ¾ tsp salt (for 6), and cook for 6 to 8 minutes. Drain. To serve, arrange asparagus on platter, season with remaining salt and with pepper, and spoon crumb mixture over top.

GRAPE AND APPLE SALAD

FOR 4	FOR 6	INGREDIENTS
sm	sm	Utensils: saucepan
med	med	mixing bowl
2 tsp	1 tbl	butter or margarine
3 tbl	¼ C	slivered almonds
2 med	2 lrg	red Delicious apples
¾ C	1 C	halved, seeded red grapes
3	5	lettuce leaves

In a small saucepan, melt butter, add the slivered almonds, and stir over low heat until browned. In a medium mixing bowl, cut, core, and dice (do not peel) apples. Cut grapes in half, seed, and add to the apples. Stir in browned almonds. Pour dressing over fruit and mix lightly. Refrigerate until ready to serve. / / Serve in a serving bowl on bed of lettuce leaves.

FOR 4	FOR 6	INGREDIENTS	INSTRUCTIONS

Dressing

FOR 4	FOR 6	INGREDIENTS
sm	sm	Utensil: mixing bowl
3 tbl	¼ C	commercial sour cream
¾ tsp	1 tsp	lemon juice
2 tsp	1 tbl	honey
¼ tsp	¼ tsp	salt
⅛ tsp	⅛ tsp	dry mustard

In a small mixing bowl, combine the sour cream, lemon juice, honey, salt, and mustard.

CRESCENT ROLLS

FOR 4	FOR 6	INGREDIENTS
med	lrg	Utensil: cookie sheet
1 tube	2 tubes	packaged refrigerator cresent dinner rolls

Preheat oven to 375°. Unroll dough and separate into 8 triangles per tube of dough. Roll up each triangle: start at wide end of triangle and roll to opposite point. Place rolls, point-side down, on an ungreased cookie sheet and curve into crescent shape. Bake at 375° for 10 to 13 minutes.

RUM BALLS

FOR 4	FOR 6	INGREDIENTS
med	med	Utensil: mixing bowl
¾ C	1¼ C	crushed vanilla wafers
⅓ C	½ C	powdered sugar
1 C	1½ C	cocoa
3 tbl	¼ C	rum
1 tbl	1½ tbl	corn syrup
3 tbl	¼ C	chopped walnuts
¼ C	⅓ C	powdered sugar

Crush vanilla wafers between sheets of waxed paper. Measure. Mix the crushed vanilla wafers with the powdered sugar and cocoa in a mixing bowl. Add the rum, corn syrup, and walnuts. Roll into 1-inch balls. Roll the balls in powdered sugar. Cover tightly and store in refrigerator. The flavor improves with age.

menu 67

Charbono†
Orange Roast Duckling
Noodles Romano
Almond Green Beans
Frozen Roquefort Salad
Bavarian Cream

† A dry Burgundy wine; serve at cool room temperature (65°)

TIMETABLE

Time	Task
*2:00 pm	Prepare Bavarian Cream
*4:00	Prepare Frozen Roquefort Salad
5:45	Prepare and roast duckling at 325°
*6:55	Prepare Noodles Romano
7:15	Place Noodles Romano in oven
7:35	Prepare Almond Green Beans
7:50	Finish Roquefort salad
8:00	Dinner is served

* May be prepared in the morning or the night before and refrigerated

---

FOR 4	FOR 6	INGREDIENTS	INSTRUCTIONS

ORANGE ROAST DUCKLING

FOR 4	FOR 6	INGREDIENTS
lrg	lrg	Utensils: roasting pan and rack
sm	sm	mixing bowl
2 3-lb	2 4-lb	ducklings, ready to cook
2 tsp	3 tsp	salt
1 tsp	1½ tsp	pepper
½ C	¾ C	orange juice
2 tbl	3 tbl	honey
1 tbl	1½ tbl	cooking oil

Rinse ducklings in cold water, inside and out. Drain dry. Season with salt and pepper, inside and out. Place on roasting rack in roaster. Combine orange juice, honey, and cooking oil in small mixing bowl. Baste ducklings with sauce. Roast ducklings about 2 hours in preheated 325° oven, basting during roasting period.

198

FOR 4	FOR 6	INGREDIENTS	INSTRUCTIONS

NOODLES ROMANO

FOR 4	FOR 6	INGREDIENTS
3 qt	4 qt	Utensils: saucepan
med	med	mixing bowl
2 qt	2 qt	baking dish
2 qt	2 qt	water
6 oz	8 oz	medium egg noodles
1 tsp	1½ tsp	salt
1 C	1½ C	cottage cheese
1 C	1½ C	commercial sour cream
2 tsp	1 tbl	minced onion
1	2	minced garlic clove
/4 tsp	½ tsp	Worcestershire sauce
3 drops	5 drops	Tabasco sauce
½ tsp	¾ tsp	salt
½ C	¾ C	Romano cheese, grated

Bring 2 quarts of water to a boil in saucepan, add salt and noodles, and cook, uncovered, for 8 to 10 minutes, or until noodles are tender. Drain in a colander, rinse gently with hot water, and place drained noodles back in saucepan. Meanwhile, combine the cottage cheese, sour cream, onion, garlic, Worcestershire sauce, Tabasco, and salt in a mixing bowl. Gently mix sauce into the noodles. Place into baking dish and sprinkle with Romano cheese. / / Bake, uncovered, for 45 minutes at 325°.

ALMOND GREEN BEANS

FOR 4	FOR 6	INGREDIENTS
sm, 1 qt	sm, 2 qt	Utensil: saucepans
½ C	¾ C	water
/4 tsp	1 tsp	salt
pkg	2 pkg	frozen green beans, 10-oz pkg
/4 C	½ C	butter or margarine
/4 C	½ C	slivered almonds
/4 tsp	½ tsp	salt
½ tbl	1 tbl	lemon juice

Bring water to a boil in larger saucepan. Add salt and green beans. Cover and bring back to a boil. Reduce heat and cook 4 to 7 minutes, or until tender. Drain. Meanwhile, heat butter in a small saucepan, add almonds, and cook over low heat until lightly browned, stirring occasionally. Remove from heat, add salt and lemon juice, and pour over drained beans. Cover to keep warm.

FROZEN ROQUEFORT SALAD

FOR 4	FOR 6	INGREDIENTS
2 sm	sm, med	Utensils: mixing bowls
1	2	ice cube tray
6 oz	8 oz	cream cheese
3 oz	4 oz	Roquefort cheese
⅓ C	½ C	mayonnaise
¾ C	1 C	heavy cream
4	6	lettuce leaves
2	3	pears
4	6	maraschino cherries, with stems

In a mixing bowl, mix cream cheese, Roquefort cheese, and mayonnaise until smooth. In a small mixing bowl, whip the cream until stiff and fold into the cheese mixture. Pour into ice cube tray and freeze about 4 hours. / / When ready to serve, rinse the lettuce leaves and drain. Wash pears, cut in half, and core. Cut frozen cheese mixture into servings and place on lettuce leaves on individual serving plates. Place a pear half, cut side down, on each cheese serving, topped with a cherry held in place with a toothpick.

BAVARIAN CREAM

FOR 4	FOR 6	INGREDIENTS
2 sm	2 sm	Utensils: mixing bowls
1 qt	2 qt	double boiler
med	med	wide mixing bowl
1 env	1½ env	unflavored gelatin
½ C	¾ C	bourbon
2	3	egg yolks
½ C	¾ C	sugar
⅛ tsp	⅛ tsp	salt
1 C	1½ C	milk
½ tsp	¾ tsp	vanilla extract
¼ tsp	¼ tsp	nutmeg
½ C	¾ C	heavy cream

Combine gelatin and bourbon in a small bowl and stir to soften gelatin. In the top of a double boiler, beat egg yolks well. Add sugar and salt. Add milk and mix well. Cook over simmering water (water should not touch the top section), stirring constantly, until mixture begins to thicken. Remove from heat, add vanilla extract, bourbon-and-gelatin mixture, and nutmeg. Stir until gelatin dissolves. Place mixture in wide mixing bowl and chill in refrigerator until slightly thickened. In a small mixing bowl, beat egg whites until stiff and fold into gelatin mixture. Beat the cream in another small mixing bowl until whipped, and fold into the gelatin mixture. Spoon into sherbet glasses and chill until firm.

menu 68

Johannisberger Riesling†
Roast Pork with Barbecue Sauce
Green Bean Casserole
Orange Salad Mold
Bakery Rolls
Pineapple Cheese Cake

TIMETABLE

*Morning	Prepare Pineapple Cheese Cake
*4:00 pm	Chill wine
*4:00	Prepare Orange Salad Mold
4:30	Place pork roast in oven at 325°
*6:30	Prepare Barbecue Sauce
6:50	Drain fat from meat and pour Barbecue Sauce over roast
*7:10	Wrap rolls in foil
*7:15	Prepare Green Bean Casserole
7:35	Place Green Bean Casserole in oven
7:35	Place rolls in oven
7:40	Unmold Orange Salad Mold onto serving plate
7:55	Arrange onion rings on top of Green Bean Casserole and return to oven
8:00	Dinner is served

† A dry Rhine wine; serve chilled (45°)   * May be prepared in the morning or the night before and refrigerated

FOR 4	FOR 6	INGREDIENTS

INSTRUCTIONS

GREEN BEAN CASSEROLE

FOR 4	FOR 6	INGREDIENTS
qt	3 qt	Utensils: saucepan
½ qt	1½ qt	baking dish
pkg	3 pkg	frozen French-style green beans
¼ C	¾ C	water
¼ tsp	¾ tsp	salt
can	1 can	canned cream of mushroom soup
can	1 can	canned fried onion rings

Bring water to a boil in saucepan. Add salt and green beans, cover, and bring back to a boil. Reduce heat and cook gently for 4 to 7 minutes, or until beans are tender. Drain. Stir in cream of mushroom soup. Pour mixture into a baking dish. / / Bake at 325° for 20 minutes. Remove from oven, cover with the canned fried onion rings, and return to oven for 5 more minutes.

ROAST PORK WITH BARBECUE SAUCE

med	Utensil: roasting pan and rack	
5 lb	pork loin roast	

Place the roast, fat side up, on a rack in an open roasting pan. Roast at 325° for 3 hours and 20 minutes. One hour before meat is done, pour off fat and cover roast with Barbecue Sauce.

Barbecue Sauce

sm	Utensil: mixing bowl
1 can	canned tomato soup
⅓ C	minced onion
⅓ C	minced celery
1	minced garlic clove
2 tbl	brown sugar, firmly packed
2 tbl	Worcestershire sauce
2 tbl	lemon juice
2 tsp	prepared mustard
4 drops	Tabasco sauce

In a small mixing bowl, combine all ingredients. Pour sauce over meat about one hour before meat is done. Baste occasionally while meat is roasting.

ORANGE SALAD MOLD

FOR 4	FOR 6	INGREDIENTS
med		Utensils: mixing bowl
2 qt		gelatin mold
1 pkg		orange gelatin
1 C		boiling water
1 can		apricots, 8 ½-oz can
1 can		pineapple tidbits, 8 ¾-oz can
2 sm		oranges
1 tbl		grated orange rind
5		lettuce leaves

Place gelatin in mixing bowl. Add boiling water and stir until gelatin has dissolved. Drain the juices from the canned fruit to make one cup of liquid, adding cold water if juices total less than one cup. Add the juices to the gelatin and refrigerate until mixture has partially set. Meanwhile, grate the orange rind and peel the oranges. Cut the orange into segments and remove the membranes. When gelatin has partially set, add the apricots, pineapple tidbits, orange segments, and grated orange rind. Turn mixture into a gelatin mold and refrigerate until firm. / / Just before serving, place washed lettuce leaves on serving plate and turn the mold out onto the bed of lettuce.

BAKERY ROLLS

FOR 4	FOR 6	INGREDIENTS
8	12	bakery rolls

Wrap rolls in aluminum foil. / / Heat for 25 minutes at 325°.

PINEAPPLE CHEESE CAKE

Crust

sm	Utensils: mixing bowl
10 in	pie plate
12	graham crackers
¼ C	melted butter or margarine
3 tbl	sugar

Crush graham crackers into small mixing bowl. Stir in melted butter and sugar. Press into bottom and sides of buttered pie plate.

Filling

med	Utensil: mixing bowl
11 oz	cream cheese
½ C	sugar
2	eggs
1 tsp	vanilla extract
1 lb 4 oz	canned crushed pineapple
⅛ tsp	cinnamon

Beat the cream cheese with a mixer until fluffy. Gradually add the sugar, eggs, and vanilla extract, beating well after each addition. Blend in drained, crushed pineapple and pour mixture into pie crust. Sprinkle with cinnamon and bake at 375° for 20 minutes. Let cool 1 hour.

Topping

sm	Utensil: mixing bowl
1 pt	commercial sour cream
3 tbl	sugar
1 tsp	vanilla extract

Mix together the sour cream, sugar, and vanilla extract. Spread over top of cake. Bake at 375° for 5 minutes. Chill at least 6 hours before serving.

menu 69

Charbono†
Roast Turkey with Dressing
Giblet Gravy
Fruit Salad
Peas and Pearl Onions
Fruit Ice Cream Mold

TIMETABLE

Day before	Prepare Fruit Ice Cream Mold
*2:00 pm	Clean, drain, and salt turkey
*2:55	Cook giblets
*3:00	Prepare dressing
‡4:00	Stuff and prepare turkey for roasting
*4:35	Prepare Fruit Salad
4:45	Place turkey in oven at 325°
7:45	Remove turkey from oven
7:45	Prepare Giblet Gravy
7:50	Cook Peas and Pearl Onions
8:00	Dinner is served

† A dry Burgundy wine; serve at cool room temperature (65°)

* May be prepared in the morning or the night before and refrigerated
‡ May be prepared in the morning

FOR 4   FOR 6   INGREDIENTS   INSTRUCTIONS

FRUIT ICE CREAM MOLD

1 qt	Utensils: circular mold
2 sm	mixing bowls
1½ pt	vanilla ice cream
1 pt	chocolate ice cream
½ C	heavy cream
1 tsp	vanilla extract
2 tbl	powdered sugar
1	egg white
3 tbl	candied fruit and peel mix.

Line inside of mold with vanilla ice cream; freeze until firm. Cover with a layer of chocolate ice cream; freeze until firm. Whip the cream in a mixing bowl and fold in the vanilla extract and powered sugar. Set aside one-half of the whipped cream to use as a topping. Beat egg white in another mixing bowl until soft peaks form; fold into the whipped cream. Then fold in chopped candied fruit. Spoon mixture into the center of the mold, cover, and freeze until firm. To serve, unmold by placing damp, hot towels around bottom of mold which has been inverted onto serving plate. Decorate with the reserved whipped cream and sprinkle with a little more candied fruit.

ROAST TURKEY WITH DRESSING

med	Utensil: roasting pan and rack
6–8 lb	turkey
1 tbl	salt
2 tbl	salad oil

Remove giblets (gizzard, heart, and liver) from turkey and set aside. Clean, wash, and drain turkey. Rub the inside of the cavity with salt. / Stuff loosely with dressing and close the large opening by inserting skewer and lacing together with cord. Tie wings in place with cord around body then wrap cord around ends of legs and tie securely to tail piece so that legs are close to body. Draw the neck skin over small cavity and fasten flat to the back of the turkey with skewer. (*Do not stuff turkey the night before*). / / Rub turkey with salad oil, sprinkle with salt and pepper and place breast side up on the rack of a roasting pan. Insert a meat thermometer between thigh and body. Roast, uncovered, about 3 hours or until thermometer registers 190°F.

Dressing

lrg	Utensils: mixing bowl
2 qt	saucepan
10 C	day-old bread cubes (or packaged dressing mix)
1 tsp	salt
2 tsp	poultry seasoning
1 lrg	onion
1 C	chopped celery
¼ C	butter
⅔ C	water
1 can	water chestnuts, 5-oz can

Place bread cubes in mixing bowl. Combine with salt and poultry seasoning. In a saucepan, combine chopped onion and celery, butter and water. Cook, stirring frequently, for about 5 minutes. Add the cooked mixture to the bread cubes and mix lightly. Drain and slice the water chestnuts and add to dressing.

GIBLET GRAVY

FOR 4	FOR 6	INGREDIENTS
	1 qt	Utensil: saucepan
		giblets from turkey
	1 tsp	salt
	4 tbl	flour
	1½ C	milk
	½ tsp	salt
	⅛ tsp	pepper

Wash giblets and cover with water in saucepan. Add salt and simmer, covered, until tender (2 to 3 hours). Drain and reserve liquid. Chop giblets into small pieces. When turkey has cooked, transfer to a serving platter, remove rack from roaster pan, and place pan on stove. Bring the turkey drippings to a boil (if just a small amount of drippings, add 1 tablespoon of butter), sprinkle in flour, and stir until brown. Gradually add milk, stirring constantly, until smooth. Add a little more milk if gravy becomes too thick. Add giblets, reserved liquid from giblets, salt, and pepper. Cook for 10 minutes, stirring constantly.

FRUIT SALAD

FOR 4	FOR 6	INGREDIENTS
	med	Utensil: mixing bowl
	½ pt	commercial sour cream
	1 tsp	sugar
	1 can	pineapple chunks, 13¼-oz can
	2 med	apples
	3	bananas

In a mixing bowl, whip the sour cream until fluffy. Beat in sugar. Drain the pineapple chunks and add the chunks to the sour cream. Clean, core and chop apples. Add to mixture. Peel and slice the bananas into mixture. Blend carefully. Transfer to a serving bowl, cover, and refrigerate until ready to serve.

PEAS AND PEARL ONIONS

FOR 4	FOR 6	INGREDIENTS
	2 qt	Utensil: saucepan
	2 pkg	frozen peas and pearl onions, 10-oz pkg
	2 tbl	water
	2 tbl	butter or margarine

In a saucepan, place the water and butter. Add vegetables, cover, and bring to a full boil over medium heat. Reduce heat to low and simmer, covered, for 5 to 7 minutes. Keep covered until ready to serve.

menu 70

Cabernet Sauvignon†
Roquefort Steak
Pasta Peas
Gooseberry Salad
Blueberry Cream Cheese Pie

TIMETABLE

Morning	Prepare Gooseberry Salad and refrigerate
*5:30 pm	Prepare dessert and refrigerate
*6:45	Prepare Pasta Peas
7:30	Bake Pasta Peas at 350°
7:30	Prepare Roquefort Steak for broiling
7:45	Open oven door, turn oven control to "broil," and broil stea
7:50	Place Gooseberry Salad on individual plates
8:00	Dinner is served

† A dry Claret wine; serve at cool room temperature (65°)

* May be prepared in the morning or the night before and refrigerated

---

FOR 4	FOR 6	INGREDIENTS
sm	sm	Utensil: mixing bowl
6 oz	9 oz	Roquefort cheese
1 tsp	1½ tsp	Worcestershire sauce
1 tsp	1½ tsp	bottled meat sauce
2 drops	3 drops	Tabasco sauce
3 lb	4½ lb	top sirloin steak
3	4	crushed garlic cloves

INSTRUCTIONS

ROQUEFORT STEAK

Cream Roquefort cheese in mixing bowl and mix in the Worcestershir
sauce, meat sauce, and Tabasco sauce. Spread the mixture on the stea
and place on broiler pan. Place the garlic cloves on the pan around th
steak. Broil steak for 5 minutes on each side (rare), 7 minutes on eacl
side (medium), or 10 minutes on each side (well done). Serve witl
drippings over steak.

FOR 4	FOR 6	INGREDIENTS
qt, 4 qt	2 qt, 4 qt	Utensils: saucepans
0 in	12 in	skillet
½ qt	1½ qt	covered casserole
oz	8 oz	small pasta shells
C	3 C	frozen peas
¼ C	1 C	chopped onion
	3	minced garlic cloves
C	¼ C	olive oil
C	½ C	butter or margarine
C	1 C	finely chopped fresh parsley
tsp	1 tsp	salt
tsp	½ tsp	ground black pepper

PASTA PEAS

According to the instructions on the package, cook the pasta shells in the large saucepan, blanch with water, and drain. Cook the peas in the smaller saucepan and drain. Sauté onion and garlic with combined olive oil and butter in the skillet for 10 minutes. Add drained pasta shells, drained peas, parsley, salt, and pepper and mix well. Place the mixture in a covered casserole and refrigerate until ready to bake. / / Bake in oven for 15 minutes. Leave in oven with door open until ready to serve.

	2 qt	Utensil: rectangular baking dish
	1 pkg	lime gelatin, 3-oz
	1 pkg	lemon gelatin, 3-oz
	2 C	hot water
	½ C	cold water
	1 lb 1 oz	canned gooseberries
	1 C	chopped celery
	½ C	slivered almonds
	½ C	grated American cheese
	6	lettuce leaves

GOOSEBERRY SALAD

Dissolve gelatin in hot water in the baking dish. Add cold water and the juice from the gooseberries. Let mixture cool until almost set. Then add chopped celery, slivered almonds, grated American cheese, and gooseberries and mix into gelatin. Place salad on lettuce leaves on individual serving dishes and refrigerate until ready to serve.

BLUEBERRY CREAM CHEESE PIE CRUMB

Crust

med	Utensils: mixing bowl	
9 in	pie pan	
2 tbl	sugar	
½ C	butter	
1 C	unsifted flour	

Combine sugar and butter in a medium mixing bowl but do not cream the mixture. Add flour and mix just enough for a dough to form. Turn dough into pie pan and pat evenly into sides and bottom. Prick well with a fork and bake in oven at 375° for 12 to 15 minutes, or until lightly browned. Let cool for 30 minutes before adding pie filling.

Pie Filling

sm, med	Utensil: mixing bowls	
3 oz	cream cheese	
½ C	powdered sugar	
½ tsp	vanilla extract	
1 C	heavy cream	
1 lb 5 oz	canned blueberry pie filling	
1 tbl	lemon juice	

In a small mixing bowl, mix together until smooth the cream cheese, powdered sugar, and vanilla extract. In a medium mixing bowl, whip cream until stiff and carefully fold in the cream cheese mixture. Pour mixture into the pie crust, spreading it evenly. Carefully blend the lemon juice into the pie filling and spoon the filling evenly over the cream cheese layer. Chill thoroughly before serving.

210

menu 71

Pinot Chardonnay†
Shish Kabobs
Spicy Rice
Creamy Orange Mold
Brandy Chocolate Cream Cake

TIMETABLE

Night	
before	Prepare meat, vegetables, and marinade; combine and refrigerate
*3:30 pm	Chill wine
*3:30	Prepare Creamy Orange Mold
*4:30	Prepare Brandy Chocolate Cream Cake
6:55	Place meat and vegetables on skewers
7:05	Prepare Spicy Rice
7:35	Unmold gelatin salad onto serving plate
7:40	Place skewers on barbecue
8:00	Dinner is served

† A dry Chablis wine; serve chilled (45°)

* May be prepared in the morning or the night before and refrigerated

FOR 4	FOR 6	INGREDIENTS
10 in		Utensil: skillet
3 tbl		olive oil
1 C		long-grain white rice
1 lrg		onion
1 pkg		dry onion soup mix
4 oz		canned mushrooms
¼ tsp		oregano
1		beef bouillon cube
½ C		chopped nuts
2 C		water

INSTRUCTIONS

SPICY RICE

Heat olive oil in skillet. Add the rice and diced onion. Sauté for about 10 minutes, stirring frequently. Add the onion soup mix, mushrooms (with the liquid in the can), oregano, crushed bouillon cube, nuts, and water. Stir, cover, and simmer for 30 minutes, or until rice is tender. (Do not lift the cover to test the rice before it has simmered 30 minutes.) Keep covered until ready to serve.

FOR 4	FOR 6	INGREDIENTS
sm	sm	Utensils: saucepan
4	6	metal skewers
2 lb	3 lb	boned lamb
3	4	green bell peppers
8	12	mushrooms
1 C	1 C	water
8	12	small white onions
8	12	cherry tomatoes
med	lrg	Utensil: mixing bowl
½ C	¾ C	olive oil
¼ C	⅓ C	red wine
2 tbl	3 tbl	lemon juice
2 tbl	3 tbl	wine vinegar
½ tsp	¾ tsp	salt
¼ tsp	⅓ tsp	pepper
⅛ tsp	¼ tsp	paprika
¼ tsp	⅓ tsp	oregano
1	2	crushed garlic clove

INSTRUCTIONS

SHISH KABOBS

Cut lamb into 2-inch chunks, removing gristle and most of the fat. Wash, seed, and cut green peppers into 2-inch pieces. Wash and remove stem from mushrooms. In a saucepan, bring 1 cup of water to a boil, add peeled onions, and cook, uncovered, for 3 minutes. Drain. Prepare the marinade, add the lamb chunks, green peppers, mushrooms, and onions. Cover and marinate in the refrigerator overnight. When ready to barbecue, alternate lamb, green pepper, mushrooms, onions, and tomatoes on skewers. Broil on charcoal grill about 3 inches from coals for about 15 to 20 minutes, or until tender. Turn skewers frequently to brown food evenly.

Marinade

Combine all ingredients in a mixing bowl. Add meat and vegetables (except for tomatoes) and marinate overnight.

212

BRANDY CHOCOLATE CREAM CAKE

lrg	Utensils: mixing bowl
2 9-in	cake pan
1 pkg	chocolate cake mix
1⅓ C	buttermilk
2	eggs

Empty cake mix into mixing bowl. Blend in the buttermilk and eggs and beat at medium speed for 3 minutes. Pour into lightly buttered and floured cake pans. Bake in preheated 350° oven for 30 to 35 minutes, or until cake springs back when touched lightly in the center. Let cake layers cool in pans for 10 minutes.

Syrup

sm	Utensil: saucepan
⅓ C	honey
⅓ C	brandy

Meanwhile, warm the honey in the saucepan over low heat. Add the ⅓ cup of brandy. Remove cakes from pans and spoon the syrup over the layers. Let cake cool completely.

Frosting

sm	Utensil: mixing bowl
2 C	heavy cream
¼ C	powdered sugar
3 tbl	brandy

Whip the cream in a small mixing bowl, then beat in the powdered sugar and add brandy gradually. Use this mixture to frost each layer and top and sides of cake. Refrigerate cake for at least one hour before serving.

CREAMY ORANGE MOLD

med		Utensils: mixing bowl
2 qt		gelatin mold
1 pkg		orange gelatin, 3 oz
1 C		boiling water
½ tsp		grated orange peel
1 C		orange juice
3 oz		cream cheese
¼ C		mayonnaise
5		lettuce leaves

Place gelatin in mixing bowl, add boiling water, and stir until the gelatin has dissolved. Add the orange peel and juice. Chill until partially set, then beat with a mixer until light and fluffy. Blend in the softened cream cheese and mayonnaise. Pour mixture into lightly oiled gelatin mold and chill until firm. / / Place lettuce leaves on serving plate and turn mold out onto lettuce just before serving.

menu 72

White Riesling†
Soy-Baked Chicken
Hot Noodles
Scalloped Asparagus
Grapefruit Salad Mold
Blueberry Crisp

TIMETABLE

*4:30 pm	Chill wine
*4:30	Prepare Grapefruit Salad Mold
6:30	Prepare Soy-Baked Chicken
6:45	Place chicken in oven at 375°
*6:45	Prepare Scalloped Asparagus
7:30	Prepare Blueberry Crisp
7:45	Place asparagus in oven
7:45	Cook noodles
7:50	Unmold gelatin salad onto serving plate
8:00	Reset oven to 400° and bake dessert
8:00	Dinner is served

† A dry Rhine wine; serve chilled (45°)   * May be prepared in the morning or the night before and refrigerated

OR 4	FOR 6	INGREDIENTS
× 12 in	10 × 14 in	Utensils: baking pan
m	sm	mixing bowl
lb	5 lb	fryer chicken parts
⅓ C	½ C	soy sauce
tbl	3 tbl	lemon juice
¼ tsp	⅓ tsp	onion powder
¼ tsp	⅓ tsp	garlic powder
¼ tsp	⅓ tsp	poultry seasoning
½ tsp	¾ tsp	paprika
tbl	3 tbl	minced fresh parsley

INSTRUCTIONS

SOY-BAKED CHICKEN

Place chicken parts, skin side down, into a baking pan. In the mixing bowl, blend the soy sauce, lemon juice, onion powder, garlic powder, and poultry seasoning. Pour this sauce over the chicken, then turn the pieces so that skin side is up. Sprinkle with paprika and bake at 375° for 1 hour and 15 minutes. Baste once with drippings. Transfer chicken to a serving dish and add cooked, hot, well-drained noodles and parsley to the chicken juices in the baking pan; mix well. Pour the noodles into another serving dish.

HOT NOODLES

FOR 4	FOR 6	INGREDIENTS
3 qt	4 qt	Utensil: saucepan
2 qt	3 qt	water
1 tsp	1 tsp	salt
6 oz	8 oz	medium-wide noodles

Bring 2 quarts of water to a boil in saucepan. Add salt and noodles and cook, uncovered, for 8 to 10 minutes, or until noodles are tender. Drain noodles in a colander and rinse with hot water.

SCALLOPED ASPARAGUS

FOR 4	FOR 6	INGREDIENTS
2 qt	2 qt	Utensils: double boiler
1 qt	1 qt	saucepan
1½ qt	2 qt	shallow baking dish
6 in	6 in	skillet
1 lb	1½ lb	asparagus
¾ tsp	1 tsp	salt
1½ tbl	2 tbl	butter or margarine
2 tbl	3 tbl	flour
1 C	1½ C	milk
½ C	¾ C	grated American cheese
2 tbl	3 tbl	butter or margarine
¼ C	⅓ C	slivered almonds
⅓ C	½ C	fresh bread chunks
⅛ tsp	¼ tsp	salt
⅛ tsp	⅛ tsp	paprika

Break off asparagus where the stalks begin to be woody and remove large scales and the skins of woody ends. Place upright into the bottom half of double boiler that is half filled with water. Add salt and invert the top half of double boiler for use as a cover. Cook for 15 to 25 minutes or until tender, but not soft.

Meanwhile, melt the butter in a saucepan, stir in the flour until smooth and add milk slowly, stirring until thickened. In a small skillet, melt butter. Add almonds and bread chunks. Stir over medium heat until lightly browned.

Grease baking dish and arrange alternate layers of asparagus, white sauce, and grated American cheese. Season with salt and paprika, top with browned almonds and bread chunks. Bake at 375° for 15 minutes (Frozen asparagus may be used. Cook according to instructions on package.)

GRAPEFRUIT SALAD MOLD

FOR 4	INGREDIENTS
2 qt	Utensils: saucepan
2 qt	gelatin mold
¾ C	water
2 env	unflavored gelatin
6 oz	canned, frozen grapefruit juice concentrate
3	ice cubes
1 lb	canned grapefruit sections
½ C	diced celery
½ C	diced, unpared red apple
5	lettuce leaves

Place cold water in saucepan, sprinkle gelatin over the water, and let stand about 5 minutes to soften. Stir over low heat until the gelatin has dissolved. Remove from heat. Add concentrated grapefruit juice and ice cubes. Stir until ice cubes have dissolved. Add grapefruit sections, celery, and apple. Turn into gelatin mold and refrigerate until firm. / / Unmold onto a bed of lettuce for serving.

BLUEBERRY CRISP

FOR 4	INGREDIENTS
2 qt	Utensils: shallow baking dish
sm	mixing bowl
2 cans	blueberrries, 15-oz can
1 tbl	lemon juice
½ C	brown sugar, firmly packed
½ C	unsifted flour
¼ tsp	salt
¼ tsp	nutmeg
¼ C	butter or margarine
1 pt	vanilla ice cream

Drain the blueberries and place them into a buttered baking dish. Sprinkle with lemon juice. In a mixing bowl, mix the brown sugar, flour, salt, and nutmeg. Cut in the softened butter until crumbly. Cover berries with the brown-sugar mixture. Bake at 400° for 15 to 20 minutes, or until bubbly. Serve warm with ice cream.

menu 73

Semillon Wine†
Stuffed Pork Loin Roast
Herb-Buttered Broccoli
Orange Rice
Vanilla Pecan Cake

TIMETABLE

*4:00 pm	Chill wine
*4:00	Prepare Vanilla Pecan Cake and refrigerate
*4:45	Prepare roast
5:20	If serving 6, put the roast in oven at 325°
5:30	Prepare rice except for cooking
6:00	If serving 4, put the roast in oven at 325°
7:30	Cook broccoli and prepare herb butter
7:45	Cook rice
8:00	Dinner is served

† A dry Sauterne wine; serve chilled (45°)   * May be prepared in the morning or the night before and refrigerated

---

FOR 4   FOR 6   INGREDIENTS   INSTRUCTIONS

STUFFED PORK LOIN ROAST

FOR 4	FOR 6	INGREDIENTS
med	med	Utensils: saucepan
med	med	baking pan
3 lb	4 lb	pork loin roast, bone in (cut into chops for stuffing)
1 tsp	1½ tsp	salt
¼ tsp	⅓ tsp	pepper
⅓ C	½ C	dried apricots, quartered
⅓ C	½ C	dried prunes, quartered
¼ C	⅓ C	port wine

When purchasing the roast, ask the butcher to cut the roast into chops suitable for stuffing. Sprinkle the roast with salt and pepper. In a saucepan, combine apricots, prunes, and wine. Cook over medium heat for 15 minutes. Drain off the liquid and use the cooked mixture to stuff between the chops. Tie the roast back into the original shape. / / Roast in 325° oven for 40 minutes per pound of roast.

218

HERB-BUTTERED BROCCOLI

FOR 4	FOR 6	INGREDIENTS
1 qt, 3 qt	1 qt, 4 qt	Utensils: saucepans
2 lb	3 lb	broccoli
1 C	1½ C	water
½ tsp	¾ tsp	salt
⅓ C	½ C	butter or margarine
3 tbl	4 tbl	lemon juice
1 sm	1 med	minced garlic clove
¼ tsp	⅓ tsp	oregano
¼ tsp	⅓ tsp	ground black pepper

Trim heavy, coarse stalks from broccoli. Boil water in larger saucepan, add salt, and place broccoli in pan with stalks down. Cover and steam the broccoli for 20 minutes, or until tender. Combine the butter, lemon juice, garlic clove, oregano, and pepper and heat until melted into sauce form. Just before serving, pour the sauce over the cooked broccoli.

ORANGE RICE

FOR 4	FOR 6	INGREDIENTS
2 qt	2 qt	Utensil: saucepan
3	5	celery stalks
1 sm	1 lrg	onion
¼ C	⅓ C	butter or margarine
5 oz	8 oz	long-grain white rice
1 C	1½ C	water
¾ C	1 C	orange juice
1½ tsp	2 tsp	salt
2 tsp	3 tsp	grated orange rind

Finely chop the celery and onion and cook in melted butter until tender, not brown. Add rice, water, orange juice, and salt. / / Cook to a boil over high heat, cover, remove from heat, and let stand for 13 to 15 minutes. Add orange rind just before serving.

VANILLA PECAN CAKE

FOR 4	FOR 6	INGREDIENTS
	lrg	Utensils: mixing bowl
	1	tube baking pan
	½ lb	butter or margarine
	2 C	sugar
	6	eggs
	1 box	vanilla wafers, 12-oz box
	½ C	milk
	1 pkg	flaked coconut, 7-oz pkg
	1 C	chopped pecans
	1 tsp	vanilla extract

Preheat oven to 300°. Cream the butter and sugar in a large mixing bowl. Beat the eggs into the mixture one at a time. Crush the vanilla wafers and add them to the creamed mixture. Add milk. Fold in coconut, pecans and vanilla extract. Turn into a greased and floured tube baking pan and bake for 1 hour 15 minutes at 300°. Cool, turn out on plate. Serve with vanilla ice cream or glaze.

Glaze

	sm	Utensil: mixing bowl
	1 C	powdered sugar
	2 tbl	milk

Blend powdered sugar in small mixing bowl with the milk. Drizzle over the cake.

menu 74

White Pinot†
Veal Parmesan
French Bread
Genoese Rice
Raspberry Salad
Grasshopper Pie

TIMETABLE
*3:00 pm   Chill wine
*3:00   Prepare Grasshopper Pie
*6:30   Prepare French Bread
*6:40   Prepare Genoese Rice
*7:15   Prepare Veal Parmesan
 7:45   Place veal in oven at 375°
 7:45   Place covered rice casserole in oven
 7:45   Place French Bread in oven
 7:50   Unmold salad onto serving plate
 8:00   Dinner is served

† A dry Chablis wine; serve chilled (45°)   * May be prepared in the morning or the night before and refrigerated

FOR 4	FOR 6	INGREDIENTS

INSTRUCTIONS

FRENCH BREAD

sm	sm	Utensil: saucepan
½ loaf	¾ loaf	French bread
3 tbl	¼ C	butter
2 tbl	3 tbl	grated Parmesan cheese

Slice bread loaf. Melt butter in saucepan and brush each slice with butter and sprinkle with grated cheese. Arrange back into original loaf form and wrap with heavy aluminum foil. / / Bake at 375° for 15 minutes.

FOR 4	FOR 6	INGREDIENTS
2	2	Utensils: small mixing bowls
12 in	12 in	skillet
2 qt	3 qt	shallow baking dish
4	6	thin veal cutlets
1	1	egg
½ tsp	¾ tsp	salt
⅛ tsp	¼ tsp	pepper
½ tsp	¾ tsp	garlic salt
½ C	¾ C	dry bread crumbs
3 tbl	4 tbl	grated Parmesan cheese
3 tbl	3 tbl	olive oil
1 tsp	1½ tsp	oregano
1 can	1 can	tomato sauce, 8-oz can
4 slices	6 slices	mozzarella cheese, sliced thin

VEAL PARMESAN

Pound cutlets with meat hammer, making them as thin as possible. Cut into small portions and dip into egg which has been beaten with salt, pepper, and garlic salt. Mix bread crumbs with all but 1 tablespoon of Parmesan cheese in a mixing bowl. After dipping the veal pieces into egg mixture, dip them into crumb mixture and brown slowly in skillet with olive oil. When veal has browned, transfer to baking dish, sprinkle with oregano, pour tomato sauce over all, and arrange mozzarella cheese slices on top. Sprinkle with the remaining Parmesan cheese. / / Bake at 375° for about 15 minutes.

GENOESE RICE

FOR 4	FOR 6	
10 in		Utensils: skillet
	4 qt	saucepan
	2 qt	covered baking dish
½ lb		diced bacon
1 tbl		butter or margarine
1 C		sliced fresh mushrooms
1 tsp		salt
¼ tsp		lemon juice
2½ C		water
2 tbl		butter or margarine
1 pkg		Italian-style rice mix
1 pkg		frozen peas
2 tbl		chopped green peppers
2 tbl		minced fresh parsley

Cook bacon in skillet until crisp and drain on paper towels. Pour off all but 1 tablespoon of bacon grease. Add butter. Sauté the mushrooms in the bacon grease-butter mixture for about 5 minutes. Season with salt and add lemon juice. Place 2 ½ cups of water in a saucepan and add butter and contents of the spice envelope in the package. Bring mixture to a boil, add rice, stir well, and bring back to a boil. Lower heat, cover pan, and cook gently for 10 minutes. Add the frozen peas to the rice, breaking up block if necessary. Cover and cook for 5 minutes, or until all liquid is absorbed and rice is cooked. Add the green pepper, bacon, and sautéed mushrooms. Place in covered baking dish. / / If prepared in advance, rice casserole may be heated for 15 minutes at 375°. Top with minced parsley just before serving.

FOR 4	FOR 6	INGREDIENTS

INSTRUCTIONS

RASPBERRY SALAD

med		Utensils: mixing bowl
2 qt		gelatin mold
1 pkg		raspberry gelatin
1 C		boiling water
1 pkg		frozen raspberries, 10-oz pkg
8½ oz		canned crushed pineapple
1		banana
½ C		chopped pecans

In a mixing bowl, dissolve gelatin in boiling water. And the frozen raspberries while mixture is hot, stirring to separate the berries. Let cool. Add pineapple, banana slices, and pecans. Pour into gelatin mold. Chill until firm. May be topped with sour cream.

GRASSHOPPER PIE

Crust

sm		Utensils: mixing bowl
sm		saucepan
9 in		pie pan or plate
16		chocolate wafer cookies
3 tbl		butter

Using a rolling pin, crush the cookies until they become fine crumbs and add to mixing bowl. Melt the butter in a saucepan and thoroughly blend into cookie crumbs. Press the mixture into the pie pan. Freeze for 20 minutes.

Filling

med		Utensils: double boiler
sm		mixing bowl
19		marshmallows, regular size
½ C		milk
¼ pt		heavy cream
¼ C		green crème de menthe

Place the marshmallows and milk in the top of the double boiler and heat until marshmallows are melted. Remove from heat and let cool. In a small mixing bowl, whip the cream. When the marshmallow mixture has cooled, add the crème de menthe. Fold in the whipped cream. Pour the filling into the pie shell and chill for 4 to 6 hours. The flavor improves if refrigerated overnight.

menu 75

Gamay Beaujolais†
Veal Scallopine Marsala
Melon and Prosciutto
Basil Tomatoes
Mushroom Pilaff
Roman Lemon Ice

TIMETABLE

*4:00 pm	Chill wine	
*4:00	Prepare Roman Lemon Ice	
*6:30	Prepare Melon and Prosciutto	
*6:45	Prepare Basil Tomatoes	
7:10	Prepare Mushroom Pilaff	
7:30	Bake Mushroom Pilaff at 350°	
7:30	Cook Veal Scallopine Marsala	
7:55	Remove cover from pilaff	
7:55	Toss Basil Tomatoes with croutons	
8:00	Dinner is served	

† A light, dry Burgundy wine; serve chilled (45°)   * May be prepared in the morning or the night before and refrigerated

---

FOR 4   FOR 6   INGREDIENTS   INSTRUCTIONS

VEAL SCALLOPINE MARSALA

FOR 4	FOR 6	INGREDIENTS
10 in	12 in	Utensil: skillet
1½ lb	2¼ lb	thinly sliced veal cutlets
⅓ tsp	½ tsp	salt
⅛ tsp	¼ tsp	pepper
1 tbl	1½ tbl	flour
2 tbl	3 tbl	butter or margarine
½ C	¾ C	Marsala wine
2 tbl	3 tbl	water

Pound thinly sliced veal cutlets with a meat hammer until very thin. Cut into pieces about 5 inches square, sprinkle with salt and pepper, and flour lightly. Melt butter in skillet, and, when hot, brown veal thoroughly on both sides over high heat. When well browned, add the wine and, keeping the flame high, let meat cook about one minute longer. Place meat in serving dish. Add water to pan. Stir and scrape bottom and sides of pan. Pour over meat and serve.

FOR 4	FOR 6	INGREDIENTS

MELON AND PROSCIUTTO

FOR 4	FOR 6	INGREDIENTS
1 med	1 lrg or 2 sm	honeydew melon
1 tbl	1½ tbl	lime juice
4 thin slices	1 thin slices	prosciutto

Cut melon into serving wedges, remove seeds, and cut off rind. Make a slice, lengthwise, in the center of each wedge, but not cutting all the way through the melon. Sprinkle lime juice into each wedge and stuff with a slice of prosciutto. Refrigerate until ready to serve. (May be served as a first course if desired.)

BASIL TOMATOES

FOR 4	FOR 6	INGREDIENTS
med	med	Utensil: serving bowl
3	4	tomatoes
½ tsp	¾ tsp	salt
¼ tsp	⅓ tsp	pepper
⅛ tsp	⅛ tsp	garlic powder
½ tsp	¾ tsp	fresh or dry sweet basil
2 tsp	1 tbl	olive oil
1 tsp	1½ tsp	water
1 C	1½ C	plain croutons

Wash, peel, and slice tomatoes into bite-size wedges. Place in serving bowl. Sprinkle with salt, pepper, garlic powder, and basil. Add olive oil and water, and toss well. Cover and refrigerate until ready to serve. / / Add croutons and toss, just before serving.

MUSHROOM PILAFF

	2 qt	Utensil: covered, flameproof baking dish
	½ C	butter
	1¼ C	brown rice
	1 coil	coiled vermicelli
	4 oz	canned mushrooms
	1 can	canned chicken consommé
	⅓ C	water
	1½	chicken bouillon cubes

Melt butter in flameproof baking dish over medium heat. Add rice and coil of vermicelli (crushed with hands). Cook over medium heat until lightly browned, about 10 minutes. Stir in the canned mushrooms and their juice, consommé, water, and bouillon cubes. Cover and place in oven at 350° for 25 minutes. Remove cover and bake 5 minutes longer. (If flameproof baking dish is not available, use a skillet to brown the rice and vermicelli, then transfer the mixture to a baking dish.)

ROMAN LEMON ICE

2 qt	2 qt	Utensils: saucepan
sm	sm	mixing bowl
1	2	freezer tray
1 C	1½ C	sugar
3 C	1 qt	water
½ C	¾ C	lemon juice
1	1	egg white
3 tbl	¼ C	sugar
2 oz	3 oz	rum

Combine sugar and water in saucepan and heat until sugar melts. Add lemon juice and strain through a very fine sieve. Freeze until mushy, stirring frequently, then remove from freezer. Beat egg white in a small mixing bowl until stiff. Add the beaten egg white and sugar to the lemon mixture and mix well. Add rum and mix. Return to freezer and freeze to ice consistency, stirring very often.

CHAPTER FOUR

Hors d'Oeuvres

APPLE DIP

2 C	applesauce
1 C	commercial sour cream
2 tbl	minced onion
1 tsp	Worcestershire sauce
½ tsp	salt

Simmer applesauce in saucepan at least 5 minutes, to evaporate some of the liquid. Chill, then combine with other ingredients and mix well. Serve as a dip for raw vegetables.

AVOCADO DIP

2	ripe, large avocados
2 tbl	lemon juice
8 oz (1 pt)	softened cream cheese (or cottage cheese)
1½ tsp	salt
3 drops	Tabasco sauce
1 tbl	grated onion

Cut avocados in half. Remove seed and peel. Cut into cubes and whip until smooth in blender. Blend in lemon juice, cheese, salt, Tabasco sauce, and onion. Serve as a dip for crackers or raw vegetables.

CHEESE CRISPS

1 C	shredded Cheddar cheese
¼ C	softened butter
½ tsp	salt
dash	cayenne
1 tbl	finely chopped chives
¾ C	sifted flour

Mix all ingredients together in mixing bowl until a smooth dough forms. Shape into a log about 1-inch in diameter. Wrap in waxed paper and chill. Slice into one-eighth inch slices, place on lightly greased cookie sheet, and bake at 350° for 10 minutes, or until lightly browned.

BACON SNACKS

Cut 10 slices of bacon in half, fry in skillet for just 5 minutes, then roll any of the listed ingredients inside. Secure rolls with toothpicks, place on cookie sheet, and bake at 400° for 10 to 12 minutes.

water chestnuts (6-oz can), drained, and
  marinated in soy sauce (¼ C)
peanut butter spread on bacon slices with 2
  walnut halves as center
pitted dates
stuffed olives
pineapple pieces
orange pieces

CHEESE MEATBALLS

1 lb	lean ground beef
4½ oz	canned deviled ham
1	egg
½ C	dry bread crumbs
¼ tsp	salt
⅛ tsp	pepper
¼ lb	blue cheese
to cover	dry red wine
2 tbl	butter

In mixing bowl, mix ground beef, with deviled ham, slightly beaten egg, bread crumbs, salt, and pepper. Form into balls about the size of walnuts, coarsely crumble the blue cheese, and push a little of the cheese into the center of each ball. Place in a china bowl and cover with wine. Let stand at least 3 hours. Remove the balls and sauté them in butter in a skillet until medium done. Add wine and simmer 5 minutes more, stirring gently. Serve in chafing dish with cocktail picks.

CLAM DIP

8 oz	softened cream cheese
2 tsp	lemon juice
1½ tsp	Worcestershire sauce
½ tsp	salt
dash	pepper
½ C	canned minced clams

In a mixing bowl, mix the cream cheese, lemon juice, Worcestershire sauce, salt, pepper, and ¼ cup of the juice from the canned clams. Stir in clams. Serve as a dip with crackers or potato chips.

CRABMEAT DIP

3 oz	softened cream cheese
2 pkg	frozen crabmeat
⅓ C	mayonnaise
1 tbl	lemon juice
1 tbl	Worcestershire sauce
2 tbl	catsup
1 tbl	grated onion
½ tsp	Tabasco sauce

Place softened cream cheese in mixing bowl. Mix in the crabmeat, add other ingredients, and blend well. Serve as a dip with crackers or potato chips.

CURRY DIP

½ C	mayonnaise
2 tbl	lemon juice
1 tsp	curry powder

Mix ingredients together in mixing bowl. Serve as a dip with seafood or raw vegetables.

HOT CHILI DIP

1 lb 12 oz	canned tomatoes
4 oz	whole green chili (canned)
¼ C	dried, minced onions
1½ lb	sharp Cheddar cheese

In a saucepan, simmer tomatoes, chopped chili, and onions for 30 minutes, stirring. Add grated cheese and serve in chafing dish.

PEANUT-GLAZED HAM PIECES

lrg slice	½-inch thick cooked ham
⅓ C	chunk-style peanut butter

Spread ham slice with a thick layer of peanut butter. Place under broiler for 2 to 3 minutes, or until the peanut butter forms a brown crust. Cut into bite-size pieces and serve with cocktail picks.

PIZZA APPETIZERS

2 C	finely chopped Cheddar cheese
¾ C	chopped onion
4½ oz	canned chopped ripe olives
¼ tsp	ground oregano
6 oz	canned tomato paste
1 tsp	garlic salt
8	small French rolls

In a mixing bowl, mix together the cheese, onion, drained olives, oregano, tomato paste, and garlic salt. Cut small French rolls in half, spread with mixture, and bake at 400° for 8 minutes.

QUICK PIZZA APPETIZERS

10½ oz	pizza sauce
8	sourdough English muffins
8 oz	mozzarella cheese

Cut English muffins in half, spoon pizza sauce onto each half, top with grated mozzarella cheese. Broil until lightly browned.

ROMANO CANAPES

4	white bread slices
½ C	mayonnaise
¼ C	grated Romano cheese
2 tbl	dried minced onion

Remove crusts from bread slices. In a mixing bowl, combine the mayonnaise, grated cheese, and onion. Spread mixture on bread slices. Broil about 5 minutes, or until lightly browned. Cut each slice into 9 squares. Serve hot.

SHERRY-BLUE DIP

⅔ C	crumbled blue cheese
3 oz	softened cream cheese
¼ C	sherry wine
1	garlic clove
¾ C	commercial sour cream

In a mixing bowl, mix the blue cheese and softened cream cheese with the sherry wine. Then combine with the minced garlic clove and sour cream. Serve as a dip with crackers or raw vegetables.

SHRIMP DIP

4½ oz	canned shrimp
1 tsp	lemon juice
1 tsp	Worcestershire sauce
½ tsp	garlic salt
½ tsp	dry mustard
½ tsp	MSG
dash	pepper
1 C	commercial sour cream

Drain shrimp well. In a mixing bowl, combine the lemon juice, Worcestershire sauce, garlic salt, dry mustard, monosodium glutamate, and pepper. Blend in the sour cream, then add shrimp. Serve as a dip with crackers or potato chips.

SHRIMP SOUP DIP

10 oz	canned frozen shrimp soup
8 oz	softened cream cheese
1 tbl	chopped, stuffed olives
1 tbl	Worcestershire sauce
dash	garlic salt
1 tbl	sherry wine

Defrost soup, blend with cream cheese in a mixing bowl. Add remaining ingredients and beat with mixer. Chill. Serve as a dip with crackers or potato chips.

TUNA PECAN SPREAD

6½ oz	canned tuna fish, drained
¼ C	chopped pecans
½ C	mayonnaise

Combine all ingredients in mixing bowl. Chill. Serve as a dip with crackers or potato chips.

TUNA CRUNCH BALLS

6½ oz	canned tuna fish, drained
2 tsp	lemon juice
2 tsp	mustard
1 tsp	dried, minced onions
¼ tsp	celery seeds
¼ tsp	mayonnaise
3 tbl	sesame seeds

Combine all ingredients, except sesame seeds, in a mixing bowl. Beat with mixer for 2 minutes. Form into small balls. Roll balls in sesame seeds. Broil for 5 minutes, or until lightly browned. Serve hot.

CHAPTER FIVE

Introduction to Wines

INTRODUCTION TO WINES

The serving of wine with meals, while a common practice in European countries for many centuries, has only recently begun to gain popularity in America. Each day, more and more American families are discovering the benefits and pleasures of good wines, and a general knowledge of wine is becoming more important for all good hosts and hostesses.

What is wine?

Wine is a natural beverage that results from the fermentation of grape juices. Since it continues to age, develop, and react as long as it exists, the qualities of the wine change right up to the moment it is consumed.

The making of wine.

Grapes are selected by the winemaker according to the flavor and quality desired. He then controls and guides the fermenting process to bring out the characteristics desired. The color is determined by the length of time the juices are allowed to ferment with the skins; the dryness is determined by the total fermenting time; and the alcoholic content is increased in some wines by the addition of brandy. A sparkling wine is produced by fermenting the wine in sealed containers to capture escaping gasses, or, in less expensive wines, the fermentation occurs in large, sealed vats.

The quality of American wines.

For many years, wine experts have expressed the opinion that European wines are far superior to wines from any other region. However, that opinion is no longer valid. In most wine competitions, American wines have won many awards for excellence, and it is now a well-established fact that, except for a few rare European wines, the fine American wines are equal in quality to all others.

Vintage years.

Since the climate in European countries varies greatly from year to year, the quality of wines produced there will also vary. Consequently, most European wines are dated to identify the year in which the wine was produced, especially if the year was a relatively good one. Since almost 90 percent of all American wines are produced in California, and the climate in California is relatively consistant from year to year, very few American wines are dated.

Premium and standard wines.

Over 90 percent of all wines produced in America and Europe are of standard grade. These wines are relatively inexpensive and are available in most grocery and liquor stores. They are normally labeled by their generic name (Burgundy, Claret, Rhine, Sauterne, etc.). The premium wines (sometimes referred to as "special," "deluxe," "estate," and "private stock") are produced from carefully selected varieties of grapes. They are fermented from the juices of the first pressing of the grapes (or natural run) and are usually labeled by their varietal name (Cabernet Sauvignon, Charbono, Folle Blanche, etc.).

Classification of American Wines:

CLASSIFICATION	GENERIC NAME	VARIETAL NAME
Appetizer Wines:	Sherry (dry to sweet) Vermouth (dry to sweet) Special natural wines	

Red Dinner Wines:	Burgundy (dry)	Barbera Charbono Gamay Pinot Noir Red Pinot
	Claret (dry)	Cabernet Cabernet Sauvignon Grignolino Zinfandel
	Vino Rosso (semisweet)	
	Rosé (dry to sweet)	
	Red Chianti (dry)	

CLASSIFICATION	GENERIC NAME	VARIETAL NAME
White Dinner Wines:	Chablis (dry)	Pinot Chardonnay Folle Blanche Pinot Blanc Chenin Blanc White Pinot
	Sauterne (dry to sweet)	Sauvignon Blanc Semillon Haute Sauterne Chateau Sauterne
	Rhine Wine (dry)	Grey Riesling Johannisberger Riesling Sylvaner Traminer White Riesling
	Others	Catawba (dry) Delaware (dry) Light Muscat (dry to sweet) White Chianti (dry)

CLASSIFICATION	GENERIC NAME	VARIETAL NAME
Dessert Wines: (Sweet)	Port	Red Port Tawny Port White Port
	Tokay	
	Muscatel	Gold Muscatel Red Muscatel Black Muscat
	Others	Angelica Madeira Marsala Cream Sherry
Sparkling Wines:	Champagne	Brut (very dry) Sec (semisweet) Doux (sweet)
	Sparkling Burgundy (semisweet to sweet)	
	Others	Sparkling Muscat (sweet) Sparkling Rosé (dry to semisweet)

Which wine with which food?

There is much controversy over which wines to serve with which foods. Those who consider themselves experts feel that each food has a specific wine that must be served with that food; or, conversely, each wine is suitable to only one particular food. Nothing could be further from the truth.

Certain customs have evolved over the years, and these customs should be used only as guides. The normal rule of serving white wine with light-colored meats and light foods, and serving red wine with red meats and heavy foods, has proven to be an excellent one to use as a general guide. Rosé wines can be served with any meal and are becoming very popular because of their versatility.

The most important rule to remember in the serving of wines is: "Serve the wine you most enjoy, and enjoy the wine you serve."

Wine serving temperature.

Again, customs dictate that white wines should be served chilled and red wines served cool (cool room temperature). The correct temperature for each wine is that temperature which brings out the characteristics of the wine most enjoyable to you. Therefore, serve the wine at the temperature you most enjoy.

Wine Selection Charts

Standard American Wine Selection Chart

MAIN COURSE	WINE	SERVING TEMPERATURE*
Beef and beef dishes	Burgundy	Cool
	Claret	Cool
	Rosé	Chilled
Chicken and chicken dishes	Chablis	Chilled
	Rhine Wine	Chilled
Curried dishes	Burgundy	Cool
	Claret	Cool
	Rosé	Chilled
Clams	Chablis	Well-chilled
Crab	Chablis	Well-chilled
	Rhine Wine	Chilled
	Sauterne	Chilled
Fish	Chablis	Chilled
	Rhine Wine	Chilled
	Rosé	Chilled
Game	Burgundy	Cool
	Claret	Cool

* Cool = 65°
Chilled = 45°
Well-chilled = 40°

MAIN COURSE	WINE	SERVING TEMPERATURE
Game fowl	Burgundy	Cool
	Chablis	Chilled
	Claret	Cool
Ham	Chablis	Chilled
	Rhine Wine	Chilled
	Rosé	Chilled
Lamb	Burgundy	Cool
	Rhine Wine	Chilled
	Rosé	Chilled
Liver	Claret	Cool
	Rosé	Chilled
Lobster	Chablis	Well-chilled
Oysters	Chablis	Well-chilled
Pasta (Italian macaroni, etc.)	Burgundy	Cool
	Chianti	Cool
	Claret	Cool
Pork	Chablis	Chilled
	Rhine Wine	Chilled
	Rosé	Chilled
	Sauterne	Chilled

MAIN COURSE	WINE	SERVING TEMPERATURE
Shrimp	Chablis	Well-chilled
	Rhine Wine	Well-chilled
Turkey	Burgundy	Cool
	Chablis	Chilled
	Claret	Cool
	Rosé	Chilled
Veal	Chablis	Chilled
	Rhine Wine	Chilled
	Rosé	Chilled
	Sauterne	Chilled

Premium American Wine Selection Chart

MAIN COURSE	WINE	SERVING TEMPERATURE
Beef roasts and steaks	Cabernet Sauvignon	Cool
	Red Pinot	Cool
	Zinfandel	Cool
Beef dishes	Barbera	Cool
	Cabernet	Cool
	Charbono	Cool
	Gamay	Cool
	Grignolino	Cool
	Pinot Noir	Cool
	Red Pinot	Cool
	Zinfandel	Cool
Chicken	Grenache Rosé	Chilled
	Grey Riesling	Chilled
	Pinot Chardonnay	Chilled
	White Riesling	Chilled
Curried dishes	Barbera	Cool
	Cabernet Sauvignon	Cool
	Gamay	Cool
	Pinot Noir	Cool
	Zinfandel	Cool

MAIN COURSE	WINE	SERVING TEMPERATURE
Clams	Chenin Blanc	Well-chilled
	Folle Blanche	Chilled
	Pinot Blanc	Chilled
	Pinot Chardonnay	Chilled
	White Pinot	Chilled
Crab	Chenin Blanc	Well-chilled
	Folle Blanche	Chilled
	Grey Riesling	Chilled
	Sauvignon Blanc	Chilled
	Semillon	Chilled
	Traminer	Chilled
	White Riesling	Chilled
Fish	Chateau Sauterne	Well-chilled
	Grey Riesling	Chilled
	Pinot Chardonnay	Chilled
	Sylvaner	Chilled
	Traminer	Chilled
	White Pinot	Chilled
Game	Cabernet Sauvignon	Cool
	Charbono	Cool
	Grignolino	Cool
	Pinot Noir	Cool
	Red Pinot	Cool

MAIN COURSE	WINE	SERVING TEMPERATURE
Game fowl	Barbera	Cool
	Cabernet Sauvignon	Cool
	Catawba	Chilled
	Charbono	Cool
	Grignolino	Cool
	Pinot Chardonnay	Chilled
Ham	Delaware	Chilled
	Gamay	Cool
	Johannisberger Riesling	Chilled
	Pinot Chardonnay	Chilled
	Traminer	Chilled
	White Chianti	Chilled
	White Pinot	Chilled
Lamb	Johannisberger Riesling	Chilled
	Pinot Chardonnay	Chilled
	Pinot Noir	Cool
	Traminer	Chilled
	White Riesling	Chilled
Liver	Barbera	Cool
	Cabernet	Cool
	Grenache Rosé	Chilled
	Grignolino	Cool
	Zinfandel	Cool

MAIN COURSE	WINE	SERVING TEMPERATURE
Lobster	Chenin Blanc	Well-chilled
	Folle Blanche	Chilled
	Grey Riesling	Chilled
	Pinot Blanc	Chilled
	Pinot Chardonnay	Chilled
Oysters	Pinot Chardonnay	Chilled
	Sylvaner	Chilled
	Traminer	Chilled
	White Pinot	Chilled
	White Riesling	Chilled
Pasta (Italian macaroni, etc.)	Barbera	Cool
	Charbono	Cool
	Chianti	Cool
	Gamay	Cool
	Grignolino	Cool
	Pinot Noir	Cool
	Zinfandel	Cool
Pork	Gamay Beaujolais	Chilled
	Johannisberger Riesling	Chilled
	Pinot Chardonnay	Chilled
	Semillon	Chilled
	Traminer	Chilled
	White Riesling	Chilled

MAIN COURSE	WINE	SERVING TEMPERATURE
Shrimp	Chenin Blanc	Well-chilled
	Folle Blanche	Chilled
	Grey Riesling	Chilled
	Semillon	Chilled
	Sylvaner	Chilled
	White Riesling	Chilled
Turkey	Barbera	Cool
	Cabernet Sauvignon	Cool
	Charbono	Cool
	Gamay	Cool
	Pinot Chardonnay	Chilled
	Red Pinot	Cool
	Zinfandel	Cool
Veal	Gamay Beaujolais	Chilled
	Grey Riesling	Chilled
	Johannisberger Riesling	Chilled
	Pinot Chardonnay	Chilled
	Sauvignon Blanc	Chilled
	Traminer	Chilled
	White Pinot	Chilled

Premium European Wine Selection Chart

MAIN COURSE	WINE	SERVING TEMPERATURE
Beef roasts and steaks	Beaujolais	Chilled
	Bordeaux, Medoc	Cool
	Chambertin	Cool
	Chassagne-Montrachet	Cool
	Château Cheval Blanc	Cool
	Château Prieure Lichine	Cool
	Hermitage	Cool
	Juliénas	Cool
	Vosne Romanée	Cool
Beef dishes	Beaune	Chilled
	Château Ausone	Cool
	Châteauneuf-Du-Pape	Cool
	Nuits St. Georges	Cool
	Volnay	Cool
	Valpolicella	Cool
Chicken	Château Ausone	Cool
	Château Cheval Blanc	Cool
	Château-Du-Bruil	Chilled
	Chinon	Chilled
	Puligny-Montrachet	Chilled
	Sancerre	Chilled
	Soave	Chilled

MAIN COURSE	WINE	SERVING TEMPERATURE
Curried dishes	Chambertin	Cool
	Nuits St. Georges	Cool
	Volnay	Cool
Clams	Pouilly Fuissé	Well-chilled
	Sancerre	Chilled
	Verdicchio	Chilled
Crab	Pouilly Fuissé	Well-chilled
	Sancerre	Chilled
	Verdicchio	Chilled
Fish	Gewurztraminer	Chilled
	Muscadet	Chilled
	Neuchâtel	Chilled
	Puligny-Montrachet	Chilled
	Sancerre	Chilled
	Verdicchio	Chilled
Game	Bordeaux, St. Emilion	Cool
	Chambertin	Cool
	Château De Lascombes	Cool
	Fleurie	Chilled

MAIN COURSE	WINE	SERVING TEMPERATURE
Game fowl	Bordeaux, St. Emilion	Cool
	Château Ausone	Cool
	Châteauneuf-Du-Pape	Cool
	Hermitage	Cool
Ham	Juliénas	Cool
	Sancerre	Chilled
Lamb	Beaujolais	Chilled
	Beaune	Chilled
	Chambertin	Cool
	Château Beychevelle	Cool
	Hermitage	Cool
	Nuits St. Georges	Cool
Liver	Beaune	Chilled
	Château Ausone	Cool
	Château Prieure Lichine	Cool
	Juliénas	Cool
Lobster	Montbazillac	Chilled
	Pouilly Fuissé	Well-chilled
	Sancerre	Chilled
	Verdicchio	Chilled

MAIN COURSE	WINE	SERVING TEMPERATURE
Oysters	Graves	Chilled
	Nuits St. Georges	Chilled
	Sancerre	Chilled
Pasta (Italian macaroni, etc.)	Chianti	Cool
	Juliénas	Cool
Pork	Fleurie	Chilled
	Gewurztraminer	Chilled
Shrimp	Pouilly Fuissé	Well-chilled
	Verdicchio	Chilled
Turkey	Bordeaux, Medoc	Cool
	Château Ausone	Cool
	Château De Lascombes	Cool
	Château Hautbrion	Cool
Veal	Château Montrachet	Cool
	Muscadet	Chilled
	Neuchâtel	Chilled
	Puligny-Montrachet	Chilled
	Sancerre	Chilled
	Verdicchio	Chilled

INDEX

Lamb:
  barbecued lamb, 154
  lamb curry, 186
  shish kabobs, 212
Lamb curry, 186
Lasagne del mondo, 189
Lemon carrots, 180
Lemon cream, 117
Lemon freeze, 136
Lemon meringue pie, 194
Lemon sauce, 110
Lemon sherbet, 93
Lemon whip, 34
Lettuce and cucumber salad, 41
Lima bean casserole, 20
Lima beans, 54
Lime-avocado salad, 89
Liver:
  liver and onions, 22
  liver in tomato sauce, 25
Liver and onions, 22
Liver in tomato sauce, 25
Lobster-crab meat casseroles, 192
Lobster newberg, 195

Marinated avocados, 69
Marinated bean salad, 81
Marinated green beans, 47
Marinated onions and tomatoes, 144
Marinated vegetables, 193

Marshmallow fruit, 131
Meatballs and rice, 30
Meatball stroganoff, 114
Meat loaf, 27
Mediterranean sea food platter, 119
Melon compote, 183
Melon and prosciutto, 226
Melon's secret, 178
Melon with roquefort, 113
Meringue pie, 90
Mexican style chili, 32
Mint sauce, 154
Minted peas, 121
Minted pineapple, 180
Mixed green salad, 187
Mocha frost, 122
Mocha lime sherbet, 55
Mocha raisin nut bars, 26
Mocha walnut torte, 36
Muffins:
  apple muffins, 21
  blueberry muffins, 50
  honey muffins, 39
  spicy orange muffins, 69
Mushroom pilaff, 227
Mushroom salisbury steak, 35

Noodles:
  buttered noodles, 6
  green sesame noodles, 1

Noodles (cont.)
  hot noodles, 109, 115
  noodles Romano, 199
Noodles Romano, 199

Orange and green salad, 152
Orange avocado salad, 169
Orange babas, 181
Orange-cranberry salad, 92
Orange glazed carrots, 28
Orange-pineapple mold, 175
Orange pork chops, 38
Orange rice, 219
Orange roast duckling, 198
Orange salad mold, 203
Orange salad with honey dressing, 138
Orange sherbet salad, 48
Oregano beef, 120

Pan browned potatoes, 160
Parsley biscuits, 124
Parsley potatoes, 118
Pasta:
  lasagne del mondo, 189
  rigatoni, 54
Pasta peas, 209
Peach almond pudding, 75
Peach ice cream pie, 162